John F. Kennedy and the New Frontier

John F. Kennedy and the New Frontier

EDITED AND WITH AN INTRODUCTION BY

Aïda DiPace Donald

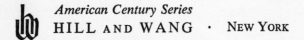

American Century Series
HILL AND WANG · NEW YORK

ISBN (clothbound edition): 0-8090-6345-X
ISBN (paperback edition): 0-8090-0084-9

Library of Congress catalog card number: 66–26031

First edition October 1966

Manufactured in the United States of America

2 3 4 5 6 7 8 9 10

For David

Contents

Introduction

In the Presidential campaign of 1960 John F. Kennedy broke through American complacency with a call to get America moving again. It had not occurred to most Americans that their country was not meeting its challenges; indeed few thought about what those challenges were. Yet in his skillful presentation of facts and figures, overlaid with a "New Frontier" philosophy of vigor, direction, and adventure, Kennedy reached the people and slipped into office. He served his country not quite three years.

This book of essays examines the nature of President Kennedy's leadership, his goals, and his accomplishments. Kennedy's own "measure of Presidential success was concrete achievement."[1] Educating a nation or musing on the quality of American life were valuable pursuits, but tangible works were suitable monuments to Presidential immortality. Perhaps because Kennedy's life was snuffed out so prematurely, historians ought not to measure the Kennedy Presidency with the same high standard Kennedy set for himself and by which he rated his immediate predecessors. But in the outpouring of writings since his tragic murder—writings both distinguished and highly informative—his advisers and long-time associates have used that high standard to assess his Presidency. It may be useful in this stage of the historiography of the Kennedy years to have in one place, in a small volume, some of those writings and other pieces on the thousand days.

With one exception all the selections in this book were written or published after November 22, 1963. They are, on the whole, analytical, logical expositions, written by distinguished commentators of diverse outlook, interests, and occupations. The book is divided into three parts: I John F. Kennedy—measures of his intellect and manner of leadership; II Kennedy and the Frontiers—appraisals of aspects of the Kennedy program; III The Kennedy Presidency—overall evaluations of Kennedy's accomplishments. Under each of these general headings the writings are organized to integrate the subject matter as much as possible. From the vast body of literature on Kennedy and the New Frontier I have chosen articles of advocacy and of criticism. However, only those pieces which are tempered by good judgment and fairness to other points of view are here included.

I

President Kennedy's leadership was so much an extension of his whole being that most writers on the New Frontier attempt to define the quality of his mind and the nature of his personality. Typical of the questions asked are: "Was he an intellectual?" "Did he project a bold vision for America?" "How and where did he apply his pragmatic approach?" "Did he educate the public to its responsibilities?" Arthur M. Schlesinger, Jr., in passages from *A Thousand Days* explores the Kennedy mind, intentions, and manner. In the following selections Richard H. Rovere, James Reston, William G. Carleton, Richard E. Neustadt, and others also concern themselves with these matters.

Most writers agree that Kennedy's intellect was critical, rational, well-balanced, detached, and richly furnished. He possessed a truly modern mind—a composite of good formal training and a superb self-education. The President understood America, its history, problems, and needs. Abroad he understood the mainsprings of change and revolution and the inevitability of more change and more revolution. His touchstone was always faith in reason and he instinctively knew where he stood in relation to contending power blocs.

But writers differ on the effectiveness of Kennedy's leadership. There can be no doubt that Kennedy himself believed that one man in motion could make a difference. He gave energetic leadership to any sphere of activity where his writ was clear and power undeniable—and he wanted results. Louis Koenig shows us how Kennedy functioned in two areas—the administration of the federal government and the leadership of the Democratic party. Kennedy as administrator, states Koenig, was tireless in reaching into all levels of government to have problems and not solutions brought to his desk and to spur the decision-making process. As party leader he was vigorous in applying "the Kennedy formula" to the Democratic organization. He "looked for the eventual dominance of urban politics over congressional politics." He projected a future based on the "combination of a program geared to urban groups and a personal political organization that mobilized local party organization. . . ."

In the field of defense Kennedy's intellect and executive talents fared best, for as commander-in-chief of the armed forces the President had the scope and power to initiate programs as well as to oversee them. Theodore C. Sorensen, McGeorge Bundy, William E. Leuchtenburg, Jerome Wiesner, and others discuss the New Frontier ideas and advances in national security, foreign policy and science.

Sorensen writes that Kennedy implemented the McNamara nuclear defense plan of deterrence plus. America's nuclear forces had to be large enough to deter aggression and to retaliate effectively after a first strike. A full "counterforce" or "first-strike" strategy was put aside for the production and development of survivable missiles like the submarine-launched Polaris and underground Minuteman. The nuclear program was rational, as well as less provocative and less expensive. The McNamara strategy further provided for greater flexibility in meeting aggression. Consequently, the armed forces were built up and made more mobile. The responses of nuclear retaliation or passivity in the face of conventionally waged wars were rejected. McNamara also attained complete control of the military establishment, an "achievement that may well stand out as the most important development of the Kennedy era," in William Leuchtenburg's estimate.

Kennedy's insatiable curiosity and determination to master

everything that came within his purview affected activities associated with defense. Jerome Wiesner relates that the President
schooled himself in the application of science to national security
and technology, initiated the moon space program, and became an
expert on the myriad problems of disarmament.

In areas where Kennedy shared responsibility with the Congress
—such as in the education of the public—and in the important role
of leading the Congress itself, the President was cautious. He
would not mount "The Bully Pulpit" like a Theodore Roosevelt,
but preferred a reasonable, nonhortatory approach. Because of
this circumspect attitude writers like Douglass Cater imply that
Kennedy was too rational, too respectful of differing points of
view, and too aware of his own place in the political balance of
forces. "Presidential leadership has other ingredients . . . as 'intuition,' 'vision,' 'conviction,' and . . . 'courage,' " Cater asserts.
". . . A prime characteristic of greatness is the ability to employ
power consciously but never too self-consciously. History reveals
that great Presidents must show a capacity not only to conserve
power but to risk squandering it when occasion demands. The nation has profited from such philanthropy." In the same vein James
Reston states that Kennedy "never really exploited his considerable
gifts as a public educator." "He did not normally like to take on
anything more than he had to tackle, no matter how worthy."

In rebuttal to these arguments Arthur Schlesinger declares that
Kennedy's "secret was timing." "In the absence of visible crisis
Presidents had to wait for some event to pierce the apathy and
command the nation's ear." ". . . If the President committed his
prestige to congressional action before the nation was ready to listen
to his arguments, he might squander the hope of later influence."
Seymour E. Harris also concludes that it would have been foolhardy for Kennedy to be too far ahead of Congress on advanced
proposals.

II

Kennedy's Presidency falls into two periods. For the first eighteen
months to two years Kennedy chose to push ideas and activities
through the executive hierarchy while maneuvering cautiously as

teacher, legislator, and diplomat. By his third year the President broke the pattern to lead daringly in all his roles as chief executive. He embraced advanced theories of economics, presented to the Congress some of the most momentous legislation in generations, and turned the tide of the cold war towards detente and control of the atom.

The clearest example of this change is in Kennedy's dealing with economic problems. Seymour E. Harris deftly reviews the political economy of the Kennedy years, focusing sharply on how New Frontiersmen got the economy rolling. The President relied on fiscal policy primarily, although the supply of money was also increased, and in his third year he subscribed to the "new" economics to sustain economic growth. Kennedy asked for a tax cut despite an expected budget deficit and was preparing a poverty program to cut into high structural unemployment and deep multigenerational poverty. Harris reminds us also that two important factors in the prolonged economic boom of the 1960's were the immense increased defense spending and the initiation of the twenty billion dollar moon space program.

A parallel shift can be seen in Kennedy's relations with Congress. Yet many writers criticize Kennedy for giving only limited attention to congressional problems and for not matching his words with deeds. Carroll Kilpatrick, James Reston, and Douglass Cater, for example, assert that Kennedy ought to have accomplished more with Congress. ". . . The most far-reaching achievement of the 87th Congress" was Kennedy's Trade Expansion Act, says Kilpatrick. His other notable successes appear side by side with notable failures. "The President's power struggle with Congress was almost equal to that of his struggle with the Communist leaders abroad." Kennedy had "top-heavy majorities" in his first Congress, continues Kilpatrick, yet he lost major bills and compromised in nearly every instance to get acts passed. Kennedy's use of public opinion to spur Congress was disappointing; the President relied heavily on press conferences but was often "content to state a conclusion rather than to use the occasion to mobilize support with strong argument"; and he tried to make the 1962 elections a "popularity contest."

James Reston writes that on the whole Kennedy did not work

"very successfully with the Congress." ". . . He didn't really know the deck on Capitol Hill. . . ." ". . . Blarneying with pompous Congressmen bored him and he simply would not take time to do it. . . ." "He had little patience for the . . . endless details of legislation." And he had "an excessive respect for the chairmen of the committees and other elders of the Congress." ". . . His domestic program was in deep trouble when he was killed and some of us despaired that Capitol Hill would ever be his field of triumph." Douglass Cater contrasts Kennedy's "courageous expectations with cautious operations." The President quietly supported the enlargement of the House Rules Committee but "enlargement was a timid . . . way of trying to tame that recalcitrant group. . . ." Kennedy lost important bills by only a few votes; and "in a number of major battles Kennedy appeared to make a display more for the record than for anticipated results."

Arthur Schlesinger and Seymour Harris declare (and Theodore Sorensen would agree) that Kennedy's relations with Congress were all that could be expected. The arithmetic of Congress was against the President and a powerful conservative coalition thwarted his aims. Strategically, the President was preparing the way in 1961 and 1962 for bills to be passed in 1964 and 1965. Tactically, he "could not afford to alienate Congressmen gratuitously if he wanted to save his less controversial bills," observes Schlesinger. ". . . The things he did get even before the 1962 election constituted a legislative record unmatched in some respects since the days of Roosevelt."[2] It is to be regretted that nowhere is there a comprehensive analysis by a Kennedy advocate of that record. In his memoir Schlesinger devotes only a few pages to Kennedy's legislative accomplishments, while Sorensen's account is episodic.[3]

In the area of civil rights Kennedy's knowledgeable, prudent bent, which made him rely on executive action, is noticeable for most of his incumbency. From the beginning he gave the Justice Department's civil rights division his full support and, with this leadership translated through his brother, Attorney General Robert F. Kennedy, the division was invigorated and enlarged in order to guarantee Negro rights. The record, as set forth by Alexander M.

Bickel and Louis Koenig, shows the President's pertinacity in implementing laws already on the books and in encouraging Negro involvement in all aspects of American life.

The limitations are also recounted. ". . . A number of new Kennedy appointees, especially among the district judges, were totally out of sympathy with the Supreme Court cases on equal protection . . . ," says Bickel. The record also shows that not until November 1962 did the President forbid racial discrimination in the sale or rental of housing financed through federal aid. And Kennedy did not propose any civil rights legislation until the summer of 1963. Then he acted only after violence, bloodshed, and mayhem exploded in Southern streets. His rights proposals, moreover, were not given top priority on the Presidential agenda, for Kennedy went off to Europe during the troubled days and, on his return, affirmed that the bill would have to share congressional attention with the tax cut.

III

In the complicated field of foreign policy President Kennedy grasped new ideas and was determined to succeed. While he was putting those ideas into practice and exercising control over his domain, he became entangled in the Cuban invasion—an operation not of his own making, though of his own choosing—and sustained a bitter defeat. His ability to assess critically his errors and needs served him well, however, for the Cuban adventure demonstrated to him the limits of American power. Moreover, it revealed the inadequacies of "expert" advice and the faults of bureaucratic decision-making. Thereafter, Kennedy insisted on detailed and fuller information, better used his extremely able appointees to sift and analyze data, and relied more on his own judgment.

Kennedy hoped that his foreign policy would relax cold-war tensions. He discarded John Foster Dulles' militant rhetoric and worked in a variety of ways to better relations with America's adversaries. The President recognized the forces of diversity and neutralism in the world and acted on the assumption that nationalism was a stronger power than Communism in shaping the destinies of underdeveloped countries. In Southeast Asia he labored to neutralize Laos, and he helped to finance U.N. military action in the Congo. On his own he expanded the Food for Peace program and organized the Peace Corps. In Latin America he created the Alliance for Progress. He constantly searched, not always successfully, for solutions to European problems. William Leuchtenburg and McGeorge Bundy especially underscore all these endeavors of Kennedy to rethink and to restructure American diplomacy.

As in economic policies and congressional relations, Kennedy's diplomacy falls into two periods. The cautious, experimental President most often relied on the resources of money and legislation already available to him. But by 1963 he cut new paths. William Carleton clearly defines the Kennedy diplomatic shift. "In foreign policy, the first two years of Kennedy were ambiguous," he comments. The President "was confronted with a new fluidity, a necessity and an opportunity for a reappraisal." "Nevertheless, . . . Kennedy seems needlessly to have fanned the tensions of the dying cold war."[4] His Inaugural Address and first State of the Union Message were alarmist; he approved the Cuban invasion; he overreacted to Khrushchev's familiar Berlin ultimatum; he misread the intent of the Common Market forces toward Great Britain. Only after Kennedy's nuclear confrontation with the Soviets in late 1962 did the President grasp the opportunities for a detente and publicly ask for a reappraisal and a redefinition of American diplomacy. Kennedy's American University speech in the summer of 1963 marked his change and, in the new circumstances, he secured the Test Ban Treaty.

It is James Reston's view that Kennedy was better on the big questions than on the small, but Reston's commentary fits into the familiar pattern of the Kennedy shift. The big problems the President disposed of so skillfully often broke near or in his third year, while lesser problems rose in his early months. Thus Kennedy's recognition of the stakes involved in the missile build-up in Cuba and his successful handling of that crisis is a triumph. A year and a half before, he had "trifled" with the Cuban crisis and bungled badly at the Bay of Pigs. On another, lesser question, the President "temporized with the Vietnamese crisis . . . never really defining his aims or reconciling his power with his objectives." Reston's "major theme" that Kennedy "was always at his best in the highest moment of crisis" does not prevent him from charging that from the fumbling over the small question of Cuba in 1961 came the missile threat of the Soviets in 1962. And it is perhaps not inappropriate to observe today that from another small question of Kennedy diplomacy—Vietnam—has emerged the greatest trial of Lyndon B. Johnson's Administration.

For Douglass Cater ambiguities abound in Kennedy's foreign policy. The Kennedy promises and performances did not jibe. "Foreign aid was to be rescued from its former stereotype as simply a way of supporting the defense effort. . . ." But "the progress of the new AID agency was frustrated. . . ." The President emphasized the "threat to Southeast Asia of a Communist takeover of Laos. . . ." Yet the Laos accord promised at best that "if the Communists kept their word the country would remain neutral." Kennedy "voiced repeated determination not to yield Allied rights" in Berlin, but "did not make a passionate protest when the Soviets erected a wall." Kennedy was cautious during the first Cuban episode and only picked up the Soviet challenge in 1962.

Writers disagree in their appraisals of Kennedy's foreign policy, but they are almost unanimous, for a variety of reasons, in their admiration of the President's handling of the Cuban missile crisis. For example, Reston and others believe that Kennedy's victory over the Soviets in October 1962 shifted the direction of the cold war. The crisis "produced the events on which Kennedy's place in history probably depends," Reston estimates. One such event was the taking of the "first really serious steps to bring atomic weapons under control." Richard Neustadt declares that the missile encounter was "the cardinal test of Kennedy as an executive in his own right and also as a student of executives abroad. . . ." Carleton sees the affair as the "high point, the turning point, in the Kennedy Administration." These and other writers look upon Kennedy's operational control of events, his understanding of Soviet psychology, and his plans for measured, increased response to Soviet moves as triumphs of statesmanship.

Even those writers who criticize some aspects of Kennedy's handling of the missile crisis stress the dynamism of his leadership. William Carleton asks whether the confrontation could have been avoided. James Reston speculates that Kennedy's youth and Bay of Pigs failure brought on the Soviet challenge. David Horowitz, a representative of New Left thought, goes beyond these assertions and finds that a pattern of provocation in Kennedy's defense and foreign policy led to the missile showdown.[5] "The mysteries attending the discovery of the build-up, the unusual nature of the crisis diplomacy, and the lack of any immediate overwhelming, military threat, all point to the existence of an important dynamic element in the planning of US policy," Horowitz charges. ". . . Having built up a sizeable missile superiority of its own, and having laid the plans for a rapid increase in this superiority in the next few years, the Kennedy Administration had waited for an opportune moment to demonstrate its nuclear superiority to the world, and with the prestige thus gained, tip the scales of the world power balance. The test was expected to come in Berlin, when Cuba presented itself." ". . . The Russians . . . [were to] be caught red-handed, faced with a predetermined show of strength and compelled to retreat."

Kennedy survived a diplomatic apprenticeship of unremitting pressure, and in his last year led his country imaginatively and boldly. His call for an end to the cold war in June 1963 was a highly intelligent response to the nuclear confrontation of the year before. His negotiation of the Test Ban Treaty in August was one of his greatest achievements. In global history the treaty may well be considered more important than the nuclear episode that prepared the way, or the contemplation of errors or personal traits that precipitated the crisis.

IV

It is not an easy task to appraise the Presidency of John F. Kennedy. The assignment is fraught with difficulties and the compass of reason is not always a steady guide. The briefest review of authors' judgments indicates how widely writers can differ. William Carleton believes than Kennedy will be known more for "intangibles . . . than for achievements in statesmanship." Douglass Cater is not much impressed with the Kennedy record because the President was too cautious and usually acted in response to challenge. Richard Neustadt declares that Kennedy will be remembered for his irreversible commitments in the nuclear field, on Negro rights, and on the economy. James Reston states that the President's two great accomplishments are the defusing of the cold war and the acceptance of the "new" economics. Richard Rovere asserts that Kennedy will be remembered for his beginnings, his style, and his appointees. Theodore Sorensen claims for Kennedy all these things and more.

America got moving again under President Kennedy but, significantly, Kennedy's great departures and accomplishments came in his third year. All the splendid qualities of mind and temper that characterized Kennedy as President came to the fore most vividly at the end. The critical, liberating spirit, which he used to create a climate for change, finally found release in significant bills and diplomatic shifts. His progressive program was deadlocked in Congress, but he looked to the future, and re-election, to carry out his mandate.

For those who lived through John F. Kennedy's years, he will remain a memorable figure. In an age of visual mass communication, it could hardly be otherwise, given the President's youth, good looks, and eloquence. The Kennedy record, on the other hand, is one of limited achievement, intangibles, and imponderables. How historians judge Kennedy will depend on whether they are interested in ideas, style, and image, or in action, grand legislative accomplishments, and reality. And historians' opinions will be shaped by their perspective. Will these arbiters of history look backward to the doldrums of the Eisenhower years or forward to the dramatic achievements of the Johnson era? For at least one historian, John F. Kennedy died with promises unfulfilled, on the outskirts of greatness, and that is one of the tragedies of our time.

Aïda DiPace Donald

Baltimore
July 1966

[1] Arthur M. Schlesinger, Jr., *A Thousand Days,* Boston: Houghton Mifflin Company, 1965, p. 675.

[2] *Ibid.,* pp. 712–13.

[3] *Ibid.,* pp. 707–13. See also Theodore C. Sorensen, *Kennedy,* New York: Harper & Row, Publishers, 1965, pp. 339–57, and the combined Kennedy and Johnson records in Appendix A.

[4] Carleton adds parenthetically: "It may be that 'needlessly' is too strong a word; perhaps Kennedy thought he needed to arouse the country to obtain a more balanced military program, more foreign economic aid, the Alliance for Progress; perhaps he thought, too, that a truculent tone was necessary to convince Khrushchev that America would stand firm under duress for its rights in Berlin."

Similarly, see Ernest R. May, "The Kennedy Presidency," *Frontier* (January 1964), pp. 16–18, for the view that Kennedy was an "opportunist" in seizing on "those moments when events had jarred the Congress's balance and made the most of them. Thus he exploited the Bay of Pigs fiasco to get money for an ambitious start on the Alliance for Progress. He made use of Yuri Gagarin's earth orbit to launch a man on the moon program that, apart from anything else, promised to pump forty billion dollars into the lagging economy. By dramatizing the Berlin crisis of 1961, he was able to reverse Eisenhower's New Look and restore some flexibility to American defense policy. By getting Congress into a state of alarm about payments balances and gold outflow, he engineered the Trade Expansion Act. And there was hope that in similar fashion he would extract from Capitol Hill a tax bill and new civil rights legislation. He showed promise of being as masterful an opportunist as Lincoln or Wilson."

[5] See also Leslie Dewart, "The Cuban Crisis Revisited," *Studies on the Left* (Spring 1965), pp. 15–40, and his footnote references; and Henry M. Pachter, *Collision Course: The Cuban Missile Crisis and Coexistence,* New York and London: Frederick A. Praeger, 1963, especially pp. 83–93.

Part I

—

JOHN F. KENNEDY

ARTHUR M. SCHLESINGER, JR.

Kennedy on the Eve

THE KENNEDY MIND: I

Kennedy was called an intellectual very seldom before 1960 and very often thereafter—a phenomenon which deserves explanation.

One cannot be sure what an intellectual is; but let us define it as a person whose primary habitat is the realm of ideas. In this sense, exceedingly few political leaders are authentic intellectuals, because the primary habitat of the political leader is the world of power. Yet the world of power itself has its intellectual and anti-intellectual sides. Some political leaders find exhilaration in ideas and in the company of those whose trade it is to deal with them. Others are rendered uneasy by ideas and uncomfortable by intellectuals.

Kennedy belonged supremely to the first class. He was a man of action who could pass easily over to the realm of ideas and confront intellectuals with perfect confidence in his capacity to hold his own. His mind was not prophetic, impassioned, mystical, ontological, utopian or ideological. It was less exuberant than Theodore Roosevelt's, less scholarly than Wilson's, less adventurous than Franklin Roosevelt's. But it had its own salient qualities—it was objective, practical, ironic, skeptical, unfettered and insatiable.

It was marked first of all, as he had noted to Jacqueline, by inexhaustible curiosity. Kennedy always wanted to know how things worked. Vague answers never contented him. This curiosity was fed by conversation but even more by reading. His childhood consolation had become an adult compulsion. He was now a fanatical reader, twelve hundred words a minute, not only at the normal times and places but at meals, in the bathtub, sometimes even when walking. Dressing in the morning, he would prop open a book on his bureau and read while he put on his shirt and tied his necktie. He read mostly history and biography, American and English. The first book he ever gave Jacqueline was the life of a Texan, Marquis James's biography of Sam Houston, *The Raven*. In addition to *Pilgrim's Way*, *Marlborough* and *Melbourne*, he particularly liked Herbert Agar's *The Price of Union*, Samuel Flagg Bemis's *John Quincy Adams*, Allan Nevins's *The Emergence of Lincoln*, Margaret Coit's *Calhoun* and Duff Cooper's *Talleyrand*. He read poetry only occasionally—Shakespeare and Byron are quoted in the looseleaf notebook he kept in 1945–46—and by this time fiction hardly at all. His wife does not remember him reading novels except for two or three Ian Fleming thrillers, though Kennedy himself listed *The Red and the Black* among his favorite books and, at some point in his life, had read most of Hemingway and a smattering of contemporary fiction—at least *The Deer Park*, *The Fires of Spring* and *The Ninth Wave*. His supposed addiction to James Bond was partly a publicity gag, like Franklin Roosevelt's supposed affection for "Home on the Range." Kennedy seldom read for distraction. He did not want to waste a single second.

He read partly for information, partly for comparison, partly for insight, partly for the sheer joy of felicitous statement. He delighted particularly in quotations which distilled the essence of an argument. He is, so far as I know, the only politician who ever quoted Madame de Staël on Meet the Press. Some quotations he carried verbatim in his mind. Others he noted down. The looseleaf notebook of 1945–46 contained propositions from Aeschylus ("In war, truth is the first casualty"), Isocrates ("Where there are a number of laws drawn up with great exactitude, it is a proof that the city is badly administered; for the inhabitants are compelled to frame laws in great numbers as a barrier against offenses"), Dante ("The hottest places in Hell are reserved for those who, in a period of moral crisis, maintain their neutrality"), Falkland ("When it is not necessary to change it is necessary not to change"), Burke ("Our patience will achieve more than our force"), Jefferson ("Widespread poverty and concentrated wealth cannot long endure side by side in a democracy"), de Maistre ("In all political systems there are relationships which it is wiser to leave undefined"), Jackson ("Individuals must give up a share of liberty to preserve the rest"), Webster ("A general equality of condition is the true basis, most certainly, of democracy"), Mill ("One person with a belief is a social power equal to ninety-nine who have only interest"), Lincoln ("Public opinion is everything. With it nothing can fail, without it nothing can succeed"), Huck Finn on *Pilgrim's Progress* ("The statements are interesting—but steep"), Chesterton ("Don't ever take a fence down until you know the reason why it was put up"), Brandeis ("Unless our financial leaders are capable of progress, the institutions which they are trying to conserve will lose their foundation"), Colonel House ("The best politics is to do the right thing"), Churchill ("The whole history of the world is summed up in the fact that, when nations are strong, they are not always just, and when they wish to be just, they are often no longer strong. . . . Let us have this blessed union of power and justice"), Lippmann ("The political art deals with matters peculiar to politics, with a complex of material circumstances, of historic deposit, of human passion, for which the problems of business or engineering do not provide an analogy"), Hindu proverbs ("I had no shoes—and I murmured until I met a man who had no feet"), Joseph P. Kennedy ("More men die of jealousy than cancer") and even John F. Kennedy:

To be a positive force for the public good in politics one must have three things; a solid moral code governing his public actions, a broad knowledge of our institutions and traditions and a specific background in the technical problems of government, and lastly he must have political appeal—the gift of winning public confidence and support.

There emerges from such quotations the impression of a moderate and dispassionate mind, committed to the arts of government, persuaded of the inevitability of change but distrustful of comprehensive plans and grandiose abstractions, skeptical of excess but admiring of purpose, determined above all to be effective.

His intelligence was fundamentally secular, or so it seemed to me. Of course, this was not entirely true. As Mary McCarthy wrote in her *Memories of a Catholic Girlhood,* "If you are born and brought up a Catholic, you have absorbed a great deal of world history and the history of ideas before you are twelve, and it is like learning a language early; the effect is indelible." Though Kennedy spent only one year of his life in a Catholic school, he assimilated a good deal of the structure of the faith, encouraged probably by his mother and sisters. He often adopted the Catholic side in historical controversy, as in the case of Mary Queen of Scots; and he showed a certain weakness for Catholic words of art, like "prudence," and a certain aversion toward bad words for Catholics, like "liberal." Nor could one doubt his devotion to his Church or the occasional solace he found in mass.

Yet he remains, as John Cogley has suggested, the first President who was a Roman Catholic rather than the first Roman Catholic President. Intellectual Catholicism in American politics has ordinarily taken two divergent forms, of which Senator Thomas J. Dodd of Connecticut and Senator Eugene McCarthy of Minnesota were contemporary representatives. Kennedy was different from either. Unlike Dodd, he lived far away from the world of the Holy Name Societies, Knights of Columbus and communion breakfasts. He discussed the princes of the American Church with the same irreverent candor with which he discussed the bosses of the Democratic party. When a dispatch from Rome during the 1960 campaign suggested Vatican doubts about his views of the proper relationship between church and state, Kennedy said, "Now I understand why Henry VIII set up his own church." His attitude toward life showed no traces of the black-and-white moralism, the pietistic rhetoric, the clericalism, the anti-intellectualism, the prudery, the fear of Protestant society, which had historically characterized parts of the Irish Catholic community in America. On the other hand, he did not, like Eugene McCarthy, seek to rescue Catholic doctrine from fundamentalism and demonstrate its relevance to the modern world. Catholic intellectuals recognized his indifference to the scholastic tradition, and some disdained him for it.

Kennedy's religion was humane rather than doctrinal. He was a Catholic as Franklin Roosevelt was an Episcopalian—because he was born into the faith, lived in it and expected to die in it. One evening at the White House he argued with considerable particularity that nine of the ten commandments were derived from nature and almost seemed to imply that all religion was so derived. He had little knowledge of or interest in the Catholic dogmatic tradition. He once wrote Cogley, "It is hard for a Harvard man to answer questions in theology. I imagine my answers will cause heartburn at Fordham and B. C. [Boston College]." One can find little organic intellectual connection between his faith and his politics. His social thought hardly resulted from a determination to apply the principles of *Rerum Novarum* to American life. He felt an immense sense of fellowship with Pope John XXIII, but this was based more on the Pope's practical character and policies than on theological considerations. Some of his Protestant advisers probably knew the encyclicals better than he did. Once during the 1960 campaign I handed him a speech draft with the comment that it was perhaps too Catholic. He said with a smile, "You Unitarians"—meaning Sorensen and myself—"keep writing Catholic speeches. I guess I am the only Protestant around here."

Still, his basic attitude was wholly compatible with the sophisticated theology of Jesuits like Father John Courtney Murray, whom he greatly admired. In the notebook he kept during his sickness, he wrote down some lines from Barbara Ward: "What disturbs the Communist rulers is not the phraseology of religion, the lip-service that may be paid to it, or the speeches and declarations made in its favor. . . . Religion which is a mere adjunct of individual purpose is a religion that even the Soviets can tolerate. What they fear is a religion that transcends frontiers and can challenge the purpose and performance of the nation-state." This was not in the midfifties the typical attitude of American Catholics; but, if Kennedy was not a typical American Catholic, his example helped create the progressive and questing American Catholicism of the sixties.

Above all, he showed that there need be no conflict between Catholicism and modernity, no bar to full Catholic participation in American society.

His detachment from traditional American Catholicism was part of the set of detachments—detachment from middle-class parochialism, detachment from the business ethos, detachment from ritualistic liberalism—which gave his perceptions their peculiar coolness, freshness and freedom, and which also led those expecting commitments of a more familiar sort to condemn him as uncommitted. In fact, he was intensely committed to a vision of America and the world, and committed with equal intensity to the use of reason and power to achieve that vision. This became apparent after he was President; and this accounts in part for the sudden realization that, far from being just a young man in a hurry, a hustler for personal authority, a Processed Politician, he was, as politicians go, an intellectual and one so peculiarly modern that it took orthodox intellectuals a little time before they began to understand him.

Another reason for the change in the intellectuals' theory of Kennedy was their gradual recognition of his desire to bring the world of power and the world of ideas together in alliance—or rather, as he himself saw it, to restore the collaboration between the two worlds which had marked the early republic. He was fascinated by the Founding Fathers and liked to harass historians by demanding that they explain how a small and underdeveloped nation could have produced men of such genius. He was particularly fascinated by the way the generation of the Founders united the instinct for ideas and the instinct for responsibility. "Our nation's first great politicians," he wrote, "—those who presided at its birth in 1776 and at its christening in 1787—included among their ranks most of the nation's first great writers and scholars." But today

the gap between the intellectual and politician seems to be growing. . . . today this link is all but gone. Where are the scholar-statesmen? The American politician of today is fearful, if not scornful, of entering the literary world with the courage of a Beveridge. And the American author and scholar of today is reluctant, if not disdainful, about entering the political world with the enthusiasm of a Woodrow Wilson.

His summons to the scholar-statesman went largely unnoticed by the intellectual community in the fifties, perhaps because he chose such improbable forums as *Vogue* and a Harvard Commencement. Only when he began as President to put his proposition into practice did the intellectual community take a fresh look at him.

THE KENNEDY MIND: II

The character of his reading and quoting emphasizes, I think, the historical grain of his intelligence. Kennedy was in many respects an historian manqué. The historical mind can be analytical, or it can be romantic. The best historians are both, Kennedy among them. *Why England Slept,* with its emphasis on impersonal forces, expressed one side; *Profiles in Courage,* with its emphasis on heroes, expressed the other. But, even in his most romantic mood, Kennedy never adopted a good-guys vs. bad-guys theory of history. He may have been a Whig,[1] but he was not a Whig historian. He had both the imagination and the objectivity which enabled him to see the point in lost causes, even in enemy fanaticisms. In a review of Liddell Hart's *Deterrent or Defense* in 1960, he praised the author's credo: "Keep strong, if possible. In any case, keep cool. Have unlimited patience. Never corner an opponent, and always assist him to save his face. Put yourself in his shoes—so as to see things through his eyes. Avoid self-righteousness like the devil—nothing is so self-blinding." Liddell Hart was addressing these remarks to statesmen; they work just as well for historians.

Kennedy rarely lost sight of other people's motives and problems. For all the presumed coolness on the surface, he had an instinctive tendency to put himself into the skins of others. Once during the 1960 campaign, Kennedy, returning to New York City on a Sunday night from a visit with Mrs. Roosevelt in Hyde Park, dropped in at Voisin's for dinner with a couple of friends. At a neighboring table, a man obviously drunk, began in a low but penetrating voice to direct a stream of unprintable comment at him. Kennedy's companions raised their own voices in the hope

[1] In the English sense, that is; in the American sense of believing in a strong Congress and a weak executive, he often emphasized to James MacGregor Burns and others, "I am no Whig!"

that he would not hear, but to no avail. Finally one made a motion
to call the headwaiter. Kennedy laid a hand on his sleeve and said,
"No, don't bother. Think how the fellow's wife must be feeling."
His friend looked and saw her flushed with embarrassment. He
later reacted with comparable dispassion to de Gaulle and Khrushchev.

He liked to quote Lincoln: "There are few things wholly evil or
wholly good. Almost everything, especially of Government policy,
is an inseparable compound of the two, so that our best judgment
of the preponderance between them is continually demanded."
When something had enough steam behind it to move people and
make an impression on history, it must have some rational explanation, and Kennedy wanted to know what that rational explanation was. The response of the fifties that it was all a struggle
between good and evil never satisfied him.

But it was not a case of *tout comprendre, tout pardonner*.
Though he saw the human struggle, not as a moralist, but as an
historian, even as an ironist, irony was never permitted to sever the
nerve of action. His mind was forever critical; but his thinking
always retained the cutting edge of decision. When he was told
something, he wanted to know what he could do about it. He was
pragmatic in the sense that he tested the meaning of a proposition
by its consequences; he was also pragmatic in the sense of being
free from metaphysics. In his response, too, to the notion of a
pluralist universe, Kennedy was a pragmatist—if one may make
sensible use of this word, which came into political vogue in the
first years of the Kennedy Administration and then was oddly
revived in the first years of the Johnson Administration with the
implication that the Kennedy years had not, after all, been pragmatic but were somehow ideological. They were not ideological,
though they could perhaps be termed intellectual.

The historical mind is rarely ideological—and, when it becomes
so, it is at the expense of history. Whether analytical or romantic,
it is committed to existence, not to essence. Kennedy was bored by
abstractions. He never took ideology very seriously, certainly not
as a means of interpreting history and even not as part of the
material of history. If he did not go the distance with de Gaulle in
reducing everything to national tradition and national interest, he
tended to give greater weight in thinking about world affairs to

national than to ideological motives. Like de Gaulle, but unlike the ideological interpreters of the cold war, he was not surprised by the split between Russia and China.

If historic conflicts infrequently pitted total good against total evil, then they infrequently concluded in total victory or total defeat. Seeing the past with an historian's eyes, Kennedy knew that ideals and institutions were stubborn, and that change took place more often by accommodation than by annihilation. His cult of courage was in this sense ethical rather than political; he saw the courage of "unyielding devotion to absolute principle" as the moral fulfillment of the individual rather than as necessarily the best way of running a government. Indeed, he took pains to emphasize in *Profiles* that politicians could also demonstrate courage "through their acceptance of compromise, through their advocacy of conciliation, through their willingness to replace conflict with cooperation." Senators who go down to defeat in vain defense of a single principle "will not be on hand to fight for that or any other principle in the future." One felt here an echo of St. Thomas: "Prudence applies principles to particular issues; consequently it does not establish moral purpose, but contrives the means thereto."

The application of principle requires both moral and intellectual insight. Kennedy had an unusual capacity to weigh the complexities of judgment—in part because of the complexities of his own perceptions. The contrast in *Profiles* between the courage of compromise and the courage of principle expressed, for example, a tension deep within Kennedy—a tension between the circumspection of his political instinct and the radicalism of his intellectual impulse; so too the contrast between the historical determinism, the deprecation of the individual and the passive view of leadership implied in *Why England Slept* and the demand in *Profiles* that the politician be prepared, on the great occasions, to "meet the challenge of courage, whatever may be the sacrifices he faces if he follows his conscience." All this expressed the interior strain between Kennedy's sense of human limitation and his sense of hope, between his skepticism about man and his readiness to say, "Man can be as big as he wants. No problem of human destiny is beyond human beings."

All these things, coexisting within him, enabled others to find in him what qualities they wanted. They could choose one side of him or the other and claim him, according to taste, as a conservative, because of his sober sense of the frailty of man, the power of institutions and the frustrations of history, or as a progressive, because of his vigorous confidence in reason, action and the future. Yet within Kennedy himself these tensions achieved reunion and reconciliation. He saw history in its massive movements as shaped by forces beyond man's control. But he felt that there were still problems which man could resolve; and in any case, whether man could resolve these problems or not, the obligation was to carry on the struggle of existence. It was in essence, Richard Goodwin later suggested, the Greek view where the hero must poise himself against the gods and, even with knowledge of the futility of the fight, press on to the end of his life until he meets his tragic fate.

THE CONTEMPORARY MAN

After Kennedy's death, Adlai Stevenson called him the "contemporary man." His youth, his vitality, his profound modernity—these were final elements in his power and potentiality as he stood on the brink of the Presidency. For Kennedy was not only the first President to be born in the twentieth century. More than that, he was the first representative in the White House of a distinctive generation, the generation which was born during the First World War, came of age during the Depression, fought in the Second World War and began its public career in the atomic age.

This was the first generation to grow up as the age of American innocence was coming to an end. To have been born nearly a decade earlier, like Lyndon Johnson, or nearly two decades earlier, like Adlai Stevenson, was to be rooted in another and simpler America. Scott Fitzgerald had written that his contemporaries grew up "to find all Gods dead, all wars fought, all faiths in man shaken." But the generation which came back from the Second World War found that gods, wars and faiths in man had, after all, survived, if in queer and somber ways. The realities of the twentieth century which had shocked their fathers now wove the fabric of their own lives. Instead of reveling in being a lost generation, they set out in one mood or another to find, if not themselves, a still point in the turning world. The predicament was even worse for the generation which had been too young to fight the war, too young to recall the age of innocence, the generation which had experienced nothing but turbulence. So in the fifties some sought security at the expense of identity and became organization men. Others sought identity at the expense of security and became beatniks. Each course created only a partial man. There was need for a way of life, a way of autonomy, between past and present, the organization man and the anarchist, the square and the beat.

It was autonomy which this humane and self-sufficient man seemed to embody. Kennedy simply could not be reduced to the usual complex of sociological generalizations. He was Irish, Catholic, New England, Harvard, Navy, Palm Beach, Democrat and so on; but no classification contained him. He had wrought an individuality which carried him beyond the definitions of class and race, region and religion. He was a free man, not just in the sense of the cold-war cliché, but in the sense that he was, as much as man can be, self-determined and not the servant of forces outside him.

This sense of wholeness and freedom gave him an extraordinary appeal not only to his own generation but even more to those who came after, the children of turbulence. Recent history had washed away the easy consolations and the old formulas. Only a few things remained on which contemporary man could rely, and most were part of himself—family, friendship, courage, reason, jokes, power, patriotism. Kennedy demonstrated the possibility of the new self-reliance. As he had liberated himself from the past, so he had liberated himself from the need to rebel against the past. He could insist on standards, admire physical courage, attend his church, love his father while disagreeing with him, love his country without self-doubt or self-consciousness. Yet, while absorbing so much of the traditional code, his sensibility was acutely contemporaneous. He voiced the disquietude of the postwar generation— the mistrust of rhetoric, the disdain for pomposity, the impatience with the postures and pieties of other days, the resignation to disappointment. And he also voiced the new generation's longings—for fulfillment in experience, for the subordination of selfish impulses to higher ideals, for a link between past and future, for adventure and valor and honor. What was forbidden were poses, histrionics, the heart on the sleeve and the tongue on the cliché. What was required was a tough, nonchalant acceptance of the harsh present and an open mind toward the unknown future.

This was Kennedy, with his deflationary wartime understatement (when asked how he became a hero, he said, "It was involuntary. They sank my boat"); his contempt for demagoguery (once during the campaign, after Kennedy had disappointed a Texas crowd by his New England restraint, Bill Attwood suggested that next time he wave his arms in the air like other politicians; Kennedy shook his head and wrote—he was saving his voice—"I always swore one thing I'd never do is——" and drew a picture of a man waving his arms in the air); his freedom from dogma, his appetite for responsibility, his instinct for novelty, his awareness and irony and control; his imperturbable sureness in his own powers, not because he considered himself infallible, but because, given the fallibility of all men, he supposed he could do the job as well as anyone else; his love of America and pride in its traditions and ideals.

Of course there was an element of legerdemain in all this. Every politician has to fake a little, and Kennedy was a politician determined to become President. He was prepared to do many things, to cut corners, to exploit people and situations, to "go go go," even to merchandise himself. But many things he would not do, phrases he would not use, people he would not exploit (never a "Jackie and I"). Even his faking had to stay within character. This sense of a personality under control, this insistence on distancing himself from displays of emotion, led some to think him indifferent or unfeeling. But only the unwary could really suppose that his "coolness" was because he felt too little. It was because he felt too much and had to compose himself for an existence filled with disorder and despair. During his Presidency, when asked about the demobilization of the reserves after the Berlin crisis, he said, "There is always an inequity in life. Some men are killed in a war and some men are wounded, and some men never leave the country. . . . Life is unfair." He said this, not with bitterness, but with the delicate knowledge of one who lives in a bitter time—a knowledge which stamped him as a son of that time. His charm and grace were not an uncovenanted gift. The Kennedy style was the triumph, hard-bought and well-earned, of a gallant and collected human being over the anguish of life.

His "coolness" was itself a new frontier. It meant freedom from the stereotyped responses of the past. It promised the deliverance of American idealism, buried deep in the national character but imprisoned by the knowingness and calculation of American society in the fifties. It held out to the young the possibility that they could become more than satisfied stockholders in a satisfied nation. It offered hope for spontaneity in a country drowning in its own passivity—passive because it had come to accept the theory of its own impotence. This was what Norman Mailer caught at Los Angeles in 1960—Kennedy's existential quality, the sense that he was in some way beyond conventional politics, that he could touch emotions and hopes thwarted by the bland and mechanized society. Unlike the other candidates, Mailer wrote that Kennedy was "mysterious." He had "the wisdom of a man who senses death within him and gambles that he can cure it by risking his life." Even his youth, his handsomeness, the beauty of his wife—these were not accidental details but necessary means of inciting the American imagination. With Kennedy, Mailer thought, there was a chance that "we as a nation would finally be loose again in the historic seas of a national psyche which was willy-nilly and at last, again, adventurous." The only question was whether the nation would be "brave enough to enlist the romantic dream of itself . . . vote for the image of the mirror of its unconscious." This was the question, I believe, which frightened the nation when it began to fall away from Kennedy in the last days before the election.

Mailer soon repudiated his portrait when, as he later complained at interminable length, Kennedy personally let him down by declining to become the hipster as President. Yet there can be no doubt that Kennedy's magic was not alone that of wealth and youth and good looks, or even of these things joined to intelligence and will. It was, more than this, the hope that he could redeem American politics by releasing American life from its various bondages to orthodoxy.

No man could have fulfilled this hope, and Kennedy certainly did not. He himself regarded the Mailer essay with skeptical appreciation.[2] He knew that as a President of the United States he had no choice but to work within the structure of government and politics—though he did not yet know how beautifully that structure was organized to prevent anything from happening. What Mailer left out was the paradox of power—that the exercise of power is necessary to fulfill purpose, yet the world of power dooms many purposes to frustration. Nonetheless the Mailer rhapsody conveys something of the exhilaration which accompanied the start of the Kennedy Presidency. The Presidency itself would show how national vitality could in fact be released—not in an existential orgasm but in the halting progression of ideas and actions which make up the fabric of history.

[2] Richard Goodwin showed him Mailer's piece after it appeared in *Esquire*. Later he asked what Kennedy thought of it. Kennedy replied enigmatically, "It really runs on, doesn't it?"

LOUIS KOENIG

Administrative Chief

President Kennedy's administrative method lay between the polarities of Eisenhower and Franklin Roosevelt, and veered decidedly toward Roosevelt. Like Franklin Roosevelt, Kennedy aimed to carve out a maximum personal role in the conduct of the Presidency, but without some of the more jagged methods and much of the dinful turmoil of the Rooseveltian model. Kennedy clearly visualized his Presidential role when he declared in his 1960 campaign that as President he would want to be "in the thick of things." Kennedy the President was true to the promise of Kennedy the candidate. He put in abundant hours at desk-side conferences and on the telephone, pursuing details well down the line of departmental hierarchy, and took a constant hand in coordination, its weight laid not merely upon top-level endeavor but upon minor affairs as well.

Kennedy's intensive involvement was more than an applied philosophy of the Presidency. It was a reflection of his personality, aptitude, and body chemistry. Kennedy personally comprised a bundle of restless curiosity, a high quotient of vigor, and an extraordinary spongelike capacity to absorb the daily torrent of government data.

To carry forward his administrative view of the Presidency, Kennedy relied upon several operating principles and expedients.

This selection is from Louis Koenig, *The Chief Executive*, pp. 174–181. © 1964 by Harcourt, Brace & World, Inc., and reprinted with their permission.

Unlike Eisenhower, who stressed institutional structure, Kennedy placed great store in personal relationships. The person—his talent, perception, and reliability—counted more than his organization. Kennedy's person-centered approach reflected his pre-Presidential career, passed chiefly in legislative politics and in political campaigning, in both of which working relationships are highly personal. Accordingly, in dealing with department secretaries and White House staff members Kennedy insisted upon direct relationships, unhampered by organization and hierarchy. He, for his part, remained highly accessible to a large circle of colleagues. "You've got one of the most accessible Presidents in history," one cabinet secretary said. "I must talk with him in person or on the phone twenty times a week," said another secretary. "I don't hesitate to call him if something important comes up—even at night or on Sunday." "I can pick up the telephone and call him at any time," said still another. "I'll call up the White House and say, 'I want ten minutes tomorrow or the next day.' "

Kennedy, dealing with the departments, did not stop with the department head but reached down the hierarchy to lesser levels. A loud, clear hint of this practice was sounded in the preinaugural period in the manner of the President-elect's selection of his foreign policy aides. He designated an Assistant Secretary and an Undersecretary of State and the Ambassador to the United Nations before selecting his Secretary of State. To underscore the principle implied in the sequence of these appointments, of direct Presidential superintendency of foreign affairs, Kennedy for his first three foreign affairs nominees, and for others after them, accompanied the public announcement of their selection with a phrase hailing the "post" as "second to none in importance." The President-elect's pointed tribute signified his intention to deal directly with second- and third-echelon subordinates. Kennedy's own assessment of his experience in the Presidency affirmed the wisdom of this tactic. In a year-end television interview in 1962, he was asked, "Is it true that during your first year, sir, you would get on the phone personally to the State Department and try to get a response to some inquiry that had been made?" "Yes," Kennedy replied, "I still do that when I can, because I think there is a great tendency in government to have papers stay on desks too long.

. . . After all, the President can't administer a department, but at least he can be a stimulant."

Kennedy injected himself at any point along the decision-making spectrum from problem-selection to final judgment. Whereas Eisenhower wanted decisions brought to him for approval, Kennedy wanted problems brought to him for decision. Eisenhower preferred a consensus to be laid before him, stated briefly and in general terms. Kennedy eschewed consensus; he wanted to know a problem's facets and alternative answers, keeping decision for himself in consultation or "dialogue," as the Administration called it, with advisers. Kennedy's keen nose for detail took him far into the interior of problems. Although interested in general principles, he was essentially a pragmatist and had, as a colleague said, "a highly operational mind." Policy separated from operations, in his view, was meaningless. His desk, not surprisingly, was piled high with reports and memoranda which he read closely. Conferring with an official, he would reach into the pile, pull out a memorandum, and resort instantaneously to a paragraph to make a point or raise a question. "President Kennedy," a colleague said, "is a desk officer at the highest level."

In another burrowing tactic, Kennedy early in his term requested each department to supply his office with twice-weekly reports on its current problems and impending decisions. The procedure was intended to enable the President to inject himself into problems before they crystallized and to further his conviction that the pathways to his desk should lay open to any important official, including those several rungs down. The reports provided the departments the rare gratification of airing complaints about each other. Hence, sometime after the procedure commenced, the Housing and Home Finance Agency complained to the President that several proposed urban renewal projects that lay partially on military land were being held up in the Defense Department. The President previously had ordered all such projects speeded up to quicken the economy's slowing pace. A White House aide, seizing the report, confronted the Defense Department with the complaint. Within forty-eight hours, that department cleared proposals that had been slumbering for months in one of the Pentagon's remoter recesses.

Kennedy's appetite for detail could not be satiated by the mere resources of Washington. He prepared himself for budget-making for fiscal 1964 by going forth from the capital for several days of intensive on-the-spot surveying of major military and civilian space installations. His itinerary took him to the Redstone and Saturn projects at Huntsville, Alabama, and a new manned-space flight center at Houston. In St. Louis he inspected the plant of the Mc-Donnell Aircraft Corporation, producer of the Mercury space capsules.

Kennedy's technique pulled innumerable matters, major and minor, out of the regular decision-action line. Officials from State, Defense, and Treasury and other agencies were constantly summoned to the White House where policy was hammered out at his desk. He launched actions on his own initiative, sometimes even without advance notice to the agencies most concerned. He startled the State Department by disclosing, in answer to a news conference question in his first year, that he planned to discuss the balance of payments problem with Heinrich von Brentano, the West German Foreign Minister, who was soon to appear in Washington. This was news to the State Department as well as to the press. Dr. Brentano was not coming in an official capacity, although he was expected to have conversations at the department. The department knew of no plan for a meeting with the President.

Kennedy entertained well-defined views of the proper role of the individual department. His tactic was to devolve upon individual department heads and on identical subordinates the responsibility for recommending policy initiatives and overseeing the execution of decisions. He took a stern view of a luxuriant bureaucratic phenomenon, the interdepartmental committee, beholding it as an intruder upon departmental responsibility and therefore something inherently bad, to be extirpated if at all possible. After several months in office he abolished a lengthy list of interdepartmental committees and reassigned many of their functions to department secretaries and other officials. Committees, being hardy administrative plants because they serve vital purposes, cannot be eliminated by mere Presidential prescription. They are an inevitable bureaucratic routine for establishing interdepartmental collaboration at the working levels. Seldom do problems of any significance appear that are not interdepartmental in their contours. The committees that Kennedy killed, not surprisingly, did not stay dead. Many on his list resumed a more or less surreptitious existence after a decent interval.

In lieu of committees the Kennedy Administration resorted to "task forces," a name appropriately suggestive of vigor and purpose. Task forces, which consisted of departmental representatives and usually one or more White House staffers, were not merely committees by another name. "They operate with a consciousness of having a mandate, often from the President himself," a participant explained. Task forces carried a sense of the importance of getting things done, which often stirred bureaucracy to faster, more constructive effort. The attendant White House staff member was a powerful reminder of the chief executive's need and interest, a bearer of his influence upon decision, not merely in the moment of final choice but along much of the journey of its formation. Departmental participants in the task forces were not altogether enthusiastic about the contribution of their White House colleagues. "When the President's man says something, you don't know whether he is speaking for himself or for his boss," a department man exclaimed. "The effect can be, and often is, to cut off discussion too soon."

Kennedy, like Roosevelt, viewed the White House staff as a personal rather than an institutional staff, a vehicle for maximizing his influence rather than its influence throughout the executive branch. Impressed that the larger a staff is the more apt it is to become institutional, Kennedy tried heroically to cut back the sizable staff he had inherited from the Eisenhower Administration, but with small success. In meting out staff assignments, Kennedy put his staff on action-forcing rather than program tasks, and gave it a mixture of fixed and general-purpose responsibilities. These expedients likewise were intended to reduce the advance of institutionalization and to keep the staff personal.

Kennedy's White House staff, unlike Eisenhower's, was not organized by hierarchy or pyramid, but like a wheel whose hub was the President and whose spokes connected him with individual aides. Five aides occupied major functional posts. The staff assistant to the President, Kenneth O'Donnell, ex-football captain and war hero, handled appointments and Presidential trips and was an omnibus "chief White House official for party politics," in touch with the Democratic National Committee and local party figures. The special counsel, Theodore C. Sorensen of Nebraska, whose association harked back to Kennedy's Senate days in 1953, had responsibilities running across the board. His office, comprising two assistants, focused Presidential objectives, planned programs, broke impasses, and passed judgment on timing. Sorensen drafted Presidential messages and speeches with high artistry and a capacity that Richard M. Nixon once hailed as "the rare gift of being an intellectual who can completely sublimate his style to another intellectual." Sorensen sat with department secretaries formulating their budget and legislative programs and attended the President's meetings with legislative leaders and pre-press conference briefings. Sorensen had an acquisitive, cosmopolitan intelligence, which, as a colleague put it, "can understand anything from sugar subsidies to bomb shelters."

McGeorge Bundy . . . was special assistant for national security affairs. Bundy, aided by a small band of assistants ("the Bundy group"), kept watch for weakness and trouble in defense and foreign policy administration and saw to remedies and repairs. In the President's behalf he occupied a central place in the stream of intelligence. He received copies of virtually all the incoming cables to the Secretaries of State and Defense and the Director of the CIA. He sorted these out and put the most important before the President.

Other key aides were the assistant for congressional relations, Lawrence F. O'Brien, a long-time Kennedy associate, the press secretary, Pierre Salinger, and Ralph Dungan, who was responsible for personnel, or "head-hunting," as he put it. Dungan maintained a permanent list of talent available for government posts, checked job recommendations from legislators, the Democratic National Committee, and the departments. Beyond this, Dungan took on roving assignments—he was Presidential overseer of foreign aid and of African and Latin-American policy. The assignments of Arthur Schlesinger, Jr., the Harvard historian, were even more diverse—he acted as a liaison between the President and United Nations Ambassador Stevenson and between the White House and the State Department on Latin-American policy, and he occasionally gave assistance with Presidential speeches.

The White House staff reaped a steady harvest of influence from Kennedy's habit of entrusting important responsibilities to individuals in whom he had confidence. Staff members, therefore, oftentimes performed functions traditionally handled by departments and diplomatic representatives. Arthur Schlesinger, Jr., of the White House staff—and not high-level State Department officials—traveled through Latin America to survey the area's requirements, gathering data and impressions that became the basis of the future aid program. Press Secretary Salinger, and not the State Department or the United States Information Agency, negotiated in Moscow an agreement for the exchange of information. The attendant publicity of such assignments stripped many of the White House staff posts of their traditional anonymity.

Kennedy deployed his White House staff as critics of departmental performance and as emergency repair crews when departmental undertakings went awry. He restored direct work-flows between departments and himself and made his staff responsible for "monitoring," but not "obstructing," departmental access to him personally. With such solid mandates, the White House staff at times became overexuberant, as suggested by a "ruling" Kennedy issued after six months in office. The White House staff, Kennedy directed, was not to "interfere" in the operations of departments or agencies. The ruling was apparently triggered by a quiet crisis in the State Department's Inter-American Division. For several months the post of Assistant Secretary of State for Inter-American Affairs lay vacant, creating a power vacuum into which the President's staff quickly moved, to the bitter resentment of State Department career men.

A key function of the White House staff was to spot political and policy weaknesses in departmental proposals. Staff members played a decisive part in heading off a tax increase which may have made sense economically, but not politically, in the Berlin build-up of July 1961; they delighted liberals by implanting several public-ownership features into the Communications Satellite bill; they knocked down a State Department proposal that action on the Trade bill be postponed for more than a year, until 1963. There was wide agreement that a large advantage of the Sorensen-Bundy service was penetrating analysis. "When Sorensen gets into something," a Budget Bureau career man said, "it gets a thorough scrubbing." It was also the lack of such a scrubbing that plunged the staff to the far depths of its worst failure, the abortive Cuban invasion in the young administration's fourth month. The staff was admittedly timid about raising questions that should have been asked. "At that point," a White House aide confessed, "we just didn't have the confidence to tell the veterans of the bureaucracy, 'Look, you're crazy.' "

In another blow at the institutionalized Presidency, Kennedy performed drastic surgery on the most advanced expression of that phenomenon, the National Security Council. He abolished the NSC's nerve- and work-center, the Planning Board, and its organ for implementing decision, the Operations Coordinating Board. Most important of all, he shunned the NSC by seldom bringing it into session. He sought counsel for major crises like Berlin of 1961 and Cuba of 1962 by bringing together an *ad hoc* group of advisers in whom he had special confidence. In lieu of the Planning Board and the OCB was the Bundy office, which greatly scaled down the former mountainous paper work.

Kennedy also largely dispensed with cabinet meetings, holding that the entire body of secretaries should be assembled only for matters of full breadth and significance. He saw no reason for the entire cabinet to ponder matters affecting only three or four departments. The cabinet, consequently, met infrequently. In the summer of 1962 various department heads, then occupied with the political campaign, happened to converge upon Chicago. There they laughingly acknowledged that what had not transpired in Washington for some months was at last happening in the Midwest, a cabinet "meeting"!

The Kennedy technique clearly maximized the President's involvement and imprint upon policy, breathed vitality into sluggish bureaucracy, and extended the reach of a highly knowledgeable President and his staff into the departments. Yet there were also disadvantages. There was feeling that Kennedy was too accessible to operating personnel, too much "in the thick of things," over-immersed in minor policy and small detail, with too little time for major business. Or again, that Kennedy's emphasis on swiftness—terse statement, quick strides from one problem to the next—resulted at times in inadequate consideration of alternatives. Much public business, like reducing the arms race or overhauling the tax system, does not permit quick, concise expression. "The system now," a frequent participant said, "favors people who know exactly what they want to do. It is tough on people who have dim misgivings—even if those misgivings happen to be very important."

One strength of the Kennedy system may also have been a weakness. His method rested upon the realistic view that the executive branch, lacking the apparatus of collective responsibility found in Great Britain, depended heavily, for action and decision, upon the President's judgment. Yet what ordinarily was plausibly realistic may have caused at times an overdependence upon the time, energy, and talent of the President. The great risk of the Kennedy method is that no single mind, even a Presidential mind, can absorb the information or muster the wisdom necessary for sound judgment of many intricate issues pouring upon the President.

The problems with which American statesmanship must deal have acquired a complexity that render them no longer fit for individual insight and judgment, no matter how perceptive. To be dealt with adequately, they must at some stage be subjected to collective study involving diverse technical skills, specialized knowledge, and organizational viewpoints. Decision without collective study is apt to be founded on inadequate information and to lack roundness of judgment.

LOUIS KOENIG

Party Chief

President Kennedy had paid considerable heed to the lessons of both Roosevelt and Eisenhower. He was deeply concerned over the fact that a party's national program supported by its Presidential candidate may falter or fail at the hands of the party's own leaders in Congress. Was the answer not to wait for the election year to initiate a purge, but to move upon the source of power ahead of time—in the state and local party organizations, where the seeds of trouble germinate?

The state party organizations are allegedly self-governing principalities, but Kennedy, who pursued his duties of party chief with zest, remorseless diligence, and ingenuity, moved upon them with aggressive enterprise. He acted principally through his personal organization—Lawrence F. O'Brien and Kenneth O'Donnell, his brother Robert and his brother-in-law Stephen E. Smith, and other associates, all of whom enjoyed close personal ties with state and local Democratic power centers in the big Northern industrial states on which Kennedy concentrated. His own organization in these states was in some ways more powerful than the regular Democratic organization. He maintained close ties with state leaders such as Jesse M. Unruh of California, city leaders such as Ray Miller of Cleveland, and local potentates such as Charles A. Buckley of the Bronx, dealing them considerable preferment. After

This selection is from Louis Koenig, *The Chief Executive,* pp. 118–122. © 1964 by Harcourt, Brace & World, Inc., and reprinted with their permission.

the 1962 elections his brother-in-law Stephen Smith, a man of
quiet competence, served the Democratic National Committee as a
trouble shooter in the key states of New York, Pennsylvania, Ohio,
and Michigan, all of which had chosen Republican governors.
Smith's chief responsibility in his uneasy capacity was to prevent
fractious Democrats from feuding with each other. His early
assignments included the laying of olive branches on such adversaries as "reform" Senator Joseph Clark of Pennsylvania and
Philadelphia "machine" leader Congressman William Green, Jr. In
Michigan Smith toiled to heal the rift between the United Auto
Workers and Democratic regulars, and in New York to quell the
party's lengthy strife and chaos.

Kennedy did much "coordinating" himself. Soon after taking
office, he worked mightily to revise the New York State Democratic leadership. He gave the cold shoulder to two top Democratic
chieftains, Carmine De Sapio, New York County leader, and
Michael Prendergast, state chairman. The more luscious patronage
appointments credited to New York were awarded to members of
a reform Democratic group dedicated to Prendergast's and De
Sapio's ouster. The President appointed as ambassador to NATO
Thomas K. Finletter, who with former Senator Herbert H. Lehman
and Mrs. Franklin Roosevelt shared the top anti-De Sapio leadership in Manhattan. Lehman's grandnephew, Jonathan B. Bingham,
was named United States Representative to the United Nations
Trusteeship Council. Francis T. P. Plimpton, appointed deputy
representative to the United Nations, was a resident of Suffolk
County, but no endorsement was sought from the Suffolk Democratic leader. John S. Stillman, Orange County Democratic chairman, who was named assistant to the Undersecretary of Commerce, was never regarded as an ally of Prendergast.

Kennedy's "cold treatment" of De Sapio and Prendergast had a
social dimension. During his inauguration ceremonies, Kennedy
pointedly distinguished between New York Democrats in good and
bad standing. Congressman Charles A. Buckley, the long-time
Bronx Democratic leader, Joseph T. Sharkey, the Brooklyn leader,
and Peter J. Crotty, the Erie County chairman, all enjoyed places
in the Presidential box at the Inaugural Ball. Prendergast and De
Sapio were among the fifteen thousand dancers who milled about

on the floor. In a visit to New York City several weeks later, Kennedy rode with James A. Farley through the city streets, visited Lehman at his apartment, interviewed Sharkey, and talked with Buckley on the telephone. De Sapio was totally ignored and Prendergast heard only from a member of the Presidential staff. By these and other means Kennedy implied he would never deal with Prendergast and De Sapio, and encouraged lesser New York Democrats to challenge their leadership.

Kennedy resorted to several expedients to advance the candidacies of legislative Democrats he viewed favorably. To further the cause of Wilkes T. Thrasher, Jr., an all-out New Frontiersman running in the Third Congressional District of Tennessee in 1962, he picked the candidate to represent him as a special ambassador at independence ceremonies in Trinidad. The scarcity of such plums underscored the importance of the President's action. As the 1962 elections neared, Kennedy seemed to take a giant step toward Roosevelt's method when he announced that he was "going to help elect Democrats" who supported his legislative program. The incumbent Representative Leonard Farbstein of Manhattan, who was running for reelection, faced a primary contest with Assemblyman Bentley Kassal, the reform Democratic candidate. In a letter to Farbstein, Kennedy praised his "clear judgment, wisdom, dedication and energy" and expressed "my personal appreciation for your sustained support of our legislative program." Farbstein made the letter public, terming it an endorsement. His opponent, Kassal, contended that it was not, that he had been assured indeed that Kennedy would not take sides in the primary. The President said no more, and Farbstein swept on to victory. Reform groups are common casualties of Presidential party decisions, especially where the rival individual or group represents power the President cherishes or respects. Farbstein, as a member of the House Foreign Affairs Committee, had been an ardent advocate of bills favorable to Israel. In turn, the Administration's attitude toward Israel is considered important by large numbers of Jewish voters in New York.

Kennedy, as other Presidents have done in by-year elections, viewed the 1962 electoral campaign not merely as an opportunity to elect Democratic legislators, but to bring his goals and programs to the people. Two years of feet-dragging by a Democratic Congress added glow to the opportunity. But while the President serves his own purposes, at least partially, his presence is cherished by the congressional candidates and the local party organizations. Kennedy's capacity to bring out the crowds gave tremendous publicity to the campaign and a great boost to campaign enthusiasm. Thanks to the perquisites of his office, the President also has campaigning facilities which no competitor can match. While out on the trail in 1962, Kennedy had an entourage of five press assistants, a reporting service that produced texts of his speeches within minutes of their delivery, and a busload of miscellaneous aides. The transportation of himself and his group was cared for by a fleet of White House automobiles, two jet airliners, a DC-7 airliner, and four Army jet-powered helicopers. Everywhere he went he was followed by forty-four reporters, photographers, and television technicians traveling by chartered plane. His chief rival campaigner, former President Eisenhower, toured in his eight-passenger aircraft unaccompanied by press parties, mimeograph machines, or helicopters.

Like other Presidents before him, Kennedy in his attentions to the states was by no means always on the side of the reformers—if support for the regulars strengthened his own position. At a Democratic fund-raising dinner in New York City, he sent Charles A. Buckley a lavish verbal bouquet, described by a Kennedy staff member as "the most personal message I've ever known in all my twelve years' association with the President." The message, which was read at the dinner, was signed significantly, by "Joe, Jack, Bobby and Teddy Kennedy." This fulsome tribute to one of the most encrusted and anachronistic of bosses brought *The New York Times* to protest the President's knowing recognition of a figure who needed to be "decried and deplored" rather than "promoted and protected." Not the least importance of Buckley was that as chairman of the House Public Works Committee he was admirably situated to help the Administration by influencing other House Democrats to vote for the President's bills. In the Pennsylvania struggle between Senator Joseph Clark, a liberal reformer, and Congressman William J. Green, an old-style political boss of Philadelphia whose habit was victory, Kennedy veered toward Green. The President needed the Congressman for the 1964 election if the 1960 contest were a guide. In 1960 Kennedy had carried Philadelphia by a 337,000 vote majority, amply assisted by Green's machine. Yet he had carried the state of Pennsylvania by only 51.2 per cent of the vote. Green's obvious usefulness led Kennedy to shower him with attentions. The Congressman visited Kennedy in Florida, sat in his box at a football game, and accompanied him in his helicopter to the funeral of Senator Robert S. Kerr in Oklahoma. Not that Kennedy was against party reform—though many party leaders thought so—but he believed that the only way to achieve it was to win over the power centers for himself first.

Publicity is another weapon a President can employ to promote his legislative party friends, and President Kennedy moved in 1963 to coordinate White House publicity with the needs of his Democratic supporters on Capitol Hill. The President brought Paul Southwick, an experienced newspaperman, into the White House from the Area Redevelopment Agency of the Commerce Department. Southwick, as part of the White House press office staff, forwarded useful news and information to the Democratic legislators with suggestions of how they might exploit the President's activities for their own publicity needs.

In another publicity gambit, Kennedy moved to wrest from the Republican party one of its proudest possessions, the observance of Abraham Lincoln's birthday. He celebrated that event in 1963, the centenary of the Emancipation Proclamation, with a White House reception for Negro and civil rights leaders and a host of Democrats, chiefly legislators who supported the Kennedy program. More than a thousand celebrants were on hand, including Negroes distinguished in endeavors ranging from law to jazz. The day was ripe with suggestion of the solid harmony between Lincoln's ideals and contemporary Democratic action. Prior to a buffet, Kennedy received at a ceremony in his office a report on civil rights progress in the hundred years since Lincoln's Emancipation Proclamation. The report noted that "as the century following emancipation draws to a close, more forces are working for the realization of civil rights for all Americans than ever before in history. Government is active in every branch and at every level, if not in every region." But, it added, with a solid air of commitment, "The final chapter in the struggle for equality has yet to be written."

Kennedy's death cut short the experiment that was to have been tested in the 1964 Presidential election and probably in the 1966 congressional election. He died in the line of duty as party leader. The purpose of his visit to Texas, which ended in his assassination, was to reduce the widening cleavage between Texan Democratic factions identified with Senator Ralph W. Yarborough and the then Vice-President Johnson. It is left for future Presidents to see whether the stalemate between the party's Presidential leadership and its congressional leadership can ever be resolved in favor of the President and the majority of the nation who support him. The Kennedy formula looked for the eventual dominance of urban politics over congressional politics. His legislative program was heavily directed toward the urban vote, and his personal political organization concentrated upon winning and holding the allegiance of the great Democratic organizations in the Northern urban states. The combination of a program geared to urban groups and a personal political organization that mobilized local party organizations conceivably could have added up to a force that Democratic legislators would have found difficult to resist after 1964.

ARTHUR M. SCHLESINGER, JR.

The Bully Pulpit

The most common criticism of Kennedy during his Presidency was that he had failed as a public educator. It was said that he concentrated on "selling" himself and his family rather than his ideas; that he was excessively preoccupied with his "image"; and that he was unwilling to convert personal popularity into political pressure for his program. He was compared invidiously with the Roosevelts, Wilson and other Presidents celebrated for their skill in rallying the electorate behind controversial policies. "He has neglected his opportunities to use the forum of the Presidency as an educational institution," wrote Carroll Kilpatrick of the *Washington Post*. "I think it is the President's fault," said Howard K. Smith of CBS-TV. ". . . Every great President has been also a great teacher and explainer. . . . Today [October 1963], in lieu of really important explanations by the President, the papers of America are full instead of the speeches of Goldwater." "He never really exploited his considerable gifts as a public educator," concluded James Reston of *The New York Times*.

Yet in later years the age of Kennedy was seen as a time of quite extraordinary transformation of national values and purposes—a transformation so far-reaching as to make the America of the sixties a considerably different society from the America of the fifties. And, instead of hearing that Kennedy did too little as a public educator, one heard more often in retrospect that he had tried to do too much too quickly, to put over too many new ideas in too short a time, that he had unnecessarily affronted the national mood and pushed ahead so fast that he lost contact with public opinion. Clearly the paradox of Kennedy and public education deserves examination.

PUBLIC EDUCATION: THE CONVENTIONAL THEORY

First impressions often crystallize into lasting stereotypes. It is instructive to recall that Kennedy had been in office for only a few weeks before the proposition about his delinquencies as a public educator was becoming a cliché in the newspapers. I discover a memorandum of mine to the President as early as March 16, 1961:

There is increasing concern among our friends in the press about the alleged failure of the Administration to do as effective a job of public information and instruction as it should and must. Lippmann had a column about this last week. Joe Alsop has been haranguing me about this over the telephone and plans to do some columns about it soon. Lester Markel is going to do a long piece about it in *The Times Magazine*.

Markel had brought his complaint directly to the President, who called me one afternoon to ask how many fireside chats Roosevelt had given. "Lester has been in here saying that I ought to go to the people more often," the President said. "He seems to think that Roosevelt gave a fireside chat once a week."

Markel's remark suggested part of the problem. Memory had left an impression of F.D.R. as incessantly on the air and of Theodore Roosevelt and Wilson constantly using the White House, in T.R.'s phrase, as a "bully pulpit." Compared to these glowing recollections, Kennedy's efforts seemed meager and perfunctory. In fact, memory considerably improved the record of the past. By the most liberal possible interpretation, Roosevelt had given only thirty fireside chats in his twelve years as President; before the war, he averaged no more than two a year.[1] In three years, Kennedy made nine television reports to the nation from the White House, therefore averaging 50 per cent higher than F.D.R.'s peacetime rate; and he gave far more public speeches each year than the Roosevelts or Wilson had given. He also held frequent private meetings at the White House with editors, businessmen, labor leaders, organization representatives and other panjandrums of the opinion mafia. And he used television and the press with skill and resource.

Like all modern Presidents, Kennedy found the newspapers a major educational instrument. Only 16 per cent had backed him in 1960; but the working press had been strongly for him. Kennedy liked newspapermen; they liked him; and he recognized that they provided him a potent means of appealing to readers over the heads of publishers. In Pierre Salinger he had an engaging and imaginative press secretary. While Salinger sometimes lacked the total knowledge of high policy which his very able predecessor under Eisenhower, James Hagerty, had enjoyed, and while newspapermen claimed he lacked Hagerty's proficiency in making their technical arrangements, he admirably conveyed Kennedy's own insouciant spirit to the White House press room, bore patiently with Kennedy's occasional outbursts against the press and prescribed an open-door policy for newspapermen in the White House and throughout the government.

The press conferences were the central forum of Presidential contact. Kennedy averaged twenty-one a year, far fewer than Roosevelt and somewhat fewer than Eisenhower. Though at times oddly resistant when the time came for another press conference, he was the most skilled Presidential practitioner in this medium since Roosevelt. Moreover, while Roosevelt's press conferences were intimate off-the-record sessions around the Presidential desk in the oval office, Kennedy's were mass public affairs, often on live television; he achieved his success under far more exacting conditions.

Success was the product of study as well as of art. Salinger organized a meticulous briefing process, drawing in predicted questions and recommended responses from information officers

[1] The breakdown is as follows: 1933, 4; 1934, 2; 1935, 1; 1936, 1; 1937, 3; 1938, 2; 1939, 1; 1940, 2; 1941, 3; 1942, 4; 1943, 4; 1944, 3; 1945, 0.

across the government. The President would then convene a press conference breakfast, ordinarily attended by Salinger, Sorensen, Bundy, Heller and Robert Manning, the State Department's Assistant Secretary for Public Affairs. Here the President would try out his answers, often tossing off replies which convulsed the breakfast table but which, alas, could not be diplomatically made on the occasion. Later in the day he would go over to the auditorium of the State Department, and the fun would begin: the forest of hands waving from the floor; the questioner recognized by a brisk jab of the Presidential forefinger; then the answer—statistics rolling off the Presidential tongue, or a sudden glint in the eye signaling the imminence of a throwaway joke, or, very occasionally, an abrupt frostiness of countenance; then the next questioner recognized almost before the answer to the first was completed—it was a superb show, always gay, often exciting, relished by the reporters and by the television audience.

One felt at times that the President missed chances to make points to the nation for fear of boring the men and women in the room by telling them things he supposed they already knew. F.D.R. had never hesitated to cast elementary statement or homely metaphor—lend-lease and the neighbor's firehose—before the sophisticates of the Washington press corps, knowing that the key phrases would filter through to the people who needed them. In Kennedy's case, the uninitiated, instead of learning something about a public issue, often only witnessed abstract and cryptic exchanges between reporter and President. Nonetheless, the conferences offered a showcase for a number of his most characteristic qualities—the intellectual speed and vivacity, the remarkable mastery of the data of government, the terse, self-mocking wit, the exhilarating personal command. Afterward he liked to relax, watch himself in action on the evening news and chat about the curious habits of the press. Once I asked him why he kept calling on the Texas newspaperwoman who had so offended him by asking about security risks in the State Department. He replied, "I always say to myself I won't call on her. But she gets up every time and waves her hand so frantically that toward the end I look down and she's the only one I seem to see."

His relations with the press, like those of all Presidents, had its ups and downs. Calvin Coolidge is the only President on record

who did not seem to care what was written about him. When
someone asked him about a savage attack by Frank Kent in the
American Mercury, he replied philosophically, "You mean that
magazine with the green cover? It was against me, so I didn't read
it." No other President was this philosophical; and Kennedy was
certainly not. He read more newspapers than anyone except
perhaps Roosevelt,[2] and very often with appreciation; but like
Presidents Hoover, Roosevelt, Truman and Eisenhower—indeed,
like most politicians—he retained an evidently inexhaustible capacity to become vastly, if briefly, annoyed by hostile articles or by
stories based on leaks. When this happened there would be
complaints to the staff, calls to reporters, searches for the sources
of stories and even the cancellation for a time of the *New York
Herald Tribune.* (This uncharacteristic act resulted from his irritation over the paper's insistence in playing the congressional investigation of Billie Sol Estes on its front page while, he believed,
studiously ignoring a concurrent investigation into stockpiling
scandals in the Eisenhower Administration.) Nor were relations
improved when the information officer of the Defense Department
talked imprudently about news as "part of the arsenal of
weaponry" and affirmed "the inherent right of the government to
lie . . . to save itself when faced with nuclear disaster."

Washington reporters, with their acute sense of contemporane-
ity, always believe that each new administration is plotting an
assault on the freedom of the press with a determination and
malignity never before seen in the republic; the iniquities of past
Presidents fade quickly in retrospect. So for a time in 1962 they
proclaimed a deep sense of grievance over the "hypersensitivity"
of the President and the Administration. For its part the Administration used to wonder about the hypersensitivity of reporters, who
seemed to feel that, if a government official dared disagree with a
story, it was an attempt to "manage" the news. When *Look* came
out with a piece detailing the indignities which newspapermen were

---

[2] And expected everyone else to do likewise. No experience was more
frequent for members of his staff than to be called by the President early in
the morning for discussion of an item in the papers; in my case the calls
regularly came before I had had a chance to read the papers. Averell
Harriman once told a congressional committee, "A man cannot serve President Kennedy unless he reads the newspaper carefully. He won't last very
long if he doesn't, in this Administration."

suffering under the reign of terror, Kennedy laughed and remarked, "This is the best example of paranoia I have seen from those fellows yet."

This guerrilla warfare between press and government was, of course, inherent in the situation; it was also a great bulwark of national freedom. Gilbert Harrison, the editor of *The New Republic,* summed the problem up accurately:

From the past 10 years in Washington, I have decided that irrespective of party or person, race, creed or color, every public official, elected or not, has the same attitude toward journalists, and it is this: "If you knew what we knew, you would not say what you do." Likewise, the attitude of the journalists is constant, and it is this: "If you knew what we knew, you would not do as you do," which is sometimes revised to read: "If you would *tell* us what you are doing and what you *mean* to do, perhaps we would not say what we say."

Each attitude is proper to the vocation of the one who holds it. Each is unyielding. If a President has never been known to telephone a critical journalist and tell him how wrong he, the President, has been, no journalist I know confesses *his* mistakes.

This was substantially the President's view. When asked what he thought of the press in the spring of 1962, he said, "Well, I am reading it more and enjoying it less—[*laughter*]—and so on, but I have not complained, nor do I plan to make any general complaints. I read and talk to myself about it, but I don't plan to issue any general statement on the press. I think that they are doing their task, as a critical branch, the fourth estate. And I am attempting to do mine. And we are going to live together for a period, and then go our separate ways." [*Laughter*] The reporters understood this; and, despite the animated exchanges of 1962 and occasional moments of mutual exasperation thereafter, the press corps regarded Kennedy with marked fondness and admiration.

PROBLEMS OF THE CONVENTIONAL THEORY

Kennedy thus used the conventional instruments of public education with freedom and skill. But he felt that press conferences and public addresses could not work for him as they had worked for the Roosevelts and Wilson—that hortatory and explicit public education was simply not suited to the mood of the 1960's. For, as a student of history, he understood that public education did not take place in a vacuum. To move a nation, a President had first to have the nation's ear; and there was no quicker way to dissipate Presidential influence than to chatter away when no one was listening.

Thus a decade of reformers and muckrakers, working in the cities and states, had given the nation's ear to Theodore Roosevelt and Wilson, and a Depression touching nearly every family in the country had given the nation's ear to Franklin Roosevelt. The early thirties in particular had been a time when visible and tangible crisis had generated a hunger for national action. With people hanging on every Presidential word, public education offered no great problem to a President who had something to say. But no President, not even one of the Roosevelts or Wilson, could create by fiat the kind of public opinion he wanted. Effectiveness in public education required leverage in the nation to begin with.

Kennedy had very little leverage. No muckraking agitation had prepared the way for his Presidency; no national economic collapse was making his constituents clamor for action. His was an invisible and intangible crisis, in some ways more profound than the one which confronted Franklin Roosevelt but bearing infinitely less heavily on the daily lives of Americans. The economy was moving forward, 95 per cent of the labor force had jobs, American troops were not fighting in foreign lands, the country was bathed in physical contentment; and, except for racial minorities, spiritual disquietude floated about without commitment to issues. This acquiescent nation had elected him President by the slimmest of margins; no one could possibly claim his victory as a mandate for radical change. "President Kennedy today," as Richard Rovere perceptively stated his problem, "is attempting to meet a challenge whose existence he and his associates are almost alone in perceiving." The President liked to recall Owen Glendower's boast in *Henry IV, Part I*—"I can call spirits from the vasty deep"—and Hotspur's reply:

> Why, so can I, or so can any man;
> But will they come when you do call for them?

The possibility that they might not come had even troubled Presidents like the Roosevelts and Wilson. Thus by the spring of 1935 a feeling had arisen that F.D.R. was falling down on the job of public education. My father was one of those urging him then to carry his case to the people as he had done in 1933. Roosevelt replied, "My difficulty is a strange and weird sense known as 'public psychology.'" To others he explained, "People tire of seeing the same name day after day in the important headlines of the papers, and the same voice night after night over the radio. . . . Individual psychology cannot, because of human weakness, be attuned for long periods of time to constant repetition of the highest note in the scale." One had to assume that Presidents had a better sense of "public psychology" than most of their critics; that was one reason why they were Presidents and their critics were critics. Moreover, once in the White House, they were in the exact center of pressure and therefore more likely to have an accurate sense of the balance of conflicting forces. If they wanted to act, as Kennedy clearly did, it was idle to suppose that only a misreading of the political situation or mere indolence was holding them back. The Presidential secret was timing. The clamor for action was part of the equation, and activist Presidents were wrong to resent such pressure (though of course they all, including Kennedy, occasionally did, because it was so often voiced by friends from whom they expected sympathy rather than complaint). And sometimes when they succumbed to the pleadings the results were hardly those one might have predicted. Throughout 1961 *The New York Times* demanded that Kennedy carry his program to the people. Then in May 1962 at a great outdoor rally the President called for the enactment of the Medicare bill, which *The Times* itself favored editorially. The speech went to thirty-two other rallies and to millions of homes throughout the country. It seemed a splendid exercise in public education and in mobilizing support for the Administration program—exactly the sort of thing *The Times* had been advocating. But *The Times* immediately responded by condemning Kennedy for employing "hippodrome tactics."

Timing remained the key. In the absence of visible crisis Presidents had to wait for some event to pierce the apathy and command the nation's ear; experience was a more potent teacher than exhortation. At moments one felt that it was nearly impossible to change people or policies in advance of disaster, because only disaster could sufficiently intimidate and overcome those with vested interests in existing people and policies. So we read every day in the newspapers about the decay of the Diem regime in Vietnam. But, so long as the Secretaries of State and Defense endorsed the policy of unconditional support of Diem, it was hard for the President to act until some dreadful blow-up made the failure of the policy manifest—and by that time it might be too late. So too in Negro rights: if the President committed his prestige to congressional action before the nation was ready to listen to his arguments, he might squander the hope of later influence. In a sense, things had to get worse before there was a possibility of putting them better. Thus Estes Kefauver's bill for the control of the marketing of drugs lingered in committee to immense public indifference until the thalidomide scandal provoked national anger and congressional action. Francis Keppel, the Commissioner of Education, used to express the hope that Congress would pass federal aid to education before some catastrophe—150 schoolchildren, for example, burned to death in a firetrap—came along to stir overdue national concern. In the fall of 1961 President Eisenhower went on television to deliver a political blast against the Administration. A few days later over dinner at the White House Kennedy noted that the Eisenhower telecast had received a rating of only 7 as against 20 each for the programs—cowboys and crime—on competing channels. "People forget this," he said, "when they expect me to go on the air all the time educating the nation. The nation will listen only if it is a moment of great urgency. They will listen after a Vienna. But they won't listen to things which bore them. That is the great trouble."

A further trouble was that a good deal of the public education doctrine was linked to the idea of bringing pressure on Capitol Hill by appealing "over the heads" of Congress to the people. Critics recalled Wilson's remark that the President had "no means of compelling Congress except through public opinion." In the broad sense this was indisputable. Kennedy himself used to point out that every member of the House "subjected himself, every two years, to the possibility that his career will . . . come to an end. He

doesn't live a charmed life. You have to remember that the hot
breath is on him also, and it is on the Senate, and it is on the
President, and it is on everyone who deals with great matters."

But the notion that this was the way activist Presidents had
managed Congress also sprang from garbled memories of Wilson
and the Roosevelts. These Presidents passed their programs much
more by party leadership within Congress than by popular pressure
against it. Very few of F.D.R.'s early fireside chats, for example,
were appeals for the enactment of pending legislation; and, when
the coalition of Southern Democrats and Republicans was joined
together, no amount of his incomparable radio persuasion could
thrust it asunder. In any case, the hot breath was not particularly
relevant to the arithmetic of Kennedy's Congress. No quantity of
fireside chats was likely to change the vote of Representative
Howard Smith, of Senator Harry Byrd, or, indeed, of most of the
other strategically placed opponents of Kennedy's program.
"There's nothing that can be done about a man from a safe
district," Kennedy used to say. "He'll vote the way he wants to."
Such men did not need the President, the Democratic party or
organized labor to keep their seats. For the 10 per cent of swing
votes in Congress, quieter forms of suasion seemed more likely to
produce the desired results.

Public education in the explicit manner of the Roosevelts and
Wilson was thus not, in Kennedy's judgment, particularly well
adapted either to the times or to his special congressional dilemma
—or to himself. This last is a subtler matter; for a period of visible
domestic crisis like 1933 would doubtless have called forth different aspects of his own personality. But a politician lives in a
continuous interaction with his age; and the chemistry of the
sixties confirmed Kennedy in temperamental traits already well
marked—an aversion to what he called "highly charged" political
positions, a scorn for histrionics, a recoil from corniness, a determination not to become a national scold or bore. These traits were
rooted partly, as Richard Neustadt has suggested, in a rationalist's
"mistrust of mass emotion as a tool in politics." Kennedy feared
overexciting people about public issues, as he came to believe that
his call for an air-raid shelter program had done during the Berlin
crisis of 1961; and he was embarrassed on the rare occasions when

he succumbed to public emotion himself, as he did when the Cuban Brigade, freed from Castro's prisons, presented its flag to him at Miami in December 1962. They were rooted too in that qualified historical fatalism which led him to doubt whether words, however winged, would by themselves change the world.

One other factor entered in, and this I find hardest of all to assess. Contrary to a widespread impression, Kennedy did not perceive himself as a partisan President, nor did he wish the country so to perceive him. He perceived himself rather as a man who, unlike the Trumans and Robert Tafts of American politics, generally saw reason on both sides of complex issues. But he knew that the impression of a highly partisan young Democratic politician ruthlessly on the make had been one reason for the narrowness of his victory in 1960. The strategy of reassurance initiated so promptly after the election represented both Kennedy's natural impulse and the only sensible response to the character of the vote. By taking a nonpartisan stance, he aimed at erasing the picture of the power-hungry young careerist and winning the national confidence he felt he lacked. As President, he replenished that strategy whenever he feared that any actions might revive the picture or weaken the confidence: thus his propitiatory course in the aftermath of the steel controversy.

At the time it seemed that Kennedy suffered from the illusion so common to new Presidents (even Roosevelt had it till 1935) that he, unlike any of his predecessors, could really be President of all the people and achieve his purposes without pain or trauma. Some of us, however, thought national argument the best way to break national apathy and communicate the reality of problems. We believed that the educational value of fights in drawing the line between the Administration and its opponents would guarantee that, even if we did not have a law, we would have an issue. So we thought him mistaken in 1962 in making the entirely respectable, safe and overrated trade expansion bill his top legislative priority instead of staging a knockdown-drag-out fight over federal aid to education or Medicare. To the President I would cite the Roosevelts, Wilson, Jackson and so on in arguing the inevitability and superiority of the politics of combat as against the politics of consensus. But, while he did not dispute the historical points, he plainly saw no reason for rushing prematurely into battle.

I think now he had deeper reasons for this than I understood at the time—that his cast of mind had a profounder source than a pragmatist's preference for a law over an issue, than a rationalist's distaste for give-'em-hell partisanship, or even than a statesman's need to hoard national confidence against the possibility that foreign crisis might require swift and unpopular Presidential decisions. I believe today that its basic source may have been an acute and anguished sense of the fragility of the membranes of civilization, stretched so thin over a nation so disparate in its composition, so tense in its interior relationships, so cunningly enmeshed in underground fears and antagonisms, so entrapped by history in the ethos of violence. In the summer of 1963 Kennedy spoke to Robert Stein of *Redbook* about the destructive instincts "that have been implanted in us growing out of the dust" and added, "We have done reasonably well—but only reasonably well" in controlling them. His hope was that it might be possible to keep the country and the world moving fast enough to prevent unreason from rending the skin of civility. But he had peered into the abyss and knew the potentiality of chaos. On another day in the summer of 1963 he concluded an informal talk with representatives of national organizations by suddenly reading them Blanche of Castile's speech from *King John*:

> The sun's o'ercast with blood; fair day, adieu!
> Which is the side that I must go withal?
> I am with both: each army hath a hand;
> And in their rage, I having hold of both,
> They whirl asunder and dismember me.

THE KENNEDY APPROACH

The fact that neither his time nor his temperament encouraged Kennedy to be a public educator in the explicit manner of the Roosevelts and Wilson did not mean that he renounced the Presidential responsibility of public education. On the contrary: he turned out to have an ability unmatched in his age to call spirits from the vasty deep; and they generally came when he called for them. But he did so in his own fashion—a fashion which so subtly permeated national attitudes and so quietly penetrated individual lives that no one realized how much he had changed things until his time was over. The essence of his attack was not admonition and remonstrance, in the earlier style, but example.

It was this which led to the familiar charge that Kennedy and his Administration were preoccupied, to use the odious word, with "image." Noting the discrepancy between Kennedy's personal popularity and the support for his policies, observers concluded that he was reluctant to spend his popularity for result. Critics compared him to a matinee idol. One Republican congressman dismissed the enthusiasm in which he was held: "It's like that of a movie actor—it's not related to legislation." Yet the Kennedy image was not, of course, anything like that of a movie actor. It was packed with a whole set of intellectual implications which were preparing the nation for legislative change as surely as Theodore Roosevelt's muckrakers or Franklin Roosevelt's Depression. In an age of pervasive contentment, his personality was the most potent instrument he had to awaken a national desire for something new and better. The extraordinary effect with which he used it became apparent only in later years: thus Howard K. Smith in retrospect pronounced Kennedy not a failure in public education but a "brilliant communicator."

Kennedy communicated, first of all, a deeply critical attitude toward the ideas and institutions which American society had come in the fifties to regard with such enormous self-satisfaction. Social criticism had fallen into disrepute during the Eisenhower decade. In some influential quarters it was almost deemed treasonous to raise doubts about the perfection of the American way of life. But the message of Kennedy's 1960 campaign had been that the American way of life was in terrible shape, that our economy was slowing down, that we were neglectful of our young and our old, callous toward our poor and our minorities, that our cities and schools and landscapes were a mess, that our motives were materialistic and ignoble and that we were fast becoming a country without purpose and without ideals. As President, he proceeded to document the indictment. In so doing, he released the nation's critical energy. Self-criticism became not only legitimate but patriotic. The McCarthy anxieties were forgotten. Critics began to question the verities again, and defenders of the status quo no longer had the heart, or nerve, to call them Communists. The President, in effect, created his own muckraking movement.

The literature of protest in the Kennedy years poked freely into sacrosanct or shadowed corners of American society—the persistence of poverty (Michael Harrington, Herman P. Miller, Ben Bagdikian, Edgar May, Harry Caudill and many others), racial inequities (a whole bookshelf), taxation (Philip Stern, Stewart Alsop), the spoiling of land, air, water and environment (Stewart Udall, Peter Blake, Howard Lewis, Lewis Herber, Donald Carr), the drug industry (Richard Harris, Morton Mintz); it even challenged such national ikons as television (Newton Minow, Merle Miller and others), the pesticide (Rachel Carson), the cigarette (Maurine Neuberger) and the funeral parlor (Jessica Mitford). There had not been such an outpouring of self-examination since the New Deal. While Presidents cannot claim entire credit for the social criticism of their day, and while in certain fields, notably Negro rights, schools and cities, the process had begun before Kennedy, nonetheless the Presidential stance has a pervasive effect on the national mood. "There wasn't a point," said a writer in the *Village Voice,* "where he didn't upset some preconception of every group in the country." Like the Roosevelts, Kennedy, by his own personal attitude, helped the nation see itself with new eyes.

Facts thus collected were one weapon in the dissolution of the established pretensions. Wit was another. The fifties had constituted probably the most humorless period in American history. A President and Vice-President who might have been invented by H. L. Mencken were viewed with invincible solemnity. Adlai Stevenson, a truly serious man who expressed part of his seriousness in humor, was regarded with suspicion. The zone of the acceptably comic had never been so contracted. In 1952 Al Capp, explaining why he was marrying Li'l Abner to Daisy Mae, said that he had decided to go in for fairy tales because the climate for humor had changed; the "fifth freedom" was gradually disappearing. "Without it," he wrote, "the other four freedoms aren't much fun, because the fifth is the freedom to laugh at each other. . . . Now there are things about America we can't kid." This gloom permeated the decade. As Corey Ford asked in 1958, "What's funny any more? Subjects we could treat lightly once are deadly serious today. Slowly but surely the wellsprings of humor are drying up. Derision is taken for disloyalty."

Part of the narrowing of the zone of laughability was no great loss. Laughing at the powerless—at the spinster or the cripple, at the Irishman or Jew or Negro—had never been wildly funny. But laughing at the powerful was one of the great points of laughing at all; and in the fifties this began to grow risky. Comedians watched one social type or group after another eliminate itself as comic material until in the end the one safe subject was the comedian himself: thus Bob Hope or Jack Benny. Only cartoonists—Jules Feiffer and Herblock especially—kept the satiric faith.

For Kennedy wit was the natural response to platitude and pomposity. He once told me that the political writers he enjoyed most were Murray Kempton and Bernard Levin, who were by way of being the Menckens of their day. His whole personal bearing communicated a delight in satire; and in his wake came an exuberant revival of American irreverence. This had had its underground beginnings at the end of the fifties in small San Francisco and Greenwich Village nightclubs—Mort Sahl and the hungry i, Mike Nichols and Elaine May—but now it flourished, bringing Art Buchwald back to the United States ("There are only four of us writing humor from Washington these days," Buchwald said. "Drew Pearson, David Lawrence, Arthur Krock and myself"), producing skits on the Kennedys themselves—Eliot Reid; Vaughn Meader and "The First Family"—and ending in the murky and ambiguous depths of black comedy. Like muckraking, satire forced the nation to take a fresh look at itself and helped prepare the ground for change.

A third component of the Kennedy image was respect for ideas. The fifties had been a decade of anti-intellectualism. For his belief in the trained intelligence Stevenson was ridiculed as an egghead. Neither ideas nor the men who had them were welcome in the places where respectable men fingered the levers of authority. But Kennedy had long hoped, as he said in January 1960, to "reopen the channels of communication between the world of thought and the seat of power." He felt this, I think, both technically essential in a world imposing novel and complex demands on policy and morally essential to assure civilized government. As President, he carried Roosevelt's brain-trust conception further than it had ever been carried before. The intellectual was no longer merely consultant or adviser but responsible official, even in areas so remote from traditional academic preoccupations as the Department of Defense. Some imports from the campuses worked out better than others; but the reversal of national form in a decade could hardly have been more spectacular. No President had ever made such systematic use of the nation's intellectual resources; and under his tutelage both academics and "practical" men discovered that they had something to learn from the other.

The combination of self-criticism, wit and ideas made up, I think, a large part of the spirit of the New Frontier. It informed the processes of government, sparkled through evenings at the White House and around town, refreshed and enlivened the world of journalism, stimulated the universities, kindled the hopes of the young and presented the nation with a new conception of itself and its potentialities. From the viewpoint of the fifties, it was almost a subversive conception, irreverent and skeptical, lacking in due respect for established propositions and potentates. Perhaps only a President who was at the same time seen as a war hero, a Roman Catholic, a tough politician and a film star could have infected the nation with so gay and disturbing a spirit. But Kennedy did exactly this with ease and grace; and, in doing so, he taught the country the possibilities of a new national style. If he did not get the results he would have liked at once, he was changing the climate in directions which would, in time, make those results inevitable.

Part II

—

KENNEDY AND THE FRONTIERS

CARROLL KILPATRICK

The Kennedy Style and Congress

John F. Kennedy campaigned for the Presidency at a time when congressional leadership was strong. He promised that if elected he would be a forceful executive, a leader of his party, the center of a vibrant, imaginative Administration eager to meet and to deal with the nation's challenging domestic and foreign problems.

To a degree which only historians will be able to define he has provided leadership in many fields. But Congress has forced him to be more pragmatic than his pragmatic philosophy would dictate and to leaven his promise to be a forceful executive with a large dash of compromise and adjustment.

The record of President Kennedy's first two years with Congress was not without notable successes. But there were notable failures as well, and the amount of energy he expended in gaining as much as he did was enormous. The President's power struggle with Congress was almost equal to that of his struggle with the Communist leaders abroad. And Congress was under the control of Democrats. Although the President was "heartened," as he said, by the results of the November election, and can look forward to slightly improved relations with the new Congress, he faces essentially the same institutional problems. The struggle will be continued in the 88th Congress.

"The Kennedy Style and Congress" is from the Winter 1963 issue of *The Virginia Quarterly Review*. Copyright © 1963 by *The Virginia Quarterly Review*, the University of Virginia. Reprinted by permission.

Indeed, it will begin on the opening day in the House of Representatives just as it began there immediately after Mr. Kennedy's inauguration nearly two years ago. By a vote of 217 to 212, the House in early 1961 increased the size of its Rules Committee from twelve to fifteen members to break the controlling power of the Republican–conservative Democratic coalition. In January, 1963, the size of the committee will revert to twelve, and conservatives now are confident that they will dominate it once again. If they are successful, they will be in a position to keep almost any bill they wish off the House floor. Another victory over the Rules Committee is a vital necessity for the President if he is to win important victories in the next two years.

The significance of this power struggle between the President and Congress is that there is nothing new about it, nor is there any easy or permanent solution in sight; but on its outcome hangs the success or failure of the Kennedy Administration. Throughout our history the legislative and executive branches have been less coordinate than rival instruments of government. From the days of the first President there has been a struggle for supremacy except when weak Presidents accepted congressional leadership.

Having called for the invigoration of the executive power, Mr. Kennedy will be judged in large part by the success with which he leads his party in Congress. He learned early in his Administration that his fundamental weakness as leader is that he heads a party which is not united behind him. It resists his leadership. He has neither the machinery, in congressional organization, patronage, or party discipline, to impose his will on his party nor the necessary popular support to win against a well-organized opposition.

That is why he campaigned in September and October more than any President has done before him for the election of a more sympathetic Congress. He said at one point during the campaign that whenever he sent a proposal on domestic affairs to Congress he knew it would be opposed by seven-eighths of the Republicans and about a fourth of the Democrats.

"We have a party which covers all parts of the country," he explained. "We include in it Wayne Morse and Strom Thurmond and Harry Byrd, men who don't agree on a good many things, particularly on domestic matters. So I usually figure that we are going to lose one-fourth of the Democrats."

In the 87th Congress, which is the one the President was talking about, Democrats controlled the Senate by 64 to 36 and the House by 262 to 174 (one vacancy). Yet with those top-heavy majorities the Administration's omnibus farm bill was lost in the House by ten votes and the medical care bill was lost in the Senate by five votes. "We passed an agricultural bill (not the omnibus bill that was killed) the other day by one vote in the House, lost it by one vote in the Senate," the President commented during the campaign.

When Congress adjourned in October, the Administration was able to boast of winning a major new foreign trade bill, a modified tax revision bill, a communication satellite measure, a strong drug labeling law, a much-modified farm bill, a new public works measure, an increase in postal rates and federal pay, and other significant measures.

But in nearly every instance the President gave ground. He made important concessions to the textile industry to win support of his trade bill, the most far-reaching achievement of the 87th Congress. He obtained far less than half a loaf in the tax revision bill Congress finally passed. He accepted amendments to the communication satellite and drug labeling law and to the postal rate and pay increase bills.

Some of these compromises may have resulted in improvements, some may have been no more than the normal give-and-take expected in a free society. But all represented retreat on the President's part.

The President's losses in the 87th Congress included medical care for the aged under social security, a bill to create a Department of Urban Affairs, a farm bill with controls on feed grains, the proposal to withhold taxes on dividends and interest, the request for authority to make limited federal income tax adjustments in accordance with changing economic conditions, federal aid for public schools, federal aid for higher education, sharp cuts in foreign aid appropriations, a rider withdrawing most-favored-nation treatment to trade with Poland and Yugoslavia, the Justice Department's new proposals to control wiretapping, a mass transportation bill, and other measures.

History may record that the most important defeat was one which was lost without a vote ever having been taken or a bill introduced. During the summer, there was strong pressure for a tax cut to bolster the economy. The President himself and the majority of his economic advisers concluded that a cut was desirable. But rather than risk an impossible battle in Congress the President decided against making the request.

That decision, in fact, was made for the President by Chairman Wilbur D. Mills of the House Ways and Means Committee. In that intra-party battle Mills exercised more power than the President, recalling Harold Laski's comment that influential members of Congress have more power than any private members of any other legislative assembly in the world.

There is no abler man in the House than Mills. But his loyalty is primarily to the voters of his rural Arkansas district, however different their interests, prejudices, and information may be from those of a majority of the American people. Mills's great power derives, of course, not from his constituents but from the system that elevates him to the Ways and Means chairmanship solely on the basis of seniority.

Students of the problem of congressional vs. Presidential power have proposed many reforms. Some have been tried in the past, such as the caucus system, and proved to be temporarily successful. Others are desirable and urgently needed today. But the President's problem, as he interprets it, is to work with what he has, much as other Presidents have done, in attempting to impose his program on a Congress jealous of its rights and endowed by the Constitution with extraordinary powers. Those who propose the most drastic reforms of Congress forget that they really are proposing a reform of the American constitutional system. Logic and right may be on their side, but logic and right, when they go against tradition in politics, are exceedingly difficult to impose.

A reform of the seniority system, which could be made without violating anything but tradition and which is urgently needed, is a case in point. There would be no constitutional barrier to such a reform, yet it would be almost as easy to transport Vermont's snows to Florida as to change this system that on occasion gives men like Mills or Chairman Harry F. Byrd of the Senate Finance Committee virtual veto power over a chief executive.

Mr. Kennedy, like his predecessors, has decided to pursue the art of the possible with the tools at hand. He may be criticized for that, but that was his decision. He knows that the Constitution-makers intended Congress to have great power. Influenced as they were by the English Whigs, by Locke's doctrine of legislative supremacy, and by Montesquieu's warning that power must be checked by power, the framers of the Constitution instituted a government of divided powers and of checks and balances that has ever made a President's burdens onerous.

When Mr. Kennedy was elected in 1960 by the narrowest of margins and with the loss of twenty Democratic seats in the House he knew that he faced a formidable challenge in his relations with Congress. Some of his advisers told him that the only way he could succeed was to take his case to the people, to use public opinion to compel Congress to do his bidding. "The Presidency is pre-eminently the people's office," said Grover Cleveland, to which Woodrow Wilson added: "He has no means of compelling Congress except through public opinion."

The President, however, followed his own inclination and the advice of the late Speaker Sam Rayburn and of Vice-President Lyndon B. Johnson when he chose to work with Congress and to try to woo its recalcitrant members by favors, pork, patronage, and charm. He never appealed over the heads of congressmen to the people except once last summer—and that was after the event—when the Senate defeated his medical care program.

In the first session of the 87th Congress, in an attempt to woo its members, the President met privately at the White House with every committee chairman. He had coffee hours with small groups from time to time. He held briefing sessions on important bills with Democratic members as well as foreign policy briefings for bipartisan groups.

These were important and made for more cordial relations. But members of Congress have a habit of listening more attentively to the dominant pressure groups from their districts than to the President. The President's brother, Edward M. Kennedy, made this clear during his campaign for the Senate in Massachusetts. He said that he would not support the President in all matters. The President's loyalty, he explained, was to the voters of fifty states whereas the loyalty of the Senator from Massachusetts was to the

voters of Massachusetts. The younger Kennedy said that he expected the President to fight for tariff cuts but that he himself
would do all he could to assure that there would be no tariff cuts
affecting Massachusetts industries. However understandable all
this may be in a representative assembly, it hardly makes for
responsible party government.

"I have a very strong feeling," Theodore Roosevelt once said
while still in the White House, "that it is a President's duty to get on
with Congress if he possibly can, and that it is a reflection upon
him if he and Congress come to a complete break." Later, he told
how he had tried repeatedly to work with the congressional
leaders. "We succeeded in working together, although with increasing friction, for some years, I pushing forward and they hanging
back," he wrote in his *Autobiography*. "Gradually, however, I was
forced to abandon the effort to persuade them to come my way,
and then I achieved results only by appealing over the heads of the
Senate and House leaders to the people, who were the masters of
both of us. I continued in this way to get results until almost the
close of my term."

Each successful President has worked out his own methods of
dealing with Congress. Jefferson, although leader of a party which
called for a stronger legislative than executive power, worked
quietly to establish his leadership. As Wilfred E. Binkley has said
in his excellent *President and Congress,* when the House of
Representatives was organized in Jefferson's first term, "it was
apparent to the discerning that lieutenants of the President occupied every key position." If as much could be said for President
Kennedy his troubles would be cut in half. Jefferson, as well as
Wilson later, effectively used the caucus to bind party members in
advance of a vote so that they would be united on the floor.
Jefferson himself is said to have presided at some meetings of the
caucus.

A few days after Woodrow Wilson's inauguration he summoned
Postmaster General Albert S. Burleson, his patronage chief and an
experienced politician, to the White House, and said: "Now,
Burleson, I want to say to you that my Administration is going to
be a progressive Administration. I am not going to advise with
reactionary or standpat Senators or Representatives in making

these appointments. I am going to appoint forward-looking men, and I am going to satisfy myself that they are honest and capable. I am not going to consult the standpatters in our party."

Burleson expressed astonishment. He replied that if the President followed such a course "your Administration is going to be a failure. It means the defeat of the measures of reform that you have next to your heart."

Burleson left the White House not knowing whether his argument had had any effect on the stubborn Presbyterian occupant. But Burleson had made an impression, as events were to demonstrate. Wilson made many compromises with the conservatives in his party to win approval of his domestic programs. He worked closely, for example, with conservatives like Representative Oscar W. Underwood, chairman of the Ways and Means Committee, who had opposed Wilson's nomination. Wilson appointed men whom his supporters cried out against as reactionaries, because that was one way to win recalcitrant Democrats in Congress.

Wilson also used other tools to persuade Congress—his skill as an orator, a much tighter party organization on Capitol Hill than exists today, and a Democratic and liberal Republican coalition that worked with him. Now President Kennedy faces a Republican and conservative Democratic coalition that works against him.

Wilson had another advantage. He came to the White House from the New Jersey Governor's office, where he had gained experience in exercising leadership over a legislature as well as over a bureaucracy. President Kennedy, the more experienced politician, came from the Senate, where the training is in compromise and adjustment rather than in the exercise of the executive talents. Perhaps this training helps to explain why the President appears to be quicker to compromise and less willing to use the vast powers of persuasion at his command.

In addition, in Wilson's day the Democratic caucus was a useful and important instrument of translating New Freedom proposals into reality. It is inconceivable that with the deep Democratic divisions that exist today an effective caucus could be instituted Arthur S. Link says in his biography of Wilson that Wilson was the leader of his party "during a time when it was consciously attempting to transform itself from a sectional, agrarian party into a truly national organization representative of all sections and classes." President Kennedy is leader of his party during a time when it is consciously divided along sectional and ideological lines and when one wing is fighting against the establishment of a truly national organization.

Link wrote of Wilson:

It is no derogation of Wilson's contribution to emphasize the circumstances that made strong leadership possible from 1913 to 1917, for his contribution in techniques was of enormous importance.

The first of these techniques was to assert the position of the President as the spokesman of the people and to use public opinion as a spur on Congress. Theodore Roosevelt had demonstrated the usefulness of this method, but Wilson used it to the fullest advantage and made it inevitable that any future President would be powerful only in so far as he established communication with the people and spoke effectively for them.

His chief instruments in achieving a position as national spokesman were of course oratory and public messages, by means of which he gave voice to the highest aspirations, first, of the American people, and then, during the war and afterward, of the people of the world.

It is in the use of public opinion to spur Congress that President Kennedy has most disappointed some of his supporters. During the long second session of the 87th Congress, which lasted from January to October, the President made three formal radio-television reports to the American people. The first was in March when he announced the resumption of nuclear testing; the second was in August when he defensively announced that he would postpone until 1963 a request to Congress to cut income taxes; the third was in October when he spoke briefly on the desegregation crisis at the University of Mississippi. Only one of these involved the President's relations with Congress, and that was the speech on taxation delivered after Congress through Chairman Mills had in effect dictated the President's position to him.

In the congressional campaign, before the President cut short his participation because of the Cuban crisis, he had an opportunity to explain his objectives, to elucidate the issues, and to arouse the people's interest in New Frontier programs. Instead, he contented himself with trying to make the election a popularity contest. His campaigning was designed to take advantage of his high personal standing with the voters and to contrast the wickedness of backward Republicans with the generosity of forward-looking Democrats.

The President has relied heavily on the press conference to influence opinion and to state his case against his critics in Congress. It is highly questionable whether the usefulness of the press conference to him has been as great as he expected. He has not used it to the full extent to explain, argue, and educate. Instead, he often has been content to state a conclusion rather than to use the occasion to mobilize support with strong argument.

That the President is capable of explaining an issue and arguing for it with force was demonstrated best of all in a notable address in December, 1961, before the National Association of Manufacturers. He spoke at length, in detail, and with great force on the reasons why he was asking Congress for broad new trade legislation. Carefully argued speeches like that one are worth more than a dozen offhand appeals for support on an issue that is never fully clarified.

Unlike Wilson and the two Roosevelts, President Kennedy has refused to go over the heads of his former colleagues on Capitol Hill. He has neglected his opportunities to use the forum of the Presidency as an educational institution. He has not used the many facilities at his command to build fires under the feet of hesitant legislators. Instead, he has sought to win them over by the elements of compromise and adjustment he learned so well in the Senate. That has been the Kennedy style in the first two years. He signed several bills distasteful to him, including the measure he had opposed to permit tax deductions for private pension funds, rather than alienate friends in Congress.

In the President's defense, it must be said that while he pressed for New Frontier domestic programs, his larger objective always was to maintain a united front on foreign affairs. Neither Wilson nor F.D.R. had to temper his actions in his first years because of overseas crises. Even when this is said, however, it has come as a surprise to the President's early supporters to see that he has not used the Presidency in a more dramatic way to deal with his party in Congress. The role of the great compromiser hardly befits his

own definition of the Presidency. And it neglects the fact that his
power with Congress rests with the people. As all the great
Presidents learned, only the people can give the chief executive
sustenance and establish him in fact as leader of his party in
Congress. Perhaps with the clearer mandate the voters gave the
President in 1962, and with the confidence gained from the Cuban
experience, his leadership will be firmer in the 88th Congress than
it was in the 87th.

SEYMOUR E. HARRIS

Economics of the Kennedy Years

LIBERAL CRITICS

President Kennedy was subjected to a steady barrage of criticism from the right and left on his economic policy. He was particularly embarrassed by the persistent attacks from his supporters on the left, among them Walter Lippmann, Senator Albert Gore, Leon Keyserling, Oscar Gass, Sidney Hyman, Robert Lekachman, Hobart Rowan, Bernard Nossiter, TRB of *The New Republic*, Walter Reuther, and even such friendly advisers as Paul Samuelson. These critics were not equally vigorous in their comments. Perhaps Keyserling and Gass were the most vocal. They found very little to praise and much to condemn in Kennedy's decisions.

Following are a few quotes from the critics:

In a carefully prepared television program in June 1961, Walter Lippmann said of President Kennedy: What he has done in the first four or five months is "first of all to carry on in all its essentials the Eisenhower economic philosophy. . . . It's like the Eisenhower Administration 30 years younger."

Leon Keyserling, in a reply to the writer in a *New Republic* article of October 9, 1961, entitled "JFK Economics: Should We All Stand Up and Cheer?" said:

These selections are from Seymour E. Harris, *Economics of the Kennedy Years and a Look Ahead*, pp. 217–230, 6–16, 258–259. Copyright © 1964 by Seymour E. Harris. Reprinted by permission of Harper & Row, Publishers.

Measuring the current recovery properly by the test of how close it is bringing us toward reasonably full utilization of manpower and other productive resources on a sustainable basis (rather than measuring it improperly by the absolute index of the upturn in production from a recessionary basis), the recovery to date has not been substantially more satisfactory than the two upturns after recessions under Eisenhower. . . . [. . . This is not an acceptable definition of recovery, but rather of goals.]

This is a mild version of some of the criticisms by Keyserling of Kennedy economics. He is particularly critical of economists like myself who consider political issues: "When economists soften their economic findings in terms of their own political judgments, they offer the President what he does not need from them."

Elsewhere Keyserling said that the President's "proposed programs fall far short even of compatibility with these excessively low goals. . . ."

In an article in *Harper's* magazine of September 1961, Hobart Rowan, one of the most able writers on the current economic scene, was especially critical of Kennedy's reluctance to spend and of his claims of fiscal integrity. He quoted Samuelson's comment "that we are in the midst of a placebo program for recovery." (A similar position was taken by Rowan in a *New Republic* article of May 25, 1963.)

After surveying Kennedy's policies in 1961, he concluded:

Yet all this falls far short of the bright promise; the nation has had to settle for a limited program which is unlikely to result in full employment or a significant rise in our economic growth rate. . . .
. . . The political strategy can be left to the politicians. . . . In the first year of this Administration too much obeisance has been paid to political feasibility. If economists do not argue cogently and forcefully for their programs, the goals they want to achieve may never become politically feasible.

Oscar Gass, perhaps the most pungent among the President's liberal critics, also had much to say of Kennedy's economic policies in a series of articles in *Commentary* in 1961 and 1962. His summary position: President Kennedy has "projected little and accomplished almost nothing."

The President was frequently criticized for failing to use the Congress more effectively. Both Gass and Hyman made this point. Gass: ". . . The legislator feels the Constitutional separation of powers not as a theorist's simplification but as a painful reality. . . ."

On interest rates, Gass used one word: "Failure."

Kennedy's political music:

> . . . I might call it *immobilism*. . . . It lacks the militant personnel and drive to pull a working bloc of Congressional supporters into participation. . . . It . . . looks for support to established Republicans, to conservative business figures. . . . It naturally finds intellectual sustenance in the politics and economics of Galbraith and Schlesinger. . . .

This criticism that the President did not appeal to the people or use Congress effectively is an often repeated charge.

Perhaps the major criticism results from the slow pace at which the President moved: Unemployment was high; excess capacity was costly; growth inadequate; and yet the President moved sluggishly in the view of critics. Most of these detractors were prepared to admit that his slight plurality in the election might help to explain the President's reluctance to plunge. But the common view was that the President paid too much attention to Congress and failed to use Congress. Some felt that he should have appealed to the country and moved far ahead of Congress. For example, Sidney Hyman, the able historian, writing in *Look* early in July 1963, suggested that it was a mistake for Kennedy to diminish his demands; he should have put the responsibility of cutting upon the Congress.

To some extent these critics had a case. The Democratic national platform promised aggressive measures to induce growth and reduce unemployment; and the President adhered to the outlines of his platform in his campaign speeches. Yet the criticism should have been directed more to the system rather than to the President. The Presidential candidate appoints a chairman of the Platform Committee who has virtually dictatorial powers. The candidate has little time to direct or supervise the writing of the platform. Moreover, and more important, it does not bind the Congress, which has little to do with the platform. Former President Eisenhower also failed to adhere to many of the policies outlined in his platform, such as his promise not to impair collective bargaining. Here again it was the system rather than the President that was at fault.

Critics should also remember the obstacles which confronted the President, some of them unexpected or more persistent than had been anticipated. Among these were the adverse balance of payments, restraining expansionist policies; the strengthening of the coalition between the Republicans and the Southern congressmen; the increased obstacles of the Rules Committee; the unfortunate incumbence of Senator Byrd and Congressman Mills in the chairmanship of the most important committees (at least, it was unfortunate for any President who would embark on expansionist programs); the collapse of the stock market in the spring of 1962; the weakening of the stimulus, available to President Eisenhower, from the large backlog of demand for consumer goods, stemming from the Depression and the war; the revolutionary economic changes in Europe; the unavailability of the degree of liberalization of housing credit available to Eisenhower; the sluggish economy inherited in 1961 and the large advance of automation; the Berlin crisis, which resulted in much larger security outlays (a favorable factor in stimulating the economy but adverse in its effects on welfare expenditures).

From 1961 the President's Committee on the State of the Economy predicted high levels of unemployment and stunted growth unless the President (and Congress) moved with energy and dispatch. But though these economists could urge the President on, irrespective of congressional attitudes, the President had to consider noneconomic factors, including congressional attitudes.

Even in the first half of 1961, the critics were demanding more audacious measures. Yet the President had moved quickly to treat the recession: He accepted a modest deficit, pressured for more credit and lower rates, accelerated federal outlays, pushed his area redevelopment program and temporary unemployment compensation program. Despite the affirmations of Keyserling and Gass, the recovery in these early months was most satisfactory, especially if allowance is made for the less than normal preceding decline. The economy began to improve rapidly, after only nine months of recession, due to the President's aggressive measures.

But the critics had a case against the President in that even as late as the Berlin crisis and the beginning of 1962, he was still excessively cautious of large expenditures and deficits. He was not prepared *adequately* to exploit fiscal instruments. But after the first eighteen months of the Kennedy Administration, the President underwent a fundamental change. He had become convinced that deficits would stimulate the economy, that with large amounts of unemployment they would not bring on inflation, and that there were some objectives much more important than the balanced budget. Having accepted and even pushed for a $10 billion tax cut which might, on top of a pretax cut $7 billion deficit, have raised the deficit to $12 billion, the President had moved way beyond his predecessors and had taken big political risks. One might have thought this would silence the critics. But it did not. I agree with the economists who say that the $11 billion tax cut is not enough to bring unemployment down to 4 per cent within the next few years and, hence, is not enough to achieve the goals of the Democratic platform. But I do not agree that the President should have asked for a $15 billion tax cut. If he had, he would probably not have received the $11 billion, and he would have lost prestige with the Congress and the country.

Another point on which the critics were wrong was their contention that the Administration's monetary policy was weak. Writing in the *Progressive,* in 1961, Keyserling said: "In monetary policy, the changes thus far do not sufficiently liberalize credit nor sufficiently reduce interest rates; the citadel of excessive Federal Reserve Board power has not been challenged by the Administration."

Gass, in an exchange with me in *Commentary,* in 1962, quoted approvingly a congressional report which said: "Monetary policy was—and continues to be—largely immobilized in a posture more suited to restraining overemployment than to stimulating recovery."

I do not agree with these statements. The Administration in a period of less than three years, during which GNP rose by the large estimated sum of about $100 billion, or about 5.5 per cent a year (in stable dollars), kept the interest rates that count at home relatively stable. The net change was minimal, and during a large part of this period below the rates at the beginning of the recovery. This was a remarkable performance, especially considering the past anti-inflationary bias of the Federal Reserve Board, and also the need of high short-term rates when the balance of payments is weak. The Kennedy Administration was against dear money, and in light of the above considerations as well as the substantial rise of federal debt which tends to raise rates, it is striking that long-term rates declined slightly—compare the more than 50 per cent rise under Eisenhower. Keyserling and Gass would do well to compare the steady rise of interest rates in the three previous recoveries from 1949 to 1960, and the stability in 1961–1963. I refer them to the Department of Commerce, *Business Cycle Developments*.

On the subject of anemic recoveries, it is worthwhile to stress that after recoveries lasting forty-five, thirty-five, and twenty-five months, the current recovery has now continued for forty months. The trend has been broken.

The President's critics concentrated on unemployment statistics as the guide to the degree of success in solving our problem. Unemployment is indeed a serious matter. Yet there were other areas of success: the growth of the economy; related, the rise of productivity; the stability of prices; the increase in welfare payments. On all these criteria, the government performed well. Even the unemployment statistics are not so depressing as they at first seem. Sam Lubell, after interviews in twenty-three cities (*Boston Globe,* July 14, 1963), found that among married persons who were unemployed, roughly 40 per cent had husband or wife working; of the unemployed, he found that 60 per cent were not concerned, for they were moving from one job to another. (This seems like a high percentage for transitional unemployment.) Nearly 10 per cent admitted they could get jobs at lower pay than they were prepared to accept.

Admittedly, the economics of national policy called for more vigorous action. In that sense the critics were right, and in trying to convince Americans of the "economic" issues, they were serving their country. But insofar as they expected policy to be based on economics alone, they were inflating the contribution and importance of purely economic considerations.

The liberal critics failed to weigh noneconomic issues adequately, and forgot that the President had to weigh all aspects of a problem. I believe that they were also wrong when they stressed the failure of the President to "use" Congress. Conflicts between the President and the Congress, each jealous of their prerogatives, have persisted for many administrations. In 1963, the critics gave the President little credit for the revolutionary change in his economic thinking and in his proposals. By concentrating on unemployment and neglecting or underestimating the gains in growth, in stability, in the balance of payments, and in welfare programs, the liberal critics did the President an injustice.

CONSERVATIVE CRITICS

President Kennedy's conservative critics charged excessive spending, excessive deficits, inflationary policies, and unwarranted intervention by the federal government. These have been the main points of attack against the Democrats since 1933, if not since 1914. When there was a conflict, for example Kennedy's tussle with the steel industry for violating an agreement, with the result of greater threats to inflation, the critics disregarded the anti-inflationary aspects of the President's approach and concentrated on his desire to control the economy.

The conservative attacks probably stem more from noneconomic than economic origins. The conservatives particularly want the free market to operate without interference by government. Naturally, their economic analysis is not unimportant, nor is it always correct. It is, for example, economically unsound to argue, as Eisenhower, Hoover, Goldwater, and others have, that the time to reduce taxes is in the highly prosperous periods, when the budget is in balance, or in surplus, and that they should not be reduced when the economy is depressed and the budget in deficit.

Let us begin with President Eisenhower who, early in 1963, wrote an important article for the *Saturday Evening Post,* called "Spending Into Trouble." The ex-President was especially critical of excessive intervention by government and of the vast expenditures and deficits. In discussing the $99 billion 1964 budget, Eisenhower described it as bigger than the wartime budget. But the

President did not say that as a percentage of GNP the federal budget in fiscal 1945 was 47 per cent; in 1964, only about 15 per cent.

I say that the time-tested rules of financial policy still apply. Spending for spending's sake is patently a false theory. No family, no business, no nation can spend itself into prosperity. . . . They and their children will pay and pay and pay. In effect, we are stealing from our grandchildren in order to satisfy our desires of today.

In taking this position, Eisenhower showed that his economics is still primitive. For he failed to take into account the large contribution made by the growth of debt and therefore of demand. Inadequacy of demand is a crucial cause of depressions and sluggish economy, and underwriting of demand helps keep the economy flourishing. Spending is no guarantee of prosperity; but it is a necessary condition.

The nonsense about the grandchildren paying the bill is discussed and dismissed in every freshman economics course in the country. I heard this as an undergraduate at Harvard in 1919. Indeed a larger debt bequeathed to our grandchildren in the year 2000 may mean more taxes, which is a burden; but the transfers are made to other (or the same) grandchildren living at that time. The crucial point is that any beneficiaries of government spending receive income and resources not at the expense of our grandchildren but at the expense of those living today. Surely the President never picked up this kind of economics from Arthur Burns or Gabriel Hauge. It sounds more like Senator Goldwater.

. . . But all of us would feel more comfortable and secure if our national leadership exercised the foresight and self-discipline to balance its budget and to begin paying back something on the national debt. . . . Imagine how much better the country would feel if it had no debt at all but a healthy surplus!

Apparently there are still important citizens who believe repayment of the debt is a crucial need. There are times when repayment may be appropriate: in periods of boom as a means of destroying money and reducing demand. But on the whole the occasion for repayment does not come often; and there have been periods—such as 1866–1893—when repayment through the destruction of currency damaged the economy. However, repayment in the 1920's was helpful.

Eisenhower also discussed inflation—he compared Truman's 47 per cent rise of prices in seven years and his of 10 per cent in eight years. But he did not mention the contribution of war and the aftermath of war to Truman's inflation nor the Republican contribution to inflation in their espousal of tax cuts in the midst of inflationary pressures in the late 1940's. Yet in the political milieu one cannot blame President Eisenhower for boasting of what appeared a much better price history.

Even Arthur Burns, one of our most able economists, who was generally on the side of the angels during the Eisenhower period, was critical of Kennedy's spending policies, as were Henry Wallich and Raymond Saulnier, other members of Eisenhower's Council of Economic Advisers. Burns, generally a very cautious economist, predicted in 1961 that the country would reach 4 per cent unemployment in the midst of 1962—and without government intervention.

Saulnier seemed to adhere to a brand of economics rather like Eisenhower's. In a speech at Miami University in Ohio, he argued that the recession in 1957–1958 had little to do with a cut of federal expenditures in 1957. This may or may not be so. But what Saulnier failed to note was that with the rise of GNP of $45 billion in 1956 and 1957, federal expenditures rose only by $5 billion and budget receipts by $9 billion. The receipts rose too much and expenditures too little. From the third quarter of 1958 to the first quarter of 1960, receipts rose by $20 billion and expenditures by $0.7 billion, with disastrous results.

It is therefore not surprising that Saulnier wrote: ". . . As a practical matter, you can't cut taxes and raise expenditures simultaneously without at some point getting into a frightful fiscal mess and I expect this fact of life to be recognized before too long."

Saulnier's last point was virtually Republican doctrine in 1963. A tax cut would be acceptable; but it should be accompanied by no rise of expenditures and by an equivalent reduction in expenditures for many. He does not recognize that what would be gained by the tax cut in stimulating demand would be lost by reduction of spending.

There was a report, on August 14, 1961, on *Comments on the Final Staff Report on Employment in the Dynamic American Economy* by the Committee of forty-eight Republican congressmen chaired by Congressman Thomas B. Curtis. In this over forty-thousand-word report, an articulate group of Republican congressmen (some more liberal than conservative) expressed their views of the Kennedy Administration directly or by implication:

A planned economy only hides unemployment. . . . Individual drive and incentive supported by sound governmental policies are the only sensible answers to the changing job situation.

[Government's contribution is mainly not through expenditures but to promote conditions] favorable to the exercise of individual enterprise and private effort.

[The federal government is] an auxiliary handmaiden rather than a partner in working together with business, labor and state and local government.

Though the committee stressed the need of solving the unemployment problem, structural unemployment received the almost exclusive attention of the Curtis Committee. Though a comment was made that fiscal policy was accepted by "the leading figures of both political parties," it received virtually no attention in the report.

Little comment is needed on some of the absurdities in the accompanying documents. One quote will suffice: ". . . the economic goal of our economy is exactly that dictated by Communist theory—to make every individual a consumer irrespective of what he contributes to production."

Perhaps the most persistent critic of the Kennedy Administration was the editor of the *Wall Street Journal*. In reply to my comment on Eisenhower vs. Kennedy, the editor wrote, in the September 25, 1961, *Journal:* ". . . judged by the criteria of prosperity, mildness of intermittent recessions, and avoidance of inflationary excesses, the Eisenhower period compares very favorably with any predecessors. . . ."

The *Journal* complains again and again of excessive public spending. In the September 11, 1961, issue: ". . . and there is only one place where it [inflation] can be created, namely in the

Government itself. . . ." Furthermore, ". . . in just a few short months it [the government] has added tremendously to federal spending. . . . It has converted previously anticipated budget surpluses into heavy deficits, and no man can see the end."

On the steel episode, the *Journal* blamed inflationary policies. If the government had not created so much money, then neither a wage nor a price rise could be inflationary. The *Journal* asked for a fiscal and monetary policy that would be sufficiently restrictive to exclude any inflation. Hence with rising wages, and rising prices induced by higher wages, the result of such restriction could be inadequacy of monetary supplies and increased unemployment. This was exactly what happened under President Eisenhower in 1955–1958, when the attempt was made to deal with a cost inflation through classical restrictions on the monetary supply: The inflation was nevertheless a record one for peacetime, and yet the rise of unemployment was disturbing.

Perhaps the best indication of the views of the conservative critics appeared in the minority reports of the Joint Economic Committee on the January *Economic Report of the President* for the years 1961, 1962, and 1963, including two papers by Arthur Burns, and an exchange between Burns and the Council of Economic Advisers. Burns's first paper was an address in Chicago, on April 21, 1961 (a summary and the exchange with the council appear in the *Morgan Guaranty Survey* of August 1961). The second paper appeared in the same publication, July 1963. It was written for the Semicentennial Lecture Series of Rice University, and was also published by the University of Chicago Press as *The Nation's Economic Objectives: Roots and Problems of Achievement*. The minority reports were more sophisticated than they had been under Eisenhower, undoubtedly due to Congressman Curtis's mobilization of economic brains and especially the help given by Arthur Burns.

Briefly, here are the criticisms and proposals of the Republicans as revealed by the six documents mentioned above.

A major charge is excessive federal spending plus especially badly timed expenditures, which could do little good and would induce inflation. The 1963 minority report would put a $95 billion ceiling on expenditures. Burns said in 1963 that the major problem facing the country was the increase in the public debt. What particularly vexed Burns was that the Kennedy Administration was committing the same errors as Eisenhower had in 1957–1958—a series of badly planned expenditures, wrongly timed and massive in amount.

A second criticism was that the Democrats depend excessively on government. The Republican Minority Committee in 1963 quoted a study by George Terborgh which showed that there was not a high correlation between government deficits and gains of GNP.

Terborgh's analysis shows that there is no general pattern to support the theory that deficits are stimulative and surpluses repressive. In fact, in the post-war period, of 51 quarters with a rising Gross National Product, Terborgh found that 28 were associated with a Federal surplus and 23 with a deficit. . . .

Recovery, in the view of the Republican minority, was the result of natural forces and the contributions of the free market. But no attempt was made to explain the long recovery of 1961–1963, with promise of many more months of rises, or of government's contribution to this recovery.

Perhaps the strongest attacks were related to the "growthmanship" of the Kennedy Administration. Both the emphasis on growth and the weapons used to reach the targets received much comment. To the Republican minority, GNP was a most inadequate measure, for it did not account for such factors as improved quality or more leisure. Moreover, the idea of a sluggish economy, or a gap, did not appeal to the minority.

In the first exchange between the President's council and Burns, the issue was largely the size of the gap in current output relative to potential output. The difference stemmed largely from disagreement on the base from which trend lines were taken. Burns's estimate of the gap was less than Heller's.

The minority of the Joint Economic Committee expressed the view that the council was overoptimistic about the gap. Excess capacity may be largely obsolescent plant; hence, the excess capacity, in the minority's view, and the gap between actual and potential output may be smaller than it seems. This position has some merit.

Some questions may also be raised concerning the council's forecast of output. It is based on the theory of substantial rises of numbers on the labor market and continued increases of productivity. When employment prospects were not favorable, the numbers seeking work tended to fall below estimates; and after two years of recovery, rises in productivity may taper off. Hence output may not rise as much as anticipated. Burns stressed such possibilities, and also a likely inflation, which might interfere with growth. Actual developments in the first three years surprised many people. Output rose much more than expected by the government; prices were much more stable than anticipated by Burns; and unemployment, in view of the rise of output, remained generally much higher than had been expected.

Although Burns was concerned over the unemployment problem, he sometimes made little of it. He did not like the 4 per cent goal. Moreover, he asked, why should not the emphasis be on the 95 or 97 per cent employed rather than the 5 or 3 per cent unemployed.

Perhaps the greatest split between the Administration and the Republican minority was on how to treat unemployment. The council stressed the deficiency of general demand; hence the need of fiscal and monetary policy to raise demand and reduce unemployment. The minority and Burns both emphasized the structural aspects of unemployment, and hence urged measures to improve the functioning of the labor market, to retrain workers, and similar measures. At times, it seemed that the minority was completely unaware of deficiency of demand. Burns sought adequate statistics on unfilled vacancies, and he would compare unfilled vacancies and unemployment, with the lower of the two indicating structural unemployment. He especially insisted that much unemployment was inevitable irrespective of deficiencies of demand. I am not unsympathetic with this approach. But I do not agree with the Burns-minority position, which greatly overdoes the significance of structural unemployment. In one report, the minority says that "full employment is reached at higher levels of unemployment." When unemployment is 6 per cent, unfilled vacancies will be substantial but certainly not a major factor. The crucial disease is insufficient demand. . . . the large reduction of employment in declining industries in recession years as against prosperous years enforces this conclusion.

Concerned over the balance of payments, the minority in 1961 urged putting a large part of the burden of defense and aid on other countries. But in 1963 the approach was entirely different. Large expenditures, substantial deficits, and easy money were held both by the minority and Burns to have serious effects upon the unfavorable balance of payments. Irresponsible finance, in their view, reduced the confidence in the dollar. All those who were critical of measures to stimulate demand through fiscal or monetary policy tended to overemphasize the effect of fiscal and monetary policy upon the balance of payments. However, the weakness of the dollar was bound to weaken pressures for expansionist measures.

On monetary policy, the minority reports consistently criticized the "nudging" or "twisting" of the Federal Reserve to create more money. Whereas the Kennedy Administration feared the effects of inadequate liquidity, and the majority of the Joint Economic Committee criticized the executive for being too cautious in creating money, the minority group and Burns often lashed out at the executive for providing easy money, with concomitant dangers of inflation and weakening of the dollar abroad. In their view, the tax cut and the large deficit were also likely to yield further inflation if the securities were sold to the banks and the Federal Reserve provided additional reserves; and to bring higher interest rates to private borrowers if sold to savers. In general, the executive was concerned that savings might be excessive; the minority thought they would be inadequate. The minority felt that keeping rates of interest down through cheap money would discourage savings.

Obviously, the conservative charge has been the reverse of the liberal: too much government, excessive concern with growth objectives, too much spending and excessive deficits, too much help to consumers, too little to savers, and too much money and excessively low rates of interest. Failure to bring full employment was another source of criticism. The Eisenhower record on government spending, though not nearly as restrictive as had been promised, was in fact mildly expansionist, and was better than the Truman record on extent of inflation. But this view ignores the relevance of war and war's aftermath under Truman, and also assumes that less federal spending is always an advantage. In relation to Kennedy, Eisenhower's inflation record was less impressive; and if the criterion of sound policy is less spending and smaller deficits, Eisenhower clearly had the edge on Kennedy. But whether Eisenhower's advantage is good for the economy is another matter.

.   .   .   .   .

THE LARGE ISSUES

Accomplishments

In the almost three years of his [Kennedy's] Administration, following the first quarter of 1961, the President could boast of an estimated rise of GNP of about $100 billion in current dollars, or an increase to 20 per cent. In stable dollars, the rise came to 5.5 per cent a year to early 1964. This was a very satisfactory rate of growth, even if measured from a low level of the first quarter of 1961. A good index of the quality of the improvement is to compare the gain of GNP with the accompanying price rise. Improvement in output is likely to be accompanied by a price rise. One is traded against the other. In the three years ending March 1964, the ratio of the percentage of GNP (real) rise to the percentage of price rise was more than 4 to 1 (estimated). This is a very satisfactory ratio. Surely a rise of GNP four times as great as the accompanying price rise indicates a successful economic policy. In the years 1952–1960, the ratio was 3 to 2. Even this advance—25 per cent gain in GNP against 16 per cent price rise—is worthwhile.

On the unemployment front the Kennedy Administration's record was less satisfactory than that of the Eisenhower Administration, despite the fact that President Kennedy was more disposed to treat economic disease than his predecessor. Unemployment is too high, considering past accomplishments, the records in Western Europe, and the objectives expressed by the President and his party.

In defense of President Kennedy, the following can be said. An increasing trend of unemployment was already apparent in the later Eisenhower years: Unemployment at cyclical peaks was rising. For certain reasons . . . the amount of additional GNP required to accompany an increase of X jobs was nearly doubled under Kennedy. In 1961, it seemed possible that an increase of GNP of $75 billion in stable prices would reduce unemployment to 4 per cent or less within three years. It is now clear that the combination of monetary and fiscal policy required to bring unemployment down to 4 per cent by 1964 or 1965 would be very difficult to achieve. As we shall see, there are limits on the contribution of monetary policy, and hence the need of greater recourse to fiscal policy. But an annual needed rise of GNP of $40 or $50 billion would require a cut in taxes plus a rise of federal spending which would not be acceptable to the Congress or their constituents. In the years 1950–1962, the average rise of GNP (1962 prices) was but $18 billion, and only in three years did the rise exceed $30 billion.

Despite the substantial rise of output, President Kennedy succeeded in stabilizing prices. Wholesale prices actually declined, and the cost of living rose little more than 1 per cent per year. For the first time since Grover Cleveland's day, a Democratic President had succeeded in stabilizing the internal value of the dollar. To be fair, one should note that the association of Democrats with inflation, aside from the greenback, silver, and populist movements of the last quarter of the nineteenth century, has been related to their unfortunate incumbency in war times. It is rather unexpected that prices, on the average, should have risen substantially more under Eisenhower than under Kennedy, and especially since the inflation under Democrats was the major economic issue raised by Eisenhower in 1962.

Among the factors responsible for the satisfactory price history under Kennedy were attempts to keep wages and prices from rising in crucial industries, the awareness that costs must be kept down in order to increase exports and reduce imports and thus strengthen the dollar, restraints on excessive increases in the monetary supply, and unusual gains in productivity, at least for 1961–1963. This stable price history prevailed despite the fact that the government and the monetary authority did not allow international deficits of a few billions each year to be reflected in related declines in the supply of money. The orthodox approach demands monetary restraints as reserves decline, the theory being that the resultant decline of money, and hence prices, would increase exports and reduce imports.

Kennedy inherited a serious balance of payments problem. At least thirty important measures were taken to correct the situation. But deficits of $2 to $3 billion continue, though the deficits are less than they were in 1959 and 1960. This problem has been much more intractable than was anticipated in 1961, though in late 1963 and early 1964 the deficit was reduced greatly.

In welfare programs, the gains were not as large as had been promised or anticipated. The President fought for advances in many programs—area redevelopment, manpower training, liberalization of old-age, survivors and disability insurance (OASDI), unemployment compensation, extension of housing programs, Medicare, mental health and retardation, transportation, development of natural resources, and several other programs. As a measure of good intentions, the Democratic Administration deserves respect for promoting numbers of programs. Welfare expenditures, though substantially greater than under Eisenhower, were not as high as had been promised. The rise of security and space outlays, the general hostility toward public expenditures in the nation, the shift of emphasis to tax reduction—all of these contributed to a slowing down of the rate of expenditures on welfare. Although the rise of outlays was not insignificant, there was a definite decline in relation to needs.

In agriculture Kennedy pushed for high farm supports and income but tried hard to cut production. Here he had only limited success. The farmers wanted higher incomes, but were not disposed to accept strong controls.

Obstacles

Kennedy's accomplishments might have been greater, but several factors worked against him. One was, of course, the close election. A second was the troublesome problem of the balance of payments, which seriously hampered expansionist policies. It was widely believed (and with some justification) that short-term interest rates had to be kept at levels competitive with those offered by foreign lenders, and also (with less justification) that federal deficits had to be kept at minimum figures. Moreover, Western Europe was emerging as a serious competitor to the United States in the production and sale of manufactured goods and in its capacity to impose trade policies harmful to the United States. A fourth item was the crisis of confidence that comes once in a generation and in 1962 brought a serious decline in stock market prices. A fifth development was the emergence of civil rights as a vital issue, and one which reduced the cooperation of Southern congressmen in the furtherance of welfare measures. A sixth point was the rising power of the House Rules Committee. A seventh factor was the sluggish economy, punctuated by anemic recoveries, that President Kennedy inherited. By 1960 the backlog of demand for capital and consumption goods following fifteen years of depression and war had been largely used up, as had the liberalization of financing terms that stimulated buying under Eisenhower. Unusual gains of productivity further increased unemployment.

Tactics

The President's detractors found many weaknesses in his approach: He had, according to some, given us the third Eisenhower Administration; his efforts were limited, for he assumed that making speeches was the equivalent of putting a program through; he appeased the Congress instead of fighting it; he accepted congressional decisions instead of appealing to the people; he compromised with the Congress even as he launched his programs and thus gave away his program even before the contest had begun. These were mainly attacks from the left; from the right the charge was that he offered too many programs, and was an irresponsible spender. Caught between the fire of the left and of the Republican right, the latter bolstered by the Democratic right, the President had little room to maneuver.

How valid are these criticisms? It would surprise most Republicans to discover that Kennedy and Eisenhower agreed on economic policy. Consider but one item: The Republicans do not insist that fiscal policy stimulates the economy, or that increased taxes and reduced spending will cure an overstimulated economy. Rather the reverse. The Republicans approve a tax cut when the economy is exuberant, that is, when taxes should be raised, not lowered.

Those who claim that Kennedy's and Eisenhower's policies were similar should compare the programs offered and those achieved. The difference between the two Presidents was substantial on achievements, but with the current functioning of the Congress, the difference was even greater in programs offered.

Was the President wrong in not appealing to the public, when the Congress thwarted him? I doubt it. Congress largely reflects the views of its constituencies. The American public is no more disposed to modern fiscal theories than is Congress. Congressmen are not asked to use the Keynesian weapons. Instead, the public's complaints are concerned with excessive taxes and spending. Otherwise, the public has a limited understanding of modern theories. Congressmen are honest when they return from a testing period at home and announce no great enthusiasm for a tax cut accompanied by a rising debt.

On at least three occasions, the President appealed to the country directly: on Medicare, on the tax cut, on foreign aid. Moreover, his numerous press conferences were meant to educate the voter. The three direct appeals were effective presentations. But they did not seem to have much effect; and any gains may have been offset by increased resentment by the Congress for his direct appeal to all the people. I suspect that the people lead the Congress on the subject of Medicare. As for tax cuts, the Congress probably reflects the views of their constituencies. I believe that the Congress is more disposed to foreign aid than are the people.

It is not really worth answering the charge of lack of effort. No President of recent times faced as many day-by-day crises, with the possible exception of Franklin Roosevelt, and yet continued to plug for his important programs.

Did the President compromise too much in submitting his programs? There may be differences of opinion here. The President should and did lead the Congress. Disagreements arise on the question of how far he should have. The blocker on the football field who leads his runner by twenty yards is hardly effective. The President's failure in putting over some legislation he proposed suggests that he was far ahead of Congress. Consider, for example, his Medicare program, proposals for permanent changes in unemployment compensation, transportation subsidies, aid to education, and agricultural policy. In each instance the President led Congress by a substantial distance; but in most cases Congress did not move. Would it have helped if the President blocked at forty yards' distance from the ball carrier rather than twenty? I think the President would then have been less effective.

Some of the President's supporters argued that he should have submitted an audacious program, and that if he received one that fell below his standards, he should have threatened a veto and, if necessary, vetoed the bill. He then would have won a moral victory. This seemed to me unwise. It would not have been sensible to veto an $11 billion tax cut because the Congress refused the suggested tax reform and because the President wanted a $15 billion tax cut, with no restraints on usual rises in spending. It was better to wait for the tax cut than to win a moral victory and repudiate the program.

Relations with the Congress

With substantial majorities in both the House and the Senate (257 Democratic House members and 178 Republican House members, and 67 and 33, respectively, in the Senate in the 88th Congress in November 1963), greater achievements might have been expected. But aside from the handicaps mentioned earlier, there are special reasons for President Kennedy's failure to achieve more. On the whole his gains were, however, substantial in the 87th Congress (1961–1962).

Among the factors accounting for the limited cooperation of the Congress were the long delays—for example, the lack of progress in putting through appropriation bills in 1963, with important bills still not acted on as late as November; the emergence of the civil rights issue, which resulted in delays in other legislation plus the growing reluctance of Southern congressmen to agree with their party on other issues; and the rising level of discipline among Republican congressmen.

Undoubtedly the executive departments and agencies are hampered by the demands Congress makes upon high officials. In 1963, the Secretary of the Treasury spent most of his time on the Hill. The long-sustained treatment of the tax bill, the debt ceiling, and the interest rate equalization tax required the presence of the Secretary and top aides on the Hill continuously, and when they were not on the Hill they were collecting material for hearings or for the elucidation of the committees writing the bills. Under Secretary Henry Fowler and Assistant Secretary Stanley Surrey had to devote virtually all their time to attempting to get a tax bill through; and yet they had to forego many of the reform provisions on which they had worked for two years.

Democratic defections greatly hampered Kennedy's legislative program. There were relatively few economic programs of the Administration that received the support of a majority of the Republicans. In 1963, for example, the only significant Administration programs which won the Republicans' support were a mental health bill, the college aid program, and the vocational education bill.

It has sometimes been said that Kennedy suffered from the change of leadership from Senator Johnson to Senator Mansfield in the Senate and Congressman Rayburn to Congressman McCormack in the House. Undoubtedly the inexperience of the new leaders increased the difficulties of obtaining approval for the Kennedy program. There was also a weakening of discipline among the Democrats coincident with new Republican strength. With time and experience, the Democratic leadership should improve. But perhaps more important than lack of leadership was the breakdown of the congressional process. In *The New York Times* of November 12, 1963, Cabell Phillips noted consternation among congressmen at the achievements of the 88th Congress. President Kennedy had received approval of but seven of his twenty-seven major legislative programs. The *Congressional Quarterly* of November 8, 1963, put the box score at eight out of twenty-five.

Some Economic Issues

Primary objectives of economic policy were increased growth and stability; but the Kennedy Administration was also concerned with equity issues. Liberalization of OASDI and of unemployment compensation, the struggle for civil rights, the extension of welfare programs generally—all of these reflected an interest in equity issues. Large outlays for welfare may contribute to equity, growth, and recovery. But under some conditions, for example, in advanced stages of recovery with low unemployment, there may be conflicts between the stability and equity objectives. At such times large outlays for welfare may well contribute to inflation. Even in conditions of unemployment, welfare financed out of taxes, e.g., the social security program, may be costly in incentives and output; but the favorable effects on demand are an offset.

I have already suggested that one has to trade gains in growth against any cost in price inflation. A 10 per cent growth rate and 1 per cent price rise per year are indeed a large achievement, but most would not welcome a 1 per cent growth rate and a 10 per cent rise in inflation. The ratio of growth and price rise, below which growth should be sacrificed in order to assure a greater degree of price stability, is to be determined on both economic and ideological grounds. For example, is the rising ratio of growth to prices, 3 to 1, or 1 to 1, the point at which it becomes desirable to sacrifice growth to price stability? Price instability beyond a certain point injures the economy (economic consideration), and is harmful to those with relatively fixed income (an ideological issue). Slow growth and price stability are costly to the economy and are accompanied by inadequate employment and, hence, mean heavy costs for a small part of the population, the unemployed.

Three major weapons are at the disposal of the economic therapists, namely, money, fiscal policy, and direct attacks on unemployment, e.g., by manpower training. An increased recourse to monetary policy means less need for fiscal policy, that is, for the employment of government tax, spending, and debt policies to treat the economy. One able economist suggested that a reduction of money rates by 1 per cent as a stimulant saves the government $12 billion of spending. The more monetary and fiscal policies are used, the less the need for structural approach.

But substituting money and fiscal policy for structural therapy is limited in its effects. General measures, e.g., more money and more spending, will cut down unemployment in depressed areas. But even with easy money and deficits of $20 billion per year, the textile towns in New England and the coal mine towns of West Virginia would still experience substantial unemployment, above the national level.

General measures to solve the structural problems beyond a certain point can be highly inflationary and wasteful. Here, it is important to encourage new industries, train workers for available jobs, encourage migration to areas where there are unfilled vacancies, and so on. That an additional job can be had at a cost to the government of $1,000–$2,000 against $10,000 or thereabouts through fiscal measures strengthens the case for the structural approach. But much unemployment and limited unfilled vacancies restrict the use of the structural approach.

The recovery in the years 1961–1963 was unique in that it did not bring the rise of money rates of preceding recoveries. Both the Federal Reserve, by controlling member bank reserves and increasing the short-term rates that could be paid on time or savings deposits, and the Treasury, through large issues of short-term securities, managed generally to keep short-term rates competitive with rates abroad. But despite the high short-term rates, long-term rates were remarkably stable.

Hence, it may be said that the recovery profited from expansionist monetary policies. The rise in the supply of money was not spectacular, though it was relatively larger than in the 1950's; but if allowance is made for the very large increase in time deposits or if one concentrates on new financing, the large contribution of increased liquidity is evident.

Fiscal policy was the major weapon of the Kennedy Administration. The rise of spending was crucial, though the increase was only partially connected with economic objectives; the major part of the rise stemmed from increased needs to assure maximum security. By 1962, tax cut policy took precedence over spending. Widespread support for the tax cut rather than spending, and the President's conversion to the theory that deficits are helpful in periods of unemployment, account for the acceptance of a policy of tax reduction not only to increase growth but also to extend the recovery and weaken recessionary forces.

In order to achieve a tax cut of substantial proportions, the Kennedy Administration had to stress modern fiscal theories. At first they urged a balancing of the budget over the business cycle, not each year. But by 1963 it was clear that they had to take a more advanced position—namely, that deficits must continue into the advanced stages of recovery so long as unemployment was still high at the top of the cycle. They hoped that large induced deficits would raise GNP sufficiently so that within a reasonable time unemployment would fall to 4 per cent or less and the budget would be balanced.

Undoubtedly the country would have been much closer to a full employment economy if the balance of payments had not been so troublesome. But the steady deficits in the balance ruled out highly expansionist monetary policies and even weakened fiscal policies to some extent. In fact, many who favored restrictionist policies and discipline on other grounds favored the adverse balance of payments as a weapon to be used against the expansionists. But there was a persistent loss of reserves. Until July 1963 the Administration depended primarily on orthodox measures: raising interest rates, curbing inflationary pressures, diverting aid dollars to American markets, borrowing in foreign markets, orthodox expansion of international reserves. But in July 1963 the government introduced its interest rate equalization tax, a measure aimed at discouraging the excessive tapping of the American capital market by foreign interests. Large improvements followed in 1963–1964.

Finally, there is the intractable unemployment problem. In the midst of a highly prosperous economy, with a GNP of $600 billion, or 20 per cent above the level at the beginning of the Kennedy Administration, the country, in late 1963, was still confronted with unemployment of about 4 million, a rate of 5.5 per cent. Because unemployment is concentrated among the young, Negroes, the unskilled, and those living in surplus labor areas, the costs of a given level of unemployment are greatly increased. No one would have anticipated early in 1961 that a *real* rise of GNP of 5.5 per cent a year would fail to bring unemployment down to 4 per cent or even lower by 1963. This was the greatest disappointment for the Kennedy Administration. (By May 1964, unemployment had fallen to 5.1 per cent.

In order to treat the unemployment problem, the President had to press for advanced fiscal policies. With unemployment at about 4 per cent, the government would have been satisfied with smaller deficits. And yet in order to cope successfully with the unemployment problem, the planned deficits would have to be even larger than the President proposed.

One problem is that rising productivity—a welcome development in itself—is a partial cause of unemployment. It is possible that the structure of productivity changes has altered so that transitional unemployment problems have become more serious. If the problem is not solved, one may be sure that labor will insist upon a solution through reduced hours for the same pay. This would be unfortunate, for costs would rise and our competitive position deteriorate.

When confronted with a question on the relation of automation and jobs in his press conference of October 31, 1963, the President said:

. . . So automation does not need to be, we hope, our enemy. What is of concern now is this combination of a rather intensive period of automation, plus the fact that our educational system is not keeping up, so that we are graduating or dropping out of high school so many millions of young men and women who are not able to operate in this new society. . . .

. . . I think machines can make life easier for men, if men do not let machines dominate men. . . .

.   .   .   .   .

A CONCLUDING COMMENT

In the years 1961–1964, the economy performed much better than was expected early in 1961. The rise of the gross national product, the improved standard of living, the reduction of poverty, the increase of jobs, the price stability—these and other indexes attest the great advances made. Both the extent of the recovery and its duration underline what can be accomplished through the government's use of simple therapeutic weapons, even while the market is allowed to operate without interference. The only comparable recovery in the twentieth century was that of the 1930's following the abysmal decline of 1930–1933.

But there were some disappointments, notably excessive unemployment and the slow response of the balance of payments to official treatment. The latter blunted the weapons used to get out of the quagmire of continued anemic recoveries. The increasing GNP required to yield a million additional jobs contributed to the stubborn unemployment problem.

The major credit for this remarkable recovery and for the increasing acceptance of modern economics belongs to President Kennedy. He had become the most literate of all Presidents in his understanding of modern economics and revealed great courage in his willingness to risk political losses in putting his economics to the test of the market place.

Because the President had so excellent and articulate a teacher as Walter Heller—supported by others in the Administration and some economists from the outside—and because he had a Secretary of the Treasury who, although he came from the field of finance, was prepared to accept modern canons of finance the impressive conversion of the President was brought about. One might consider earlier secretaries of the Treasury, such as Morgenthau, Snyder, Humphrey, Anderson—and speculate on the resultant economic policies under their incumbencies.

In the Kennedy Administration the budget, which under Eisenhower had been an instrument for keeping spending down, became what it should be, a plan to help achieve stability and growth. It would be unfortunate if—as seems possible now—the budget should once more become an instrument that merely restricts spending and allocates limited resources among claimants, and not an instrument for molding fiscal policy. But budget directors David Bell and Kermit Gordon, trained in Keynesian economics, certainly understand the true functions of a budget.

In economic engineering, President Johnson in 1964 largely

followed through on the Kennedy program. Indeed, he cut the 1965 budget more than Kennedy would have—the ultimate size of the budget is still a matter of dispute—and he modified the spending structure, with more funds for welfare and less for defense. His dealings with the Congress showed great skill.

As far as one can gather from history, current statements, and comments from high officials in Washington, President Johnson, even less than Kennedy, will allow the Federal Reserve Board to weigh the objective of stability excessively against that of growth. Unsupportable restrictions on monetary creation are less likely than under Kennedy. Whereas the late President urged and persuaded Martin, President Johnson is more likely to tell Martin what he expects. He is not likely to be persuaded by any dubious themes of the independence of the Federal Reserve.

In the later 1960's, unemployment will probably continue to plague the economic practitioners. Should the recovery end in 1965—either as a result of the amount of inflation and the excesses of prosperity, or through misguided monetary and fiscal policy—then unemployment may well become even more troublesome than in the years 1960–1964. And the solution may be to divide the work, that is, resort to reduced hours, which may have unfortunate effects on output.

THEODORE C. SORENSEN

The Arrows

THE NUCLEAR DETERRENT

In three years Kennedy's build-up of the most powerful military force in human history—the largest and swiftest build-up in this country's peacetime history, at a cost of some $17 billion in additional appropriations—provided him, as he put it, with a versatile arsenal "ranging from the most massive deterrents to the most subtle influences." The most massive deterrent was our strategic nuclear force. Beginning with that first Defense Message of March, 1961, the President sharply increased the production and development of the submarine-launched Polaris and the underground Minuteman missiles. By emphasizing the survivability of these weapons, he emphasized both the futility of any attempt to find and knock them out and their second-strike, nonprovocative, time-granting nature. (They were in sharp contrast, for example, with the vulnerable Jupiter missiles located near the Soviet Union in prior years, easy targets requiring hair-trigger Presidential decisions.) Having warned in the campaign against "tempting" Soviet leaders "with the possibility of catching our aircraft and unprotected missiles on the ground in a gigantic 'Pearl Harbor,' " he placed more nuclear-armed bombers—our chief deterrent until the long-range missile program was completed—on a stand-by fifteen-minute alert basis.

These selections are from Theodore C. Sorensen, *Kennedy*, pp. 608–610, 624–627. Copyright © 1965 by Theodore C. Sorensen. Reprinted by permission of Harper & Row, Publishers.

Even more reassuring than these increases was a clearer definition of exactly what was meant by, and needed for, "deterrence,"
namely: a nuclear force sufficiently large and secure (1), in
general, to give any rational decision-maker in the enemy camp the
strongest possible incentive not to launch an attack by denying him
all prospect of victory or even survival and (2), specifically, under
the most pessimistic assumptions, to enable that portion of our
force which could survive the most serious possible attack to
destroy (a), if necessary, the aggressor's cities and population and
(b), enough of his remaining military strength, while still retaining
some reserve of our own, to convince him that he could neither
complete our destruction nor win the war.

How was this point of deterrence to be determined in concrete
figures? asked the skeptics. All the factors contained variables and
uncertainties. But, within a reasonable range, McNamara made
the first systematic effort to calculate this level on the basis of our
best estimates of the size and nature of Soviet attack forces and the
performance capabilities of our own retaliatory forces. The estimates used in these calculations were based on public information,
reports from Soviet defectors and modern as well as traditional
intelligence methods.

In our budget review sessions, McNamara in effect acknowledged that he was agreeing to a nuclear force above the level of
pure deterrence, but that the additions could be justified as forces
to limit the Soviet's ability to do further damage should deterrence
fail. He and Kennedy agreed, however, that to go further and seek
a "first-strike" capability—designed theoretically to render the
enemy incapable of damaging us severely, the kind of capability
advocated in some Air Force quarters—was not only unnecessarily
expensive and provocative but not really feasible. An enemy could
always protect or conceal enough missile power to inflict at least
thirty to fifty million fatalities on this country, especially by using
more submarine-launched missiles. And he could easily offset our
attempts to outbuild him by increasing his own forces as he saw
ours grow.

Recognizing the infeasibility of a preemptive first-strike or full
"counterforce" capability, Kennedy and McNamara could see as
no one else could the insecurity of an endless, unlimited arms race,

and the waste of indiscriminately adding tens of billions of dollars' worth of nuclear weapons as requested by the individual service chiefs. "There is a limit to how much we need . . . to have a successful deterrent," said the President. "When we start to talk about the megatonnage we could bring into a nuclear war, we are talking about annihilation. How many times do you have to hit a target with nuclear weapons?" He looked forward to a leveling off of defense spending and the allocation of more funds to domestic needs.

But these same calculations of deterrence also enabled Kennedy and McNamara to see clearly the folly of unilateral disarmament, and the irrelevance of complaints that we already had enough to "overkill" every Soviet citizen several times. Because our safety as a second-strike nation required a great enough force to survive a first strike and still retaliate effectively, and because our strategy required enough weapons to destroy all important enemy targets, there was no absolute level of sufficiency. The concept of deterrence, moreover, required not only superior forces but a degree of superiority that would, when made known—and the Kennedy Administration took unprecedented steps to make it known—convince all Allies and adversaries of that fact.

.   .   .   .   .

CONVENTIONAL AND UNCONVENTIONAL FORCES

No degree of nuclear superiority and no amount of civil defense shelters would have increased John Kennedy's appetite for nuclear war or his willingness to use nuclear weapons. It was a responsibility he was coolly prepared to meet, if meet it he must. But he deeply believed, as he once privately remarked, that any actual resort to nuclear missiles would represent not the ultimate weapon but "the ultimate failure"—a failure of deterrent, a failure of diplomacy, a failure of reason.

A superior nuclear deterrent, moreover, had a limited military value in the 1960's. It could deter a nuclear attack. It could probably deter a massive conventional attack on a strategic area such as Europe. But it was not clear that it could deter anything else. And for at least a decade the most active and constant Communist threat to free world security was not a nuclear attack at the center but a nonnuclear nibble on the periphery—intimidation against West Berlin, a conventional attack in the Straits of Formosa, an invasion in South Korea, an insurrection in Laos, rebellion in the Congo, infiltration in Latin America and guerrillas in Vietnam.

Khrushchev's speech on January 6, 1961, threatened not to destroy or invade new areas and populations but to impose his system upon them through continued "salami" tactics—through piecemeal expansion of the Communist domain one slice at a time—through limited warfare, subversion or political aggression in areas where our nuclear deterrent was not usable both because our security was not directly in danger and because massive weapons were inappropriate. If we lacked the conventional capacity to withstand these tactics effectively, we could be faced with a choice of launching a virtually suicidal nuclear war or retreating.

Unfortunately, in the 1950's, as the Communists increasingly achieved a military posture that made the threat of massive retaliation less and less credible, the United States had moved increasingly to a strategy based on that threat. Kennedy inherited in 1961 a 1956 National Security Council directive relying chiefly on nuclear retaliation to any Communist action larger than a brush fire in general and to any serious Soviet military action whatsoever in Western Europe. "If you could win a big one," Eisenhower had said, "you would certainly win a little one." Because NATO strategy had a similar basis, no serious effort had been made to bring its force levels up to full strength, and our own Army had been sharply reduced in size.

This doctrine bore little relation to the realities. Frequently, when conferring about some limited struggle, the President would ask, "What are my big bombs going to do to solve that problem?" There was no acceptable answer. Even the tactical nuclear weapons supposedly designed for "limited" wars were not an answer. The Kennedy Administration increased the development and deployment of those weapons worldwide, and by 60 per cent in Western Europe alone. The President understandably preferred that we hold the edge in such weapons rather than the Soviets. But he was skeptical about the possibility of ever confining any nuclear exchange to the tactical level, and he was concerned about the thousands of such weapons theoretically under his control that were in the hands of lower-level commanders. For some of these "small" weapons carried a punch five times more powerful than the bomb that destroyed Hiroshima. Those ready for use in Europe alone had a combined explosive strength more than ten thousand times as great as those used to end the Second World War. If that was tactical, what was strategic—and what would be the effect of their use in heavily populated Europe on the people we were supposedly saving? Once an exchange of these weapons started, the President was convinced, there was no well-defined dividing line that would keep the big bombs out.

This analysis of our predicament produced the new Kennedy-McNamara doctrine on conventional forces—a more radical change in strategy even than the augmenting and defining of the nuclear deterrent. The essence of this doctrine was choice: If the President was to have a balanced range of forces from which to select the most appropriate response for each situation—if this country was to be able to confine a limited challenge to the local and nonnuclear level, without permitting a Communist victory—then it was necessary to build our own nonnuclear forces to the point where any aggressor would be confronted with the same poor choice Kennedy wanted to avoid: humiliation or escalation. A limited Communist conventional action, in short, could best be deterred by a capacity to respond effectively in kind.

Obviously this doctrine did not downgrade nuclear power. But Kennedy's experiences in Berlin in 1961 and Cuba in 1962 demonstrated to his satisfaction that the best deterrent was a combination of both conventional and nuclear forces. At times, he commented, "A line of destroyers in a quarantine or a division of well-equipped men on a border may be more useful to our real security than the multiplication of awesome weapons beyond all rational need."

The new approach began immediately upon the Administration's taking office. It was consistent with the President's senatorial and campaign speeches on a "military policy to make all forms of

Communist aggression irrational and unattractive." It was articulated in books he admired by Maxwell Taylor, James Gavin and the British analyst B. H. Liddell Hart. It was urged by Secretary Rusk as essential to our diplomacy. It was recommended by Secretary McNamara as a part of his build-up of options. It was represented in Kennedy's first State of the Union Message authorizing a rapid increase in airlift. It was emphasized by the ammunition, personnel and other increases in his March 1961 Defense Message. It was expanded considerably in his May 1961 special State of the Union Message, in which all his defense recommendations were in the nonnuclear field. It was stressed in his efforts to strengthen local forces through the military assistance program. And it was, finally, the heart and hard core of his military response to the 1961 Berlin crisis.

McGEORGE BUNDY

The Presidency and the Peace

It is with some sense of temerity that a member of the White House staff undertakes to comment on the large topic of the Presidency and the Peace. Loyalty and affection are so normal in such service that detachment is difficult. Nevertheless the importance of the topic and the enforced familiarity of close experience with the Presidential task may justify a set of comments whose underlying motive is to express a conviction that is as obvious as the daylight, in general, and as fresh as every sunrise, in particular: a conviction that the American Presidency, for better, not for worse, has now become the world's best hope of preventing the unexampled castastrophe of general nuclear war.

Moreover, both charity and sorrow can be good lenses for perception, and it may therefore be possible to consider the subject without impropriety by focusing upon the years of John F. Kennedy. The tragedy which has moved his Administration from politics to history may allow to his critics and excuse in his friends some generosity in the assessment of his three years. His death revealed his greatness, and the grief of the world was less for his tragedy than for its own—in that he had shown his spreading grasp of his duty to mankind as Chief Executive for Peace.

To focus on the Kennedy years is not to forget those before, and still less the firm continuation after November 22. The Presidents of the nuclear age before Mr. Kennedy also made the service of peace the first of their purposes, and the determined commitment of President Johnson to this same end, matured in decades of direct knowledge of our nuclear world, has been made plain in his own words and actions already. Indeed one purpose of a retrospective assessment is to clarify purposes which are as important to the President today as to the President last year.

A President in search of Peace has many powers, but none is more relevant or more effective than his power as commander-in-chief. The President is keeping the peace as long as he keeps his own nuclear power in check, and with it the nuclear power of others. This most obvious of his powers, apparently so simple and so negative, can be used for peace in a number of ways.

The prerequisite, of course, is that this power should exist, and that there should be confidence in its future as well as its present effectiveness. Nothing is more dangerous to the peace than weakness in the ultimate deterrent strength of the United States. In the quarter-century that man has known the atom could be split, each American decision to enlarge its power has been the President's alone. More subtly but with just as great importance, the choices of methods of delivery and their rate of development have also been Presidential.

As important as having strength is being known to have it; and here if anything the Presidential authority and responsibility are still more clear. This is the lesson of Sputnik, and of the "missile gap" which was forecast and feared by responsible and well-informed men both in and out of government between 1957 and 1961. There was ground for doubt and need for rapid action; the ground and the need were recognized, and important steps were taken, but an appearance of complacency led to an appearance of weakness, with considerable costs abroad. These costs would surely have been greater had it not been for the remarkable personal standing of President Eisenhower.

At the beginning of the Kennedy Administration there was need both for further action and for a reestablishment of confidence. The new President himself had feared the missile gap and had pressed his concern in the campaign. It was with honest surprise and relief that in 1961 he found the situation much less dangerous than the best evidence available to the Senate had indicated the year before. His Administration moved at once to correct the public impression, and thereafter, throughout his term, he encouraged and supported policies of action and of exposition which aimed to ensure not merely that American strategic power was sufficient—but that its sufficiency was recognized.

The adequacy of American strategic strength is a matter of such transcendent importance that it must always be a legitimate topic of political debate. "How much is enough?" is a question on which honest men will differ, and interested parties will find room and reason for their claims. Thus it is natural that in the present political year we have ranging shots already from the fringes, some saying that our strength is too little and others that it is too great. Just as it is the responsibility of the commander-in-chief to ensure the adequacy of our strength, so it is his task, either directly or through his principal defense officers, to meet and overcome such criticism. The present Administration will not be lax in the exposition of the real situation, and no one who has closely examined the present and prospective balance of strategic strength can doubt that this year any assertion that we are weak will be found wanting to the point of irresponsibility.

There is an equal obligation to meet the arguments of those who think we are too strong. When these arguments grow out of fundamentally different views on the purpose and meaning of effective strategic strength, it may be necessary to agree to disagree. "Unilateral disarmament" is a tainted term, but it does embody something of what is desired by most of those who criticize our present strength as gravely excessive. The Presidents of the nuclear age have recognized that the law of diminishing returns applies to strategic missiles as to all other commodities; they have also agreed with President Johnson's comment that our nuclear defense expenditures can never be justified as a W.P.A. for selected towns or states. But they have all rejected the gamble of limiting our strategic strength in terms of any absolute concept of what is enough. They have measured our strength against that of the Soviet Union and have aimed at strategic superiority; that superiority has had different meanings at different stages, but seen from the White House its value for peace has never been small.

Yet even in this rejection of the underlying arguments which move so many of those who find our strength excessive, a President who cares for peace will respect their general concern. It is entirely true that nuclear strength can be provocative, that it is full of the hazard of accident or misuse, and that it imposes upon its commander, in his own interest as in that of mankind, a passion for prudence. All the Presidents of the nuclear age have understood this responsibility and have sought to meet it by insisting on disciplined and responsible control of this power. In the case of President Kennedy the pressing need was that as the number and variety of weapons systems increased, there should be ever more searching attention to effective command and control. To him this was a better answer to the dangers of accident than some arbitrary limitation of numbers; a thousand well-controlled and safely designed missiles could be less dangerous than a hundred of lower quality, as well as more effective in deterrence.

A related point was the President's powerful aversion to those nuclear weapons which could be used effectively only in a first strike. In 1961 and 1962 he faced a series of judgments on major systems; he always preferred the system which could survive an attack, as against the system which might provoke one. In the same way and for related reasons he preferred the system which was on the high seas or at home to that which required a base abroad and evoked a real or pretended charge of encirclement from Moscow.

The commander-in-chief must be strong, then, but also restrained. And as his strength must be recognized, so must his restraint. The doctrine of "massive retaliation" was never as absolute as Mr. Dulles at first made it seem, and its real weakness lay not in the undoubted fact that against certain kinds of aggression a nuclear response would be necessary, but in the appearance of a bomb-rattling menace which it created. The Presidency does well to avoid this appearance; in the Kennedy Administration the rule was that statements of strength and will should be made as calmly as possible. The President himself watched constantly to prevent the appearance of belligerence, and when the White House watch nodded—as in one magazine account in which a single phrase out of context was seized upon by Soviet propaganda—he made his dissatisfaction plain.

A similar discipline was enforced throughout the Administration upon both civil and military officials. Those who have read speech drafts for clearance know how seldom there is need for major change, and how often divergence between Presidential purposes and a speaker's draft can be corrected by revision which reconciles the real purposes of both. And again it is not only the act of coordination but the appearance of it which is helpful. The nuclear age multiplies the mistrust that peaceable men must feel toward military men who appear not to be under effective control, and nothing adds more to a President's reputation abroad than recognition that he is commander-in-chief in fact as well as in name.

Yet the Kennedy years show again, as the terms of strong Presidents have shown before, that harmony, not conflict, is the normal relation between the Armed Services and the Presidency. The maintenance of clear Presidential control over military policy and over public statements gave rise to some criticism, and intermittently there were assertions that this or that military need was being overridden—this or that viewpoint silenced. Energy and strength in the Office of the Secretary of Defense produced similar worries, and challenges to cherished privileges were not unresisted. But the center of emphasis belongs on the fact that the Presidency has these powers in this country; a President who uses them firmly, with a defensible concept of the national security, can count on the support of the officers and men of the Armed Forces. The American tradition of civilian control is strong and the tradition of loyalty among professional officers high; the services are eager for a strong and active commander-in-chief. The armed strength of the United States, if handled with firmness and prudence, is a great force for peace.

II

The President who seeks peace must have a clear view of the Soviet Union. The one great weakness of Franklin Roosevelt was that he did not; he had not the advantage of living, as all his successors have, through the realities of the years after 1945. Nothing is gained for peace by forgetting Czechoslovakia or Hungary or the recurrent menace to Berlin, or Korea or Southeast Asia or any of the dozens of times and places where Communists with help from Moscow have sought to put an end to liberty.

Mr. Kennedy had this clear view. He had it before he became President; he confirmed it in his first state papers; he understood not only the unrelenting ambition and the ruthlessness of Communism, but also the weakness and disarray of much of the non-Communist world. And for almost two of his three years—from the very beginning until the offensive weapons were gone from Cuba—he had an exposure to Communist pressure in Berlin, in Laos, and in the Caribbean which could only confirm the somber estimate with which he entered office.

Against these pressures he was firm, and to meet them more effectively he greatly strengthened the defenses of the United States—not merely in strategic weapons for basic deterrence, but also in forces designed more precisely to meet the hazards of each point of pressure. The reserves who were called up for Berlin never fired a shot in anger, but military service by Americans has seldom made a more effective contribution to the defense of freedom and the keeping of peace. The new kinds of strength deployed to South Vietnam have not finished that hard job, but they have prevented an otherwise certain defeat and kept the door open for a victory which in the end can be won only by the Vietnamese themselves. And never in any country did President Kennedy leave it in doubt that Communist subversion is always the enemy of freedom, and of freedom's friends, the Americans.

Yet always—and again from the beginning—he put equal emphasis on the readiness of the United States to reach honorable settlement of all differences, the respect of the United States for the reality of Soviet strength, and the insistence of the United States that both sides accept and meet their joint responsibility for peace.

He rejected the stale rhetoric of the cold war; he insisted not on the innate wickedness of Communism but on its evil effects. The Communist world was seldom if ever "the enemy." Characteristically, as in his Inaugural Address, the President used a circumlocution whose unaccustomed clumsiness was proof that it was carefully chosen: "those nations who would make themselves our adversary." Characteristically, too, what he there offered them was a request "to begin anew the quest for peace."

And he pressed in this same direction himself. In Laos, in Berlin, and most persistently of all in the search for a test ban, the

President's powers, from beginning to end, were used toward the goal of agreement. Agreement must never be surrender; that would be no service to peace. The firmness of the United States under pressure was made plain both in Berlin and in Southeast Asia. But firmness was a means to honorable settlement, not an end in itself. Harboring no illusion about the difficulty of success, the President nevertheless persevered. He was convinced that at the least it was essential to leave no doubt, in all these issues, of the good will and peaceful purpose of the United States. If there were to be a continued arms race, or a test of strength, it must be plain where the responsibility lay. But the larger truth, as he saw it, was that in these areas of difference there was real advantage to both sides in reliable agreement—if only the other side could be brought to see its own real interests, free of ambition that would be resisted, and of fear that was unjustified.

In 1961 and 1962 the invitation to seek peace together met a thin response. True, the threat to Berlin, so noisy in 1961, and so sharpened by the confession of Communist bankruptcy which was the Wall, seemed slightly milder in 1962. And an agreement was reached on Laos, imperfect in its terms and in its execution, but much better than no agreement at all. It was in Laos above all that one could see the advantage to both sides of even the most incomplete disengagement, as against a tightening and sharpening of confrontation.

But no agreement at all had come in the field nearest the President's heart—that of limiting the nuclear danger. On the contrary, Soviet tests had led inexorably to American tests. It was somehow a measure of the Kennedy temper and purpose that of all the Soviet provocations of these two years it was the resumption of testing that disappointed him most.

III

The Cuban missile crisis was the most important single event of the Kennedy Presidency. As the President himself pointed out afterward, it was the first direct test between the Soviet Union and the United States in which nuclear weapons were the issue.

Although vast amounts have been written about the crisis, we still have no solid account of one half of it—the Soviet side. What is not known of one side limits our ability to assess action on the other, and this limitation should warn us against judgments that this act more than that, or one advantage more than another, was decisive. It does not prevent a more general judgment of the main elements contributing to success.

What is at once astonishing and wholly natural is the degree to which the clear components of this success are precisely those to which the Presidency had been bent and not only in the Kennedy Administration: strength, restraint, and respect for the opinions of mankind.

That strength counted we cannot doubt—though it is typical of the uncertainties of assessment that the partisans of specific kinds of strength remained persuaded, afterward as before, of the peculiar value of their preferred weapons. Believers in nuclear dissuasion as an all-purpose strategy asserted the predominant role of strategic superiority; believers in the need for conventional strength, while not usually denying the role of SAC in the success, were convinced that what mattered most was usable nonnuclear strength at the point of contest. Interesting as this argument may be, it can have no certain conclusion. Prudence argues for a judgment that all kinds of military strength were relevant. The existence of adequate and rapidly deployable strength, at all levels, was the direct result of the reinforcement of balanced defenses begun in 1961.

A further element of strength in this crisis was the firmness and clarity of the Presidential decision to insist on the withdrawal of the missiles. This was not merely a matter of one speech or even of one decision from a week of heavy argument. It was a position clearly stated, and internationally understood, well before the crisis broke. It was reinforced in its power, and the Communist position correspondingly weakened, by the repeated Soviet assertions that no such weapons were or would be placed in Cuba.

The strength of this position, like the strength of the available military force, was reinforced by its disciplined relation to a policy of restraint. That nuclear weapons should not be strewn around as counters in a contest for face was a proposition commanding wide support. Any impulse to discount or disregard the direct threat to the United States, as a problem for the Americans to solve, was deeply undercut by awareness of the difference between American and Soviet standards of nuclear responsibility as revealed in this moment of danger.

More broadly, the strength and restraint of the American position in October stood in striking contrast to the position in which others found themselves. As a first consequence, and to a degree that exceeded predictions, the allies of the United States both in this hemisphere and in Europe were clear in their support, though in public comment, especially in the United Kingdom, there was evidence of the difficulties we should have faced if we had been less clearly strong, restrained, and right.

It can be argued, of course, that in this crisis the opinions even of close allies were not crucial, and it does seem probable that such critical decisions as the turn-around of arms-bearing ships and the announcement that the missiles would be removed were not determined by O.A.S. votes or by world opinion. This particular crisis might have been successfully resolved even in the face of doubt and division among allies whose immediate power at the point of contest was negligible.

But so narrow a judgment neglects two great hazards. Immediately, a serious division among the allies might have provoked action elsewhere, most dangerously at Berlin (and indeed in all the postwar annals of the bravery of West Berlin there is no moment in which the courage and strength of the Berliners—and indeed of all free Germans—have been more important in discouraging adventure). And even if no such adventure had been attempted, the position after the crisis would not have been one in which "the quest for peace" could easily be led from Washington. It was and is the central meaning of this affair that a major threat to peace and freedom was removed by means which strengthened the prospects of both.

The October crisis came out better than President Kennedy or any of his associates had expected. The analysis suggested above would not have been compelling in the discussions of the week of October 15, and the predominant reaction in Washington on October 28 was one of simple and enormous relief. In the weeks after the crisis, attention was diverted, first by backstairs gossip over who gave what advice, and then by a renewal of political debate over Cuba, a problem of another order of meaning than the missile crisis, and one which had rightly been left essentially as it was, while the major threat was removed. And finally, it was far from clear, in the immediate aftermath, that "those who had made themselves our adversary" in such a sudden and shocking way would now be ready for a different relation.

But what is important for our present purposes is that what shaped American action in this crisis—what set and sustained the tempered response, both to danger and to success—was the President. And while the man in the office was Kennedy, with a taste and style of his own, I think it is right to claim that the office as well as the man was embodied in the resolution, restraint, and responsibility that governed in these weeks.

IV

As the great disappointment of 1961 was the renewal of testing, so the great satisfaction of 1963 was the limited test-ban treaty.

The withdrawal of missiles from Cuba did more than end a specific crisis of great gravity. It also signaled an acceptance by the Soviet government, for the present at least, of the existing nuclear balance. In that balance there is American superiority, as we have seen, but it is a superiority that does not permit any lack of respect for the strength of the Soviet Union. No safer balance appears possible at present. No overwhelmingly one-sided margin is open to either side, and it was one lesson of the Cuban affair—as of many others since 1945—that it was well for peace that Communist strength should be matched with a margin. But the purpose of this margin must still be peace, and the aim of policy must still be to get beyond conflicting interests to the great common need for a safer prospect of survival. This is the meaning of the limited test-ban treaty.

If the missile crisis was the proof of American strength in conflict, the test-ban treaty was the proof of American readiness to work for this common purpose. And whatever the moving forces on the Soviet side, in the non-Communist world the Presidency was the necessary center of action. A special and distinguished role was played by the British Prime Minister, but Mr. Macmillan would be the first to recognize that it was mainly through his close relation to two Presidents that he was able to make the British contribution effective. It is only the American President who can carry the American Senate and the American people in any agreement on arms control, and it is only with American participation that any such agreement can have meaning for the Soviet government.

Unless a President uses these powers with energy, arms control agreements are improbable. The momentum of the arms race—the power at work to keep it going almost without conscious new decision—is enormous. Military men in all countries find it hard to approve any arms control proposal which is not either safely improbable or clearly unbalanced in their own favor. In the United States only a strong commander-in-chief with a strong Secretary of Defense is in a position to press steadily for recognition that the arms race itself is now a threat to national security. Only the President can ensure that good proposals are kept alive even after a first rejection, and that new possibilities are constantly considered—so that there may always be as many proposals as possible on the table waiting for the moment of Soviet readiness. The readiness to meet all threats must be matched by a demonstrated readiness to reach agreement.

In the case of the limited test ban it was President Kennedy himself who reached the conclusion in the spring of 1963 that the United States would not be the first to make further atmospheric tests. That quite personal decision, recognized at the time as fully within the Presidential power, and announced in an address on peace whose power and conviction were immediately recognized, is as likely an immediate cause as any for the announcement, less than a month later, that the Soviet government would now be willing to sign an agreement which had been open for two years. There followed a period of negotiation and then a debate on ratification, and in these again the Presidency was central. The test-ban treaty, as we have all told each other a hundred times, is only one step, and President Johnson has made clear his determination to seek further steps with all the energy and imagination the government can command. Meanwhile the lesson of the test ban is that no step at all can be taken in this field unless the President himself works for it. A President indifferent to arms control, or easily discouraged by Soviet intransigence or irresponsibility, or inclined to a narrow military view of the arms race, would be a guarantee against agreed limitation of armaments. Conversely, where there is zeal in the search for agreement, refusal to accept initial disappointment as final, a cool and balanced assessment of the risks of agreement against the risks of unlimited competition, and a firm use of the powers of the office, the Presidency can become—as in this case—an instrument of hope for all men everywhere.

V

In concentrating attention upon the great requirements of strength and a love for peace, and in using as examples such very large matters as the missile crisis and the test-ban treaty, I do not pretend to have exhausted the connections between the Presidency and the Peace, even as they showed themselves in the short Kennedy years. There is more in the Presidency than the special powers of the commander-in-chief or the special responsibility for pressing the hard cause of disarmament. There is more, too, than a need for understanding of Soviet realities. The Presidency is a powerful element in the strength or weakness of the United Nations, as every Secretary-General has known. The Presidency remains the headquarters of the Great Alliance, as even the most separated of national leaders has recognized. The Presidency is an indispensable stimulus to Progress in the Americas. The Presidency must make the hard choices of commitment that have brought both honor and difficulty, as in Korea in 1950, or in South Vietnam in 1954. The White House visit and the White House photograph are elements of democratic electioneering not just in the United States, but wherever the name of the American President can bring a cheer. The death of a President men loved has shown how wide this larger constituency is. Allies, neutrals, and even adversaries attend to the Presidency. When the American President shows that he can understand and respect the opinions and hopes of distant nations, when he proves able to represent the interests of his own people without neglecting the interests of others, when in his own person he represents decency, hope, and freedom—then he is strengthened in his duty to be the leader of man's quest for peace in the age of nuclear weapons. And this strength will be at least as important in meeting danger as in pursuing hope.

The Administration in Washington, led now by President Johnson, will face new problems and make new decisions, and as time passes the new imprint of a strong mind and heart will be felt increasingly—in the Presidency, in the government, and in the world. President Kennedy would have been the last to suppose that the purely personal characteristics of any President, however loved and mourned, could or should continue to determine the work of the Presidency after his death. President Johnson will conduct the office in his own way. Yet the short space of three months is enough to show plainly that the pursuit of peace remains his central concern, while the effective transfer from one Administration to the next has reflected the fact that loyalty to President Kennedy and loyalty to President Johnson are not merely naturally compatible, but logically necessary as a part of a larger loyalty to their common purpose.

And as we remember John Kennedy, let us separate the essential from the complementary. The youth, the grace, and the wit were wonderful, but they were not the center. There lay courage, vision, humanity, and strength, tested on the path to the office, and tempered by the office itself. It is these qualities, applied to the greatest issues, that belong not only to the man but to the job.

It is my own conviction that this kind of President and this kind of Presidency reflect the general will of Americans. Temperate use of strength, respect for honest difference, sympathy for those in need, and a readiness to go our share of the distance—these qualities, which I have described in phrases borrowed from our new President, are qualities of the American people. They have their opposites in our character too, but these are what we honor; these we expect of our Presidents. In the terrible shock of President Kennedy's death there were many—perhaps too many—who saw the foul deeds of a few days in Dallas, and not the dead

President himself, as the embodiment of the real America. They were wrong. As a man, as a President, as a servant of the Peace, he was what we are, and his achievement belongs to us all. Strengthened by his service the Presidency continues, and so does the quest for Peace.

DAVID HOROWITZ

Showdown: The Cuban Crisis

The United States' response to the Soviet emplacement of missiles in Cuba was clear, vigorous and decisive. On October 22, President Kennedy went on TV to inform the nation, the Russians and the world, that he had ordered a blockade[1] of Cuba to prevent additional missile equipment from arriving on the island, and that if the preparation of the missile sites did not cease, and the missiles were not withdrawn, "further action" would be taken. This action could either have meant expansion of the embargo to include petroleum shipments or an air strike. By the end of the crisis week, this latter alternative had become a real possibility.[2]

In his address, President Kennedy charged:

. . . this secret,[3] swift,[4] extraordinary build-up of Communist missiles—in an area well known to have a special and historical relationship to the United States and the nations of the Western Hemisphere, in violation of Soviet assurances,[5] and in defiance of American

---

[1] The President's word was "quarantine," but throughout the planning stages, the action was termed "blockade" by those involved, and this is clearly what it was. For this account, I have drawn on the detailed, day-by-day story of the crisis compiled by the Washington Bureau of *The New York Times,* and printed in the International Edition, November 6, 1962.

[2] *Ibid.* This air strike would probably have been against the Cuban anti-aircraft batteries which had shot down one U-2 plane and fired on others.

[3] But cf. the *Wall Street Journal,* October 24: ". . . the authorities here almost all accept one key assumption: That Mr. Khrushchev must have assumed his Cuban missile sites would soon be discovered. 'The Russians seem almost to have gone out of their way to call attention to them,' said

This selection is from David Horowitz, *The Free World Colossus,* pp. 382–397. Copyright © 1965 by David Horowitz. Reprinted by permission of Hill & Wang, Inc., Publishers.

and Hemispheric policy—this sudden, clandestine decision to station strategic weapons for the first time outside of Soviet soil—is a deliberately provocative and unjustified change in the *status quo* which cannot be accepted by this country, if our courage and our commitments are ever to be trusted again by either friend or foe.[6]

Thus did President Kennedy justify the extreme U.S. action in response to the Soviet maneuver, namely, a naval blockade, which was, in fact, an act of war and hence violated the U.N. charter and the very O.A.S. treaties which the President invoked as bases for United States' concern.[7] The action taken by the United States was even more momentous in that by engaging a test of will with the Soviet Union, it was risking a test of strength, and this test of strength would have involved not only the lives and destinies of the Soviet and American peoples, but hundreds of millions of people in other countries whose governments had no role in the decisions which had led up to, or, afterward, which shaped the crisis.

---

one authority who has studied the photographic evidence." Cf. also K. S. Karol, *New Statesman,* November 2, 1962. "Many military men have been astonished by the openness of Soviet preparations in Cuba, under the constant surveillance of US aircraft. It is possible, then, that the dispatch of Soviet missiles should be compared with the reinforcement of the US Berlin garrison at the time of the last crisis there. In Berlin, Kennedy wished to emphasize that American lives would be involved, so making world war certain in the event of a Soviet thrust."

[4] But cf. Hanson Baldwin, *The New York Times,* Int. Edn., November 1, 1962: "Considerable mystery, in the opinion of Congress and military men, still surrounds *the Administration's sudden decision* to impose a blockade of Cuba after a missile build-up that must have started weeks or months ago . . . The question that arises . . . is whether the Intelligence data that must have been collected throughout the summer and early fall was accurately evaluated, or whether policy dictated the intelligence estimated or turned them aside." [Emphasis added.]

[5] I.e., Gromyko's assurances on October 18, that the missiles were for defensive purposes. This is by no means a clear issue, however, a fact emphasized by the following passage from the above-cited Baldwin article: "Military men point out that many Administration officials, including a high State Department official, were emphatically denying the existence of any offensive Soviet missiles in Cuba until just before the President's speech."

[6] *The New York Times,* Int. Edn., October 23, 1962.

[7] It has been argued by Arthur Larson and others that because the U.S. move was an act of self-defense, it was in keeping with the principles of the U.N. Charter. But this assumes that the emplacement of missiles in Cuba altered the nuclear balance of power. Such an assumption is not warranted by the facts. See below.

Therefore, it is of more than passing importance that the nature of the Soviet provocation be understood. For the Cuban crisis provides the first real basis for estimating what the nuclear future may be like without some sort of general disengagement. It is interesting to note in this regard, that the substantive issue involved in the Cuban crisis was not understood at the time and that a general misimpression has persisted in the aftermath. This mistaken view holds that the United States was alarmed because the presence of missiles in Cuba upset or significantly altered the military balance of power, i.e., the nuclear status quo.

It would seem that in this case the wish has been father to the thought, that people would like to think that thermonuclear war will be precipitated (barring accident) only when the security of one of the great powers is threatened, or when some similarly clear-cut issue involving self-defense is at stake. In addition to the confusion caused by wishful thinking, Ambassador Stevenson's remarks (October 23) before the U.N. may have unintentionally served to mislead many people:

When the Soviet Union sends thousands of military technicians to its satellite in the Western Hemisphere—when it sends jet bombers capable of delivering nuclear weapons—when it installs in Cuba missiles capable of carrying atomic warheads and of obliterating the Panama Canal, Mexico City and Washington—. . . this clearly is a threat to the hemisphere. And when it thus *upsets the precarious balance in the world,* it is a threat to the whole world.

Stevenson avoided saying "upsets the precarious *balance of terror* in the world" or even balance of *power,* just as President Kennedy avoided any reference to a *balance* of nuclear forces in his statement, and with good reason. For if the nuclear background developed to this point in the manner in which we have described it, then the forty-two Soviet missiles in Cuba[8] would have had no effect at all on the overall nuclear balance (except, possibly, to make it more stable).

That this was in fact the case was made clear by Deputy

---

[8] Deputy Defense Secretary Gilpatric, quoted in *The New York Times,* Int. Edn., November 12, 1962.

Defense Secretary Gilpatric on a television program November 11. According to *The New York Times* of November 12:

. . . Mr. Gilpatric made two observations on the over-all missile capability of the United States compared with that of the Soviet Union.

First, he said, defense officials believe that the United States has a measurable margin of superiority in strategic weapons.

Second, in alluding to the Soviet missile build-up in Cuba, he said: *"I don't believe that we were under any greater threat from the Soviet Union's power, taken in its totality, after this than before."*[9] [Emphasis added.]

What, then, was at stake in the Soviet emplacement of missiles in Cuba? What challenge or threat necessitated a U.S. action which not only violated fundamental international law, but risked a general nuclear holocaust as well?[10] It could not have been the mere fact of the Soviet build-up, because that had been going on since July.[11] It was evidently not the material presence of "offensive" missiles, since if we are able to believe Deputy Defense Secretary Gilpatric and the evidence of the Institute of Strategic Studies, as well as the previous statements of Gilpatric and McNamara of the relative missiles strengths of the two nuclear giants, the U.S. was under no greater threat from the Soviet's power, taken in its totality, after the emplacement of missiles than before. What then was the nature of the Soviet provocation?

The answer to these questions was revealed by President

[9] The Institute for Strategic Studies made the following estimates of long-range missile strengths of the two powers for the end of October 1962: Soviet Union 75 ICBMs; US 450–500 missiles capable of being fired more than 2,000 miles. *The New York Times*, Int. Edn., November 9, 1962.

[10] The main risk was not simply that of a decision by the U.S.S.R. to engage in such a war, but in the crisis generally getting out of hand. Thus *The New York Times'* account of the crisis reports that on Saturday, October 27, "the possibility of having to knock out hostile antiaircraft batteries on the island was very real, and *there was doubt about how much longer the crisis could be carefully controlled* . . . They sat with an over-all confidence in the nation's nuclear superiority over the Soviet Union [*sic*], but this was little comfort if the Russians chose to go to a war that neither side could win. The President gravely remarked that evening that it seemed to him to be touch and go, that it could now go 'either way.' " [Emphasis added.]

[11] *The New York Times*, Int. Edn., November 6, 1962.

Kennedy himself during a television interview on December 17, 1962:

[The Russians] were planning in November to open to the world the fact that they had these missiles so close to the United States. Not that they were intending to fire them, because if they were going to get into a nuclear struggle they have their own missiles in the Soviet Union. But it would have *politically* changed the balance of power, *it would have appeared to—and appearances contribute to reality.*

Thus, it seems it was a *political* balance of power that was actually in danger of being upset, and this political balance was a question of appearances—prestige, presumably—the political consequences of what would appear in the eyes of the world and domestic critics of the Kennedy Administration[12] to be a Soviet act of defiance, perpetrated with impunity. Not to have forced the Russians into retreat would have been appeasement, a sign that the U.S. would not stand up to Soviet power when challenged, and it would therefore have opened the door to further challenges, perhaps over Berlin. This explains why Khrushchev's offer on Saturday, October 27, to exchange the missile bases in Turkey for the bases in Cuba was turned down. And indeed, *The New York Times'* account of the rejection indicates the political-prestige nature of the decision:

Such a proposal had already been rejected as unacceptable; though the Turkey missile base had *no great military* value, it was of *great symbolic* importance to a stout ally. To bargain Turkey's safety [i.e. to *apparently* bargain Turkey's safety—D. H.] would have meant shocking and perhaps shaking the Western alliance. [Emphasis added.]

[12] On October 15, Eisenhower delivered a speech in which he charged that the Kennedy Administration's foreign policy had not been "firm." In the eight years of his own Administration, Eisenhower declared, "We witnessed no abdication of responsibility. We accepted no compromise of pledged word or withdrawal from principle. No [Berlin] walls were built. No foreign bases [i.e. in Cuba] were established. One was ended [i.e. in Guatemala] and incipient wars were blocked." *The New York Times,* Int. Edn., October 16, 1962. On the other hand, domestic pressure on Kennedy to do something about Cuba should not be overemphasized. Three separate polls, including a Gallup poll, taken a week before the crisis, indicated that there had been no increase in public support for an invasion of Cuba since April 1961 (or 15 months before the Soviet build-up began). According to the Gallup poll, 24 per cent favored invasion, 63 per cent were opposed, while 13 per cent had no opinion.

The military insignificance of the Turkish missile base and the symbolic importance of not bargaining with the Soviets was emphasized in a front-page story in *The New York Times*, less than three months later, on January 21, 1963:

The Turkish Government has responded favorably to proposals that the United States remove its Jupiter missile bases. . . .

The removal of these Jupiter missiles was under consideration here *some time before* the crisis last fall over the emplacement of Soviet missiles in Cuba. [Emphasis added.]

The fact that the removal of the Turkish missile bases had been considered *before* the Cuban crisis raises the question as to why there was a crisis at all. Why, for example, was not the Soviet Ambassador given an ultimatum *in private,* before the presence of the missiles was disclosed to the world and the prestige of the United States had been put on the line?[13] Such a move would have been *normal* diplomatic procedure (and was actually proposed by Stevenson).[14] As James Reston wrote on October 27:[15]

The new Kennedy style of diplomacy is now operating in the Cuban crisis. It is highly personal and national. It is power diplomacy in the old classic European sense that prevailed before the great men worried much about consulting with allies or parliaments or international organizations. . . .

[The President] did not follow the normal diplomatic practice of giving his antagonist a quiet escape from fighting or withdrawing, but let the Soviet Foreign Minister leave the White House without a hint of what was coming and then announced the blockade on the television.

While generally approving Kennedy's "power play," Reston expressed certain reservations about its wisdom:

This brisk and sudden diplomacy, however, cannot be pursued without cost. The political reaction within the nation and the alliance has been

[13] Since both Cuba and the ships coming to Cuba were under constant surveillance, it would have been simple for the Kennedy Administration to be very precise in framing an ultimatum or deal, and very secure about verifying Soviet compliance.

[14] Henry M. Pachter, *Collision Course,* 1963, p. 30.

[15] *The New York Times,* Int. Edn., October 26, 1962.

gratifying to the Administration, but it is misleading because it is not the same as private reaction.

Privately, there are several misgivings. First, many people find it hard to believe that the offensive Soviet missile sites in Cuba suddenly mushroomed over the weekend, and accordingly, there is considerable suspicion either that the official intelligence was not so good as maintained, or the Administration withheld the facts.

Second, many diplomats within the alliance still think it was wrong to confront Khrushchev publicly with the choice of fighting or withdrawing, especially since the security of many other unconsulted nations was involved. . . .

The mysteries attending the discovery of the build-up, the unusual nature of the crisis diplomacy, and the lack of any immediate overwhelming military threat, all point to the existence of an important dynamic element in the planning of U.S. policy. Further evidence that motives behind the U.S. action in the Cuban crisis were dynamic and not only responsive in character, was offered at the time in a remarkable series of articles by the informed *New York Times* analyst, C. L. Sulzberger (appearing on October 20, 22 and 24).[16] In a retrospective glance, four months later,[17] Sulzberger summarized his previous conclusions in the following way:

Some weeks before the Cuban confrontation, Washington decided that Khrushchev's cold-war offensive, begun in 1957, was petering out. It therefore resolved on a showdown with Russia at a time and place of its own choosing. Khrushchev, with his Caribbean missile game, surprisingly[18] also seemed to seek a test. He chose a time, October, that seems to have suited us. History will judge for whom Cuba was the right place.

In his October 21 article, written from Paris *before* the announcement of the blockade, Sulzberger traced the history of the cold war as seen by the Kennedy Administration and indicated the calculated reasons why a showdown was considered important by

---

[16] International Edition, datelines: Paris, October 19, 21 and 23.

[17] International Edition, February 25, 1963, dateline: February 24.

[18] "Surprisingly" because his power situation was so weak. This suggests that Khrushchev's move was a miscalculation. Cf. James Reston, *The New York Times*, Int. Edn., October 24, "Khrushchev's Mistake on Cuba."

the leadership (Sulzberger felt that this showdown would be in Berlin, further indicating the unlikeliness that he knew about the imminent Cuban clash). "Washington," he wrote, "is convinced a moment of truth is approaching over Berlin, and that the West cannot afford to dodge this confrontation; that if we now face and surmount the crisis, the international balance will begin to swing our way." Because of this conviction, Sulzberger observed, Washington "is . . . emphasizing a paramountcy of leadership" that causes some "ripples of disquiet" among the Allies, who wish to avoid a confrontation over Berlin. "Nevertheless, we see this as a chance to turn Russia's second cold war offensive."

Russia's first "offensive," according to Sulzberger, was launched by Stalin in Greece fifteen years earlier, "halted there, blocked in Berlin and finally checked by 1951 battlefield victories in Korea."[19] Russia's second, or "Khrushchev offensive," dated from the launching of Sputnik, "when Moscow hoped to trade missile prestige [*sic, not* superiority or power] against new real estate." In this offensive, Communism "failed to win the Arab world, Guinea, or the Congo." While these failures were being registered, moreover, "pressures built up inside the Communist world." Khrushchev tried to deal with these pressures—satellite unrest, the split with China, Russia's food crisis—but, as of October 1962, had found "no panacea." "The United States is consequently convinced that Khrushchev is up against vast difficulties and seeking some kind of triumph to advertise . . . we believe it is necessary to take risks in warning Khrushchev, letting him see clearly what he is up against."

On October 23[20] Sulzberger concluded his series with an analysis of the Cuban crisis which had begun the day before. "The new trend in United States policy described in previous columns," he began, "has now culminated in a showdown with Russia. That is the real meaning of the Cuban crisis. President Kennedy decided to move against Khrushchev's cold-war offensive at a time and

---

[19] Sulzberger's reference to 1951 victories indicates that he believes that the Chinese entered the Korean War as part of Stalin's offensive rather than as a result of MacArthur's provocation. As with his statement about Greece, this is untenable before the facts.

[20] *The New York Times,* Int. Edn., October 24.

place of his own choosing. . . . This calculated risk has presumably been taken for the calculated reasons previously analyzed.
Washington seems to feel this is the time to check and reverse
Khrushchev's cold-war offensive. We have opted to force the issue
ourselves without prior approval of our allies and there are going
to be uneasy diplomatic moments. . . .

". . . Some of our leaders have been hinting this for weeks.[21]
They knew what they were talking about. One must assume it was
they who planned the showdown that has started." [Emphasis
added.]

In other words, having built a sizeable missile superiority of its
own, and having laid the plans for a rapid increase in this
superiority in the next few years, the Kennedy Administration had
waited for an opportune moment to demonstrate its nuclear superiority to the world, and with the prestige thus gained, tip the
scales of the world power balance. The test was expected to come
in Berlin, when Cuba presented itself.

Even if Sulzberger weren't as close to the inner circles in
Washington as he is, the handling of the crisis by the United States
leadership would point to the same conclusion, namely, that once
the information about the Soviet build-up was received, the only
response considered was one that would precipitate a showdown.[22]

According to official accounts, the key aerial photographs were
developed on October 15. On October 16, the President called a
meeting of the Executive Committee of the National Security
Council.[23] The results of this meeting were summarized in The
New York Times' account as follows:

---

[21] On September 24, Kennedy obtained authorization to call up 150,000
reservists. "General Curtis Le May ordered supplies to be flown to Florida,
that mission was to be completed by October 10, and the tactical Air
Command was to be combat-ready by October 20. . . . Do these dates
indicate that the Chief of Staff of the Air Force expected the crisis at the
end of October?"—Pachter, p. 7n.

[22] "Most significant [of proposals to avoid a crisis] was Stevenson's proposal to present Khrushchev with a secret ultimatum. . . . The difference
between his way of thinking and Kennedy's . . . [is that]: Kennedy and the
majority of the Executive Committee felt it necessary to have a public
showdown with Khrushchev."—Pachter, pp. 91–92.

[23] It was actually an ad hoc committee which became known as the
Executive Committee. Its members included Vice-President Johnson, Secre-
tary Rusk, Secretary of Defense McNamara, Secretary of Treasury Dillion,
Attorney General Kennedy, Undersecretary Ball, Deputy Secretary of

At this first meeting the President and his advisors were not yet clear on what was to be their objective to get the offensive weapons out of Cuba. Some talked, rather, about getting Premier Castro out.

The meeting produced two immediate decisions. One was to intensify air surveillance of Cuba. The second was that action should await further knowledge, *but should come as close as possible to disclosure of the Russian bases*—which could not be long delayed. [Emphasis added.]

In other words, the one point on which all were agreed was that the Russians should be caught red-handed, faced with a predetermined show of strength and compelled to retreat. The only question was the nature of the action to be taken, air strike or blockade.[24] On Friday, October 19, an air strike was ruled out, and it was decided to use a blockade:

Attorney General Kennedy argued against a strike on moral grounds. . . . For the United States to attack a small country like Cuba without warning, he said, would irreparably hurt our reputation in the world—and our own conscience.

The moral argument won general assent. . . .

The blockade proposal was recognized as one raising most serious dangers. As recently as October 6, Vice-President Johnson had warned that "stopping a Russian ship is an act of war."

By the end of the afternoon meeting the blockade was clearly the indicated answer.

Fortunately, the immediate danger of precipitating a thermonuclear war was avoided, and on October 28, the crisis ended, as the Soviet Union agreed to withdraw its missiles in return for a United States guarantee not to invade Cuba. In this curious way, the United States won a prestige victory over its Soviet opponent.

Defense Gilpatric, General Carter, Assistant Secretary of State Martin, General Taylor, McGeorge Bundy and Theodore Sorensen. These were joined by Alexis Johnson, John McCone, Dean Acheson and Llewellyn Thompson.

[24] "Invasion was not considered as a possible first action. It would take too long to mount. Surprise would be impossible. The effect on world opinion was certain to be unfavorable. The Soviet response might rapidly 'escalate' the affair." "But the air strike did win significant support. So did a blockade." *The New York Times'* account of events of Wednesday, October 17.

By agreeing to withdraw the missiles, Khrushchev lifted the threat of nuclear annihilation from millions whose nations were not involved in the dispute, and hence who tended to view the Cuba base as comparable to U.S. bases in Turkey, as well as from those nations who were. And though his action of putting the missiles there in the first place in general drew harsh criticism, his withdrawal of the missiles in the face of U.S. intransigence[25] gave him an opportunity to demonstrate moderation and rationality which he would not otherwise have had. Moreover, the "price" that the U.S. paid to have the Soviets withdraw their missiles, namely, an agreement not to invade Cuba, was surely one of the strangest facets of the whole affair. For it meant nothing less than that the United States officially recognized that it would, in fact, contemplate aggression against a sovereign state, and therefore that the Soviet build-up in Cuba had legitimate defensive purposes from the *Cuban* point of view.[26] In retrospect, it would seem that the Soviet Union also gained a "prestige victory."

But Kennedy's triumph, particularly within the Western Alliance and at home, was evident and impressive. From Washington's point of view, the central gain was in dispelling the illusion that the United States would not fight for its vital interests. This was considered to be important not only from the standpoint of the Allies' morale, but from the standpoint of making it clear to Khrushchev that the United States could not be faced down in areas such as Berlin.

It should further be noted that Kennedy immediately acted to restrain those who might want to see the advantage in the Cuban

---

[25] The mediating proposals of U.N. Secretary General U Thant to stop both missile preparations and blockade, had been rejected by the U.S. and accepted by the Soviet Union.

[26] Cf. the *Washington Star* and *Washington Daily News* of October 29 and 30. The former stated: "Authoritative sources warned today against any feeling that the agreement with the Soviet Union will lead to 'peaceful coexistence' with Fidel Castro's Cuba. . . . Once the first phase of actually dismantling and removing the Soviet weapons is completed, they said that the hemisphere and Cubans can get on with the more 'limited' phase of actually getting rid of the Castro régime. . . . At a forty-five minute briefing in the State Department yesterday, Secretary of State Rusk told the nineteen Latin American Ambassadors . . . not to exaggerate the extent of the U.S. guarantee against invading Cuba." Both articles cited in *I. F. Stone's Weekly,* November 5, 1962.

crisis pressed by further displays of power. After an interview with the President on October 28, the day the crisis ended, James Reston reported:

President Kennedy is looking at the Cuban crisis not as a great victory but merely as an honorable accommodation in a single isolated area of the cold war. . . .

The President is not even drawing general conclusions from this special case about the tactics of dealing with the Soviet Union in the future. To be specific, while he may be equally bold again in risking conflict in support of vital national interests, he is rejecting the conclusion of the traditional "hard-liners" that the way to deal with Moscow everywhere in the world is to be "tough," as in Cuba. . . .[27]

But if Kennedy was now eager to emphasize the limits of U.S. power in dealing with the Communists, and thus forestall the pressures of his right wing, the months following the Cuban crisis saw him take an increasingly assertive attitude towards the Western Alliance. In December, the U.S. abruptly announced cancellation of the program to build Skybolt missiles on which Britain had based its long-range plans for maintaining an independent nuclear deterrent. In February, an undiplomatic note accused the Canadian government of failing to produce a "practical" plan for joint defense. Partly as a result of this note, and the ensuing reaction, the Canadian government fell.

If there was little question about the vigor of the new post-Cuba diplomacy, however, there were many uncertainties about its direction. As one European observer wrote:

The series of successes in the last quarter of 1962 has confirmed the Kennedy Administration in its good opinion of its foreign policy. . . .

An intoxicating certainty of power is the prevailing mood. It is only when specific questions of how this power will be used in relations with enemies and allies that there is uncertainty. . . .

In East-West relations there is a new self-assurance, but hardly a sign of new ideas. The Administration which was going out of its way to warn of an impending Berlin crisis, now appears to think Cuba has made a Berlin crisis unlikely, or at least milder when it comes.

But as Mr. Dean Acheson pointed out in the meat of the speech which caused such indignation in Britain, there is now no American

27 *The New York Times,* Int. Edn., October 29, 1962.

policy in central Europe beyond an exhortation to stand firm on Berlin. . . .[28]

As we have seen, however, firmness and the development of power was itself a policy for Kennedy, who believed that strengthening the forces of freedom (to use Acheson's phrase) would induce the Soviets to become reasonable and accept a settlement on "reasonable" terms.

Kennedy's policy after Cuba was, in fact, very consistent with the assumption that only two power centers (East and West) existed in Europe, and that so long as the balance was not tipped heavily against the East, it would not settle for a status quo meaning less than domination. For after Cuba, Kennedy moved to give the NATO powers a nuclear force of Polaris submarines under terms that would weld them into unity while integrating them as an arm of U.S. striking power. The net effect would be a stronger "Atlantic" front against the Communist bloc.

Significantly, as the new year began, Kennedy was rebuffed in his design for European economic and military (and eventual political) unity interdependent with the United States, by de Gaulle, who reaffirmed his intention to build an independent nuclear force for France, and on January 14, vetoed Britain's entry into the Common Market.

Kennedy's reaction to de Gaulle's rebuff was significant, in that he did not emphasize the danger of independent nuclear forces and the spread of nuclear weapons, but rather stressed the threat to the Western Alliance and to the world in any weakening of the power bloc of the West:

It would be well to remind all concerned of the hard and fast realities of this nation's relationship with Europe—

The reality of danger is that all free men and nations live under the constant threat of Communist advance. Although presently in some disarray, the Communist apparatus controls more than one billion people, and it daily confronts Europe and the United States with hundreds of missiles, scores of divisions, and the purposes of domination.

[28] Godfrey Hodgson in the *London Observer,* December 30, 1962; cf. also James Reston in *The New York Times,* Int. Edn., December 27, 1962.

The reality of power is that the resources essential to defense against this danger are concentrated overwhelmingly in the nations of the Atlantic Alliance. In unity this Alliance has ample strength to hold back the expansion of Communism until such time as it loses its force and momentum. Acting alone, neither the United States nor Europe could be certain of success and survival. The reality of purposes, therefore, is that that which serves to unite us is right, and what tends to divide us is wrong. . . .[29]

Since de Gaulle had not indicated any intention to withdraw from the NATO Alliance, or to make a separate accommodation with the Soviets, Kennedy's picture of the world situation represented a strange estimate both of the balance of forces and the present dangers. For it is inconceivable that Kennedy considered real, or immediate, the danger of a Soviet advance in Europe in any military sense. As of January, the conventional strength of the Western bloc was larger than that of the Soviet bloc by 8.1 million to 7.3 million men.[30] Politically, the Communist bloc was being rent by the Sino-Soviet schism; economically, the East was beset by significant problems. When Kennedy spoke, the general estimate in the West was that Khrushchev's recent statement had indicated the Berlin question would not be pressed. The Russians had been cooperative in tying up the loose ends of the Cuban crisis. Khrushchev had waged a vigorous post-Cuba campaign against the militancy of the Chinese and for the policy of peaceful coexistence. Clearly, Kennedy's concern could not have been the weakness of the Western Alliance, but rather the fact that it would not have *enough* strength to force the Soviets into "fruitful negotiations."[31]

On the other hand, all indications pointed to the conclusion that U.S. missile superiority would no more induce a relinquishing of

[29] *The New York Times,* Int. Edn., January 25, 1963.

[30] P. M. S. Blackett, "The First Real Chance for Disarmament," *Harper's,* January 1963. "The total forces of the Warsaw Pact, including the Soviet Union, number about 4½ million, against 5 million men in the active armed forces of Nato." *London Observer,* December 15, 1963.

[31] For Kennedy's far-ranging optimism about the world power balance at this time, cf. the President's State of the Union Message, January 14, 1963.

Soviet positions in 1963, than had atomic monopoly or H-bomb superiority before. As in previous stages of the cold war, it would induce, rather, a Soviet move to offset the superiority. Thus, in January it was reported that observers in Washington believed "that the Russians may be attempting to compensate with [a] 'big bang' for their inferiority in missile numbers." A "very few" fifty to one hundred megaton bombs "delivered in a promiscuous pattern of nationwide bombing could paralyze any nation, and could destroy or damage all except the most heavily protected military installations. Damage and casualties caused would probably be so great as to be crippling." *"Any President,"* the report continued, *"would hesitate to invoke the threat of nuclear weapons, as we did in the Cuban crisis or even to take extremely strong action if he felt that several giant megaton weapons could be delivered on the United States."* Thus, even a small number of these weapons "mated to the powerful but few Russian ICBMs," though not sufficient to "save" the Soviet Union in a nuclear war, "might well serve, as apparently they are intended to serve, as a means of neutralizing the present superiority of the United States in numbers of ICBMs and in over-all nuclear delivery capacity."[32] And, on February 22, *The New York Times* (International Edition) reported:

The commander-in-chief of the Soviet strategic rocket forces said today [February 21] the Soviet could launch rockets from satellites at a command from the earth.[33]

[32] Hanson Baldwin, *The New York Times,* Int. Edn., January 10, 1963: "I will tell you a secret: Our scientists have worked out a 100 megaton bomb . . . we can use such a weapon only outside the confines of Europe. I am saying this in order that there should be a more realistic appreciation of what horrifying means of destruction there exist . . . Comrades, to put it in a nutshell, as I have already said during the session of the Supreme Soviet of the USSR, it is not advisable to be in a hurry for the other world. Nobody ever returned from there to report that one lives better there than here. We do not want a kingdom in heaven but a kingdom on earth, a kingdom of labor. This is the kind of kingdom we are fighting for and without stinting our efforts we shall go on fighting for it."—Nikita S. Khrushchev, to the Communist Party Congress in East Berlin, January 16, 1963; *The New York Times,* Int. Edn., January 17, 1963.

[33] For a corroborating account and discussion of the implications of the new weapon, cf. Tom Margerison in the *London Sunday Times,* February 24, 1963.

Henry Kissinger, for one, had warned the previous summer[34] that the time when all of the Soviet Union's missiles could be destroyed by a counter-force blow was limited. Dispersal, hardening of bases, and the development of missile firing submarines would make it impossible in the future to know where all of an enemy's missiles were, and hence to be free from a devastating retaliatory blow.

In the end of January, Secretary of Defense McNamara appeared before the House Armed Services Committee, and made acceptance of the impending stalemate official, declaring that "regardless of what kind of strategic forces we build . . . we could not preclude casualties counted in the tens of millions."[35]

Thus, Kennedy's two-year attempt to gain a decisive lead in the arms race (requiring a 20 per cent increase in the military budget) produced the same results as previous attempts: a new stage of the arms race, a further increase in the number of nuclear weapons, and consequently, a more difficult world to disarm. But the Cuban crisis added to the lessons of previous years, by presenting mankind with an unforgettable glimpse into the perils of a nuclear future,[36] a future dominated by the immense gap between man's revolutionary technological means, and his traditional, limited, political and ethical outlook. It was a lesson which underscored the President's own warning to the U.N. General Assembly, in September 1961, when he said:

The weapons of war must be abolished before they abolish us. . . . The risks inherent in disarmament pale in comparison to the risks inherent in an unlimited arms race.

[34] Henry A. Kissinger, "The Unsolved Problems of European Defense," *Foreign Affairs*, July 1962.

[35] *Time*, February 15, 1963. The Air Force promptly attacked this "no win" policy of accepting nuclear stalemate as a dangerous one. Cf. *The New York Times*, Int. Edn., February 1, 1963.

[36] Consider, for example, what might have happened if the "showdown" had occurred over Berlin.

WILLIAM E. LEUCHTENBURG

President Kennedy and the
End of the Postwar World

John Fitzgerald Kennedy was elected President of the
United States in 1960 at a time when America's fortunes in world
affairs had sunk to a low point. In the Truman era, the United
States had shown brilliant resourcefulness in foreign policy—in the
Marshall Plan, the Berlin airlift, NATO, and the creation of new
instrumentalities like Point Four. Under Eisenhower, the initiative
had been lost to the Soviet Union. The U.S.S.R. had penetrated into
areas of the world where Soviet influence had hitherto been
unknown—from the African jungles to the Western Hemisphere.
Ninety miles off the Florida coast, the Soviet Union boasted a
satellite on the island of Cuba.

In parts of the world where the United States had taken its
predominance for granted, America's prestige had become badly
impaired. In Latin America, the good will created by the Good
Neighbor policy had been dissipated. When Vice-President Nixon
toured South America, he was stoned in Peru and spat upon in
Caracas. After being mobbed in the Venezuelan capital, he had to
abandon his tour; a convoy of soldiers sped him in a bulletproof
limousine to the airport. In the Far East, Japan had been regarded

as an American enclave since the end of World War II. But in June, 1960, an emergency session of the Japanese cabinet resolved to inform President Eisenhower that anti-American feeling was so intense that he would have to cancel his proposed visit there.

On May 5, 1960, only eleven days before a scheduled summit meeting, the United States was embarrassed by the revelation that a U-2 plane had been shot down over Soviet territory and, to make matters worse, the government was tricked into a deception. (Before Khrushchev revealed that the Russians had Francis Gary Powers alive, a State Department press officer claimed: "There was absolutely no—N-O—no deliberate attempt to violate Soviet air space, and there never has been.") At Paris, the Soviet Premier threatened the United States with "devastating" rocket assaults, and deliberately insulted President Eisenhower by withdrawing his invitation to the President to visit the Soviet Union. His rhetoric was even more insulting; American "aggressors," Khrushchev raged, should be treated as a boy would handle an erring cat: "We would catch such a cat by the tail and bang its head against the wall."

In the 1960 campaign, Kennedy made the most of the Republican President's discomfiture. He jeered that the President, who had been elected to office on his promise to go to Korea, was ending his years in office unable to go to Japan. Kennedy charged that the Soviet Union had outdistanced the United States in space; that America's armed forces were outmatched by those of the U.S.S.R.; and that the foreign policy of the United States was at a standstill.

Kennedy based his 1960 campaign on a single theme: "I think it's time America started moving again." It was on the pledge to get America "moving again" that Senator Kennedy was elected. And it is on his success or failure to carry out this pledge that Kennedy's performance as President will ultimately be judged. While it is still much too early to make a final assessment of Kennedy's Presidency, it is possible now to examine the President's first three years in office to see how far he has come toward fulfilling his pledge to turn the tide of events.

From the outset, Kennedy faced the same hard fact that had confronted each of his predecessors in the postwar era—that in foreign relations the country has only a narrow range of options, and that with each succeeding year, the range has become narrower. In trying to start the country in new directions in foreign policy, Kennedy immediately ran up against the ineluctable fact of the cold war.

Ever since 1947, the cold war had been the dominant theme of American life. At times, the United States had seemed almost obsessed with the belief that it was locked in an apocalyptic struggle with Soviet Russia for control of the world. Even the comic strips were implicated in the cold war. Buz Sawyer was busy coping with "the sinister machinations of a World Power"; Terry, who once outmaneuvered the pirates, now chalked up exploits against the Red Chinese; Joe Palooka outfoxed the Communists to rescue an American scientist in Austria; Winnie was incarcerated in a Soviet hoosegow; and Daddy Warbucks and his buddies blew up "enemy" planes carrying H-bombs.

In some parts of the world Kennedy inherited problems which he found intractable. On the morning before his inauguration, he went to the White House to confer with President Eisenhower. One by one, the two men discussed the unresolved problems the new President would face. Of all the subjects, it was Southeast Asia that dominated the discussion. As Eisenhower looked at the map of that region, he wrinkled his brow and muttered: "This is one of the problems I'm leaving you that I'm not happy about. We may have to fight."

In Southeast Asia, the United States was trapped into fighting a parody of the cold war. From 1954 to 1960, American military aid to Laos accounted for almost half that country's national income. But the soldiers of the Royal Lao Army had little taste for fighting and its leaders had a highly developed talent for corruption. Many of the people of the tiny kingdom did not have the foggiest notion of the meaning of communism or democracy. (One survey revealed that 90 per cent of Laotians believe the world is flat.)

Even more embarrassing was America's other client regime in Southeast Asia, Vietnam. Diem's regime in that country was a naked tyranny, and Diem's air force employed napalm against the enemy. In Vietnam, where American helicopters were involved in the fighting, the cold war occasionally flared into a hot war.

Kennedy was as troubled as his critics over the loss of life and over the character of Diem's regime. But he, like Eisenhower, was just as firmly convinced that if the United States permitted these governments to fall, the Communists might overrun all of Southeast Asia. Such an event would not only hurt the cause of the free world but would escalate the dangers of nuclear war.

In Southeast Asia, Kennedy has had to settle for a holding action. Up to now, he has been able to avoid either a Communist triumph or a major war. He has shown himself more willing than Eisenhower to countenance a solution in Southeast Asia which would neutralize the region and less insistent on an outright triumph for the West. But there are grave doubts about whether a disengagement based on genuine neutrality can be achieved. And with each passing day the barbarities of the Diem regime bring increasing pressure on the President to cut America's ties to the Vietnamese government, even at the risk of a Communist takeover.*

In Cuba Kennedy inherited from his predecessor not only a problem as vexing as that of Southeast Asia but a plan of action as well. When he took office, the new President was surprised to learn that the Eisenhower Administration had developed a plan for an invasion of the island by Cuban refugees who were being trained by the United States, and that the plan had reached an advanced stage. Kennedy would have been well advised to have disavowed the stratagem. But he himself had taken a jingoistic stance toward Castro during the campaign, and there was something about the audacity of the scheme that appealed to the spirit of the New Frontiersmen. After consulting with his military and civilian advisers, the President permitted the conspirators to go ahead.

The invasion of the Bay of Pigs on the southern coast of Cuba proved a total fiasco. The United States was condemned for attempting to unseat the government of a weaker nation, and laughed at for botching the job. Walter Lippmann observed bluntly: "It was not feasible to overthrow Castro with fourteen hundred refugees, and it was unlawful to attempt it." The blunder dealt a blow to the President's self-confidence. One aide remarked:

---

* Editor's note: this was written before the *coup d'état* in South Vietnam took place.

"This is the first time Jack Kennedy ever lost anything." Afterwards, the President himself reflected: "All the mysteries about the Bay of Pigs have been solved but one—how could everybody involved have thought such a plan would succeed. I don't know the answer, and I don't know anybody else who does."

It is doubtful whether Kennedy will ever recover fully the good will he lost by this enterprise. Yet what is most striking about the Bay of Pigs affair is that it represents an approach to foreign policy quite out of keeping with the spirit of most of the Kennedy program. The attempt by force of arms to dislodge Castro was consistent with the views of men like John Foster Dulles and such Kennedy critics as Senator Barry Goldwater who have insisted that there was "no substitute for victory" in the cold war. But, save for the Bay of Pigs abortion, Kennedy has been operating on quite different assumptions.

Kennedy has made clear that, unlike Dulles and Goldwater, he does not expect to make the world over in the American image. In November, 1961, the President declared: "We must face the fact that the United States is neither omnipotent nor omniscient—that we are only six per cent of the world's population—that we cannot impose our will upon the other ninety-four per cent of mankind— that we cannot right every wrong or reverse every adversity—and that therefore there cannot be an American solution to every world problem."

Kennedy has been much more aware than his predecessor of the end of the postwar world. He is sensitive to the fact that the bipolar world of 1947 has been breaking apart in both East and West, and that this rapid pace of change has had special consequences for America's system of alliances. No longer could Western Europe be taken for granted. The creation of the Common Market had ruptured the Atlantic world by establishing an organization in which neither Britain nor America was a member. The unity of NATO was threatened by France's insistence on nuclear independence.

Europeans bluntly informed the new President that Europe was now an independent power center which was no longer willing to accept America as the unchallenged leader of one-half of the world. Viscount Hailsham, a leader sympathetic to the United

States, warned Kennedy that he was not to think of himself as the "commander-in-chief of the forces of the free world." No one doubted the influence, initiative, or integrity of the United States, he stated, but he asked: "Have the Americans paused to reflect that an alliance in which all the advanced and sophisticated technologies were left to one of the partners, and the rest were relegated to supply a modest contribution of Scotch whisky and compact cars . . . would not ultimately succeed in retaining the loyalty of European electors?"

Kennedy has attempted to adapt American policies to the new phenomenon of an independent Europe, thus far with mixed success. As a counterproposal to the rise of an economically independent Europe, the President advanced the Grand Design for Atlantic Partnership. He envisaged the creation of an economic community which would not only improve America's trading position but which would be able to cope with the task of aiding the development of the southern continents. To pave the way for the United States to join with Europe in a free trade movement, Kennedy won from Congress a Trade Expansion Act in 1962 that gave the President power to lower tariff barriers in return for trade concessions to the United States. But when de Gaulle blackballed Britain from admission to the Common Market, he darkened prospects for the Grand Design.

The United States met frustration too in its attempt to revamp NATO to take cognizance of Europe's desire for a larger role in determining nuclear policy. Europeans were reluctant to agree that only the President of the United States could have his finger on the trigger of any nuclear force, and they were increasingly unwilling to be the foot soldiers of a nuclear war. A West German asked: "Do you think they're going to stand and fight with rifles against the Russian atom bombs?" Nor has de Gaulle been willing to forego an independent nuclear force for France. But if Kennedy has not been able to win endorsement in Europe for his economic and military proposals, he has at least won respect by showing far more alertness than his predecessor to the need to adjust American policy to the end of the postwar world.

Kennedy has also shown much more patience than his predecessor with neutralist rejection of a world divided into two armed camps, and much less insistence that they choose sides in the cold war. Unlike Eisenhower and Dulles, he has not tried to build military alliances throughout the world. Rather he has been willing to recognize the usefulness of independent neutrals as a break-water against Communist expansion and has been content to encourage the development of stable and economically viable governments which would be independent of either the Western or Soviet blocs. A State Department official explained: "We seek to build a community of independent nations, their governments increasingly responsive to the consent of the governed, cooperating of their own free will in their areas of interdependence, settling their disputes by peaceful means."

But this does not mean that Kennedy has been content merely to mark time. He has given particular attention to sponsoring innovations that would win the good will of the emerging nations. He has offered an expanded Food for Peace program; revamped foreign aid to give greater emphasis to economic as distinguished from military assistance; and has chosen envoys to the nations of the Southern Hemisphere who were sympathetic to the aspirations of the new nations.

Four months after the Bay of Pigs mishap, the United States unveiled the most ambitious program it had ever directed toward Latin America—the Alliance for Progress. Under the *Alianza,* the United States adopted a new goal for foreign aid: social change. Countries were encouraged to undertake reforms to erase griev-ances that Castroism might exploit. If they would agree to basic reforms of their social structure, the United States committed itself for a ten-year period to assist in achieving such specific goals as agrarian reform, full employment, price stability, low-cost housing, and an annual economic growth rate of at least 2.5 per cent. One writer noted: "It is a monumental commitment which for size and complexity makes the Marshall Plan look puny by comparison."

Even friends of the *Alianza* conceded it got off to a slow start. When the first anniversary of the Alliance arrived, Washington decided to "mark" rather than "celebrate" the occasion. The engineering of social change is a formidable goal. To achieve success, the United States may have to persuade governments to adopt reforms which may very well result in turning these governments out of office. Moreover, the United States continued to pursue economic policies which threatened to undo the good that the Alliance might achieve. Nonetheless, the Alliance for Progress marked an important stride forward from America's past policies south of the border.

The *Alianza* was only one of a number of Kennedy programs aimed at convincing the people of the Southern Hemisphere that the United States was not just a power engaged in the cold war but a country warmly sympathetic to the aspirations of the peoples of the new nations. Of all of Kennedy's innovations, no agency conveyed this feeling so well as the newly created Peace Corps. Only a few thousand in all, the members of the Peace Corps have made their presence felt by the example they have set. They have taught schools in Ghana and in the Philippines, built roads in Tanganyika and Chile, fought a typhoid epidemic in St. Lucia, and given instruction in midwifery in Colombia. Seven fishermen out of the port of Gloucester instructed Togo's fishermen. A Brooklyn boy taught Dominican villagers how to raise chickens, and another volunteer gave lessons in advanced Greek to African schoolchildren. In Bolivia, a young American couple adopted a leper colony.

Kennedy also has emphasized innovation and flexibility in his approach to national defense. To be sure, he has been even more determined than his predecessors to build up America's military strength. "For only when our arms are sufficient beyond doubt can we be certain beyond doubt that they will never be employed," the President stated. But Kennedy has abandoned the Dulles doctrine of massive retaliation and aimed instead to achieve a new flexibility for America's Armed Forces. The United States, Kennedy believes, should not be left with a choice between annihilation and humiliation.

Kennedy's Secretary of Defense, the auto magnate Robert McNamara, shares the President's conviction that the United States needs a military posture appropriate to fighting a wide variety of conflicts—not only a dreaded nuclear engagement, but brushfire wars, guerrilla wars, and paramilitary struggles. McNamara has proved a real find. Under the leadership of "McNamara and his band" in the Defense Department, the country has markedly improved its capacity to fight both conventional and unconventional wars. No less important, McNamara has asserted the authority of the civilian Secretary of Defense over the entire military establishment. In an era when Americans are growingly alarmed by the rise of the "garrison state," McNamara's achievement may well stand out as the most important development of the Kennedy era.

It was to take some time for the world to recognize that Kennedy had departed on a different course from that followed by Eisenhower and Dulles. Twice in Kennedy's first twenty months in office, he confronted crises which threatened to plunge the world into nuclear war. His willingness to risk war first over Berlin and then over the Soviet missiles in Cuba seemed to many observers not unlike Dulles' brinksmanship. In fact, Kennedy was pursuing as peaceful a course as events would permit. He refused to act except under extreme provocation; took pains not to confront the Soviets with a situation from which they could not retreat; and limited his own actions to those required by the particular crisis. He never operated on the premise that the only acceptable solution was one that would result in total victory for the United States.

Kennedy faced the first crisis less than six months after he took office when he traveled to Vienna for his first meeting with Khrushchev. In Vienna in June, 1961, the Soviet Premier blustered that before the year was out he planned to make a peace treaty with East Germany which would extinguish Western rights of access to West Berlin.

Kennedy met the crisis with cool determination. If Khrushchev persisted in his intentions, the President told the Soviet Premier bluntly, "it will be a cold winter." Kennedy asked for increased military appropriation; ordered draft calls doubled and tripled; and requested authority to call reservists to active duty. To provide a symbolic reinforcement of West Berlin, he ordered an armored U.S. troop convoy to roll 110 miles across the Autobahn through Communist-held sections of Germany. At border points in Berlin, American tanks confronted Soviet tanks.

As the Berlin crisis mounted, the United States was swept by a frenzy of fallout-shelter building. For a season, family fallout-shelter construction became a thriving business. *The New York Times* ran a two-page ad from Hammacher Schlemmer for

"Shelters for Living"—one room would cost about $14,000. In Dallas, the Lone Star Steel Company marketed a shelter with a window painted on the wall showing an outdoor scene; it even came equipped with a shade that could be pulled down at night.

As American communities began to burrow underground that summer, some Americans showed the effects of the Soviet's war of nerves. In Santa Barbara, "Minute Man" vigilantes underwent training as guerrilla fighters and cached water in the California hills. Each vigilante had one hundred rounds of ammunition for every weapon he owned. Clergymen justified the right of the head of a family to shoot down neighbors who wanted to share his shelter. Thirty New Yorkers set out on a motor caravan to northern California in quest of a sanctuary from nuclear war. (They settled in Chico, less than seven miles from a Titan missile pad.)

By fall, the crisis was easing, not only because Kennedy showed firmness but because he was no less determined to avoid a nuclear showdown. When the President returned from Vienna, his first step had been to call for an estimate of the number of Americans who might die in a nuclear exchange. (The answer: seventy million.) While Kennedy was determined to compel the U.S.S.R. to back down from its ultimatum, he also wished to minimize the risks of nuclear war. He even ignored the provocation of the construction of the Berlin Wall. Although he was urged to approve the use of force to knock down the Wall, he permitted East Germany to seal the border and halt the flow of refugees into West Berlin.

Kennedy showed this same combination of firmness and willingness to compromise when an even more serious crisis developed in Cuba several months later. In the summer of 1962, vessels boldly displaying the hammer and sickle steamed brazenly into Cuban ports with cargoes of Soviet arms. They unloaded missiles, MIG fighters, and patrol boats, as well as technicians and instructors. Republican senators clamored for Presidential action, but so long as reconnaissance showed no evidence of offensive missiles, Kennedy refused to risk a calamitous war to curb the Soviets.

The President adopted a hard line with the U.S.S.R. only when he learned that, despite solemn assurances to the contrary from the

Soviet envoy, the U.S.S.R. was speeding the completion of offensive missile sites on the island. With full recognition of the grave
risks involved, Kennedy saw no choice but to deliver the Soviet
Union a blunt ultimatum. But he refused to sanction other alternatives. He would not approve the bombing of the missile sites,
because this smacked too much of a "Pearl Harbor" tactic, and
because it would accelerate the danger of war. Nor would he
sanction the use of force to dislodge the Castro regime, although
by now even Senator William Fulbright, who had courageously
opposed the Bay of Pigs scheme, believed the United States should
invade Cuba and eradicate the Castro menace.

When the Soviet vessels turned around and headed back to port,
and the missile bases were dismantled, and the missiles crated and
withdrawn, Kennedy scored a stunning victory. Yet even at his
moment of triumph, Kennedy made clear that he disagreed with
those who claimed that if America took a firm enough stand with
the Russians, the Soviets would always back down. The U.S.S.R.,
he recognized, could afford to back down in Cuba; it would not
always do so, especially if its own national security was at stake. If
the United States should make but one critical mistake about
Soviet intentions, the President warned, "there will be 140 million
deaths within the first eighteen hours."

For the past year, the President has been under constant
pressure to take action against Castro. In Ohio, car stickers jeer:
"Cheer up, they're only 90 miles away." But after its one unhappy
experience, the Administration has refused to employ force against
Castro. Offensive missile sites were a direct threat to the United
States; a Red regime in one Latin American nation was not.
Although the government sought to isolate Cuba economically and
politically, it was determined to avoid an armed clash in the
Caribbean. To this end, it has not only refused to encourage an
invasion of Cuba but has actively intervened to block attempts by
Cuban exiles to launch raids from American territory.

In his conduct of foreign policy, Kennedy has never been
satisfied with the limited goal of safeguarding the free areas of the
world, while avoiding a thermonuclear showdown. He has had a
larger aim in view—to take the first steps toward curbing the
nuclear arms race that threatens the universe with Doomsday. In

his 1960 campaign, Kennedy pledged "a supreme effort to break the log jam on disarmament and nuclear tests." "The world," he declared, "was not meant to be a prison in which man awaits his executioner."

Once in office the new President directed his efforts both toward reaching an arms agreement and toward effecting a *rapprochement* with the Soviet Union. In a speech to the United Nations in September, 1961, President Kennedy declared that the world faced a choice: disarmament, or a planet turned into "a flaming funeral pyre." Even more striking was an address he delivered at American University. The President urged: "Let us reexamine our attitude toward the Soviet Union." The American people, he declared, should not see "only a distorted and desperate view of the other side." One writer commented: "For the first time in eight years, a President was speaking of American policy without making the cold war the paramount matter of concern. . . . Indeed, he spoke at times of the cold war as if it hardly existed any longer."

Unhappily, the Soviet negotiators showed no interest in the arms parley at Geneva, and in August, 1961, the U.S.S.R. resumed atmospheric testing. In October, it ostentatiously exploded a nuclear device nearly three thousand times larger than the Hiroshima bomb. For more than two years, arms control negotiations foundered, as they had in the past, on the U.S.S.R.'s insistence that disarmament be agreed upon without effective controls, and its refusal to take even the first steps toward arms limitation.

In 1963, the log jam was broken. Within the United States, there was increased disillusionment with a foreign policy which rested, in the words of Harrison Salisbury, on "a parity of horror." Civil defense officials found Americans apathetic and disenchanted. "Shelters aren't worth a darn," commented a Toledo man. "With these modern missile weapons, by the time I found an air raid shelter I'd be done for." In Seattle, a university official explained: "The average citizen is not too concerned. He feels that if the atomic bomb is dropped—who wants to be around afterward?" The state of Oregon launched an outright rebellion against civil defense. Portland wiped out its civil defense program which a city commissioner declared would prove "useless" in a nuclear war. Four days later, the state government abolished the state's civil defense operation. "I'm delighted it happened," declared a Portland housewife. "I hope Oregon will become a pacesetter for the rest of the nation."

Much more important in making possible a limited agreement on arms was a change of attitude in the Soviet Union. No one knows what caused this change, but Khrushchev may well have shared President Kennedy's dismay at the rise of new members of the nuclear club like France and the possibility that yet more nations would soon possess a nuclear bomb. (The President warned: "I ask you to stop and think for a moment what it would mean to have nuclear weapons in many hands—in the hands of countries large and small, stable and unstable, responsible and irresponsible, scattered throughout the world. There would be no rest for anyone, no stability, no real security, and no chance of effective disarmament.") More particularly, the Soviet Premier must have been disturbed by the growing breach with Red China and its consequences for nuclear politics.

In Moscow in July, 1963, the United States, Great Britain and the U.S.S.R. reached an agreement providing for a limited ban on nuclear testing. While some were skeptical about how much effect the treaty would have, others saw a "historical breakthrough." For the first time in the history of The Bomb, agreement had been reached on controlling it. The pact, President Kennedy claimed, was "an important opening wedge in our effort to 'get the genie back in the bottle.'"

As Khrushchev, Secretary Rusk and Lord Home walked into the Kremlin ballroom to celebrate the signing of the test-ban treaty, the Soviet band struck up Gershwin's "Love Walked In." In fact, it is questionable whether the pact marks the beginning of a prolonged period of Soviet-American amity, and it is not even clear that the treaty will slow down the arms race appreciably. Even if it did, the United States, with some fifty thousand nuclear bombs and warheads, had enough destructive material stockpiled to demolish the Soviet Union several times over, and no one doubts that the U.S.S.R. has the power to "overkill" the United States.

Yet once the limited nuclear test ban had been achieved, new hopes burgeoned that the arms race could be brought under control, and the United States began to explore the possibilities of a limited disengagement in Central Europe. Within a brief period after the negotiation of the pact, President Kennedy proposed a Soviet-American effort to explore the moon and agreed to permit the U.S.S.R. to purchase American wheat. Today there is a stronger current of realistic optimism, however subdued, than at any time since the onset of the cold war.

The question remains: has Kennedy gotten the country "moving again" in foreign affairs? If the state of the nation's prestige abroad is taken as a critical test surely the answer must be affirmative. There is a sharp contrast between the Tokyo and South American rioting of the Eisenhower years and the greetings Kennedy and his emissaries have received, even if the change is less a consequence of the President's own policies than the "Kennedy luck." When Kennedy traveled to Latin America, he was greeted warmly. When Vice-President Lyndon Johnson returned from a tour of Southeast Asia, he reported: "We never heard a hostile voice, never shook a hostile hand."

For all the anxiety over Berlin and the unrest in Algeria and Vietnam, the world shows a happier countenance than it did when Kennedy took office. Trouble spots like the Congo now have achieved a measure of stability. There is a new confidence in America's military strength and, after Alan Shepard soared into space and back again, of America's ability to keep stride with Soviet achievements in space. Most important, the apocalyptic vision of a war of annihilation has been receding, and there is hope of new departures in foreign affairs.

There are limits to how much any one administration can hope to achieve in foreign policy in a world dominated by a nuclear balance of terror. No doubt there is much more the Kennedy Administration could do, and as in the Cuban fiasco, much it should not have done. No doubt too much of the improvement in world affairs is the result of forces, such as the Sino-Soviet struggle, which owe nothing to the President's initiative. But in the short time the President has been in office, he can justly claim that in foreign affairs he has come a long way toward fulfilling his pledge. The country is once more on the move.

ALEXANDER M. BICKEL

Civil Rights: A New Era Opens

PREVIEW: THE PRESIDENCY AND CIVIL RIGHTS

The principle of a self-starting, creative expansive discharge of the Presidential office was one of the most insistent themes in John F. Kennedy's 1960 campaign. The theme recurred with particular frequency in his discussions of civil rights. In his second television debate with Richard Nixon, Kennedy said that some civil rights objectives could be achieved by unaided executive action, and he emphasized, quoting F.D.R., that the Presidency is "above all, a place of moral leadership." But just what exactly, as of 1960, were the powers of the President affecting civil rights?

There is always a tendency to exaggerate what one man in the White House can possibly direct, or even know. There is, indeed, as Thomas Reed Powell once wrote in another connection, a certain "unwarranted animism" in the use of the phrase "the Administration." This much it is necessary to say by way of caution. But the President *can* generally summon great, immediate, and effective power, provided two things are true. One, that the President conceives it to be one of his missions, domestically as well as internationally, to initiate policy and to carry it into effect on his own responsibility, and to reach out boldly until he is

These selections are from Alexander M. Bickel, *Politics and the Warren Court*, pp. 49–74. Copyright © 1960, 1962 by Alexander M. Bickel. Reprinted by permission of Harper & Row, Publishers.

stopped by the retaining wall of a countervailing power, such as Congress. Retaining walls there are, and there are, God knows, enough of them; a President need not begin by worrying that he will be allowed to go too far without being stopped. Kennedy certainly so conceived the office in his campaign, and Nixon professed to also. Eisenhower, with a few exceptions (viz., the so-called inflation issue in 1958–59), did not, as Taft and Harding and Coolidge and Hoover before him had not. Two, it must be true that the President is willing, for a time at least, to devote a disproportionate share of his total effort to a domestic problem on which he wishes to exert the full reach of his power and influence. The decisions and the leadership that are called for cannot be delegated. The sources of the authority and of the drive that are both necessary cannot be separated. What is involved is not administration but creative work on the frontiers of power, and the President must be willing to immerse himself in it for a time. He cannot do so with respect to many matters at once.

If these two conditions are met, the opportunities are great. In attempting to analyze them as they bear on civil rights and as they opened up for John Kennedy in 1960, one may put to one side two distinct Presidential functions: (1) recommending legislation to Congress and (2) executing authority specifically conferred by Congress. The one is generally well understood, though there was reason to doubt sometimes that Eisenhower quite grasped its significance. The other is delegable and is indeed often delegated by Congress itself to cabinet officers and the like, acting under the direction of the President. Kennedy justly complained in campaign speeches that only six suits were started by the Eisenhower Administration under the Civil Rights Acts of 1957 and 1960, which deal with the right to vote. The Civil Rights Division of the Department of Justice was organized tardily and poorly, and run without distinction. Its record under Eisenhower was laughable when compared, for example, with that of the same department's Antitrust Division. This was in part owing, perhaps, to certain hostile attitudes in Congress that manifested themselves in regard to both appropriations and nominations. It was owing in the largest part to complacent administration. The cure lay in the appointment of vigorous, dedicated men at cabinet and subcabinet levels. It did not demand the exertion of much more Presidential leadership than that.

There was something, however, that the President and only the President could do about the subject matter of the 1957 and 1960 acts. He was uniquely in a position to draw attention to the problem of voting rights, not by comfortable homilies but by pointing to specific, glaring abuses until the whole nation blushed. And he could heighten the importance and prestige of the Civil Rights Commission, created and given investigative powers by the 1957 act, by associating it in the public mind with his own person and office. Eisenhower took an unconscionable time making the necessary appointments to the Commission after Congress had created it, and he pretty much ignored it afterward. When the Commission met with defiance in the South, the government's law officers in due course vindicated it in court. That was as it should be. But the President did not react, as he could have, by appealing to public opinion on his own and indicating that it was not some miscellaneous bureaucrats who had been flouted but the President's trusted appointees and delegates.

President Eisenhower's failure to react in this fashion is worth stressing because it was attributable not only to temperament but to an aspect of the conception of the passive Presidency which was of particular importance with respect to civil rights. At least until 1964 basic civil rights policy was constitutional and therefore judge-made. Eisenhower generally took the position that it is not for the President to have public views on matters that are in process of being decided by the courts, and also, as in the instance of the school segregation decision, that it is no less improper for the President to speak his own mind after the courts have acted. This is the mechanistic view of the doctrine of separation of powers, the view, to borrow a witticism of Chief Justice Taft's, that the machinery of government is really machinery. It was not the attitude of Theodore Roosevelt or even of President Taft, both of whom felt free to have convictions about the meaning of the Sherman Antitrust Act and about the constitutionality of an income tax before and after the courts announced their opinions. It was not Franklin Roosevelt's conception, as it had not been Jackson's. And it was not Lincoln's, who had a few public thoughts about the *Dred Scott* case.

The President, of course, must take the lead in obeying and in urging and in the end enforcing obedience to judicial decrees. But, as Lincoln pointed out long ago, it is one thing—and quite inadmissible—to resist a specific court decision. It is quite another to reject it (or to accept and support it) as what he called a "political rule," governing the behavior of the other branches of the government on cognate matters.[1] This is a distinction crucial to a true view of the doctrine of separation of powers. It follows that a President, while obliged to enforce, was free to deplore the Supreme Court's decisions on schools or on the investigative powers of the Civil Rights Commission. If so minded, however, he was free also to accept such decisions, and to use his "place of moral leadership," and exploit his unique access to the minds and hearts of the American people, in order to support the Court's actions. If so minded, moreover, he had the power to make the principle underlying the Court's decisions the "political rule" of his Administration. John Kennedy was so minded. This was his conception of the office of President. He was prepared, it seemed, to make of the principle of equal protection a "political rule," but would he find it possible to devote the necessary disproportionate share of his energies to its effectuation?

In planning for the first few months of 1961, the first choice that had to be made was between unaided executive action, on the one hand, and executive activation of the legislature, on the other. Both would be necessary in the longer run. But immediately? This was going to be a time, to be sure, of heightened—yet not limit-less—energies, and a peak time of executive effectiveness in legislative leadership. But it would be also a short and crowded time of competing priorities, all high; and the risk to the quantity and quality of the total legislative program that would inhere in asking immediately for civil rights legislation was obvious and familiar.

To have assessed this risk was not to conclude the choice. But it happened also that a number of immediate needs could be met by the President acting on his own; and that meeting them vigorously

---

[1] See P. M. Angle, ed., *Created Equal?—The Complete Lincoln-Douglas Debates of 1858* 23, 36, 56–58, 78, 333 (1958); R. P. Basler, ed., *The Collected Works of Abraham Lincoln,* Vols. 2 and 3, pp. 495, 516, 255 (1953); A. M. Bickel, *The Least Dangerous Branch* 259–62 (1962).

and imaginatively would amount to a fresh start on civil rights, a hopeful and it might be even a spectacular start. Moreover, and this was most important, it was reasonable to expect that the assumption of Presidential responsibility would alter the shape and posture of things so as vastly to enhance the chances of far-reaching congressional action when the time for that did come.

Assuming, then, that no new legislation would be sought initially, and that an attempt would be made to exert executive power to the fullest, what actions were open to President Kennedy as his Administration began? The initial step in the assumption of Presidential responsibility could fittingly be issuance soon after inauguration not of one or more executive orders—though they also would be needed—but of a Proclamation. We have not ceased to live by symbols, and it would not be purposeless thus to call to mind the grandest traditions of the office and the boldest actions of its great occupants. The President could review the history of Negro rights (and wrongs) since Lincoln's Proclamation: the Civil War Amendments, the largely ineffectual Reconstruction Civil Rights Acts, the forward movement in modern constitutional litigation to the climax of the segregation cases of 1954 and their progeny, and the Civil Rights Acts of 1957 and 1960. He could then proclaim his purpose to protect and defend, to apply and to extend recent legislative and judicial policies throughout the realm of executive power. And he could announce that he proposed, in the language of the Constitution, to "take care that the laws be faithfully executed" as follows:

Public education. The Civil Rights Commission, in its 1959 report, noted that many school districts attempting to evolve a desegregation plan had "no established and qualified source to which to turn for information and advice." The Commission proposed that it be given statutory authority to act as a clearinghouse for such information and advice, and also to act as a mediation and conciliation service helping school boards work out plans.[2] A bill by Senator Paul H. Douglas, of Illinois, would have given similar authority to the Department of Health, Education and Welfare. But the Office of Education in that department dates

[2] U.S. Commission on Civil Rights, *With Liberty and Justice for All* 133 (1959).

back to a statute of 1867, and the description of its duties makes remarkable reading. The office is "to collect statistics and facts showing the condition and progress of education in the several States . . . to diffuse such information respecting the organization and management of schools . . . and shall . . . promote the cause of education throughout the country."[3]

The authority was there for the President to use. He could direct the Office of Education to extend technical assistance to districts seeking to desegregate their schools, and, beyond that, to "promote the cause of education" by working out desegregation plans for districts that had taken no initiative of their own. The Office could collect and make readily available the lessons of experience on such matters as the maintenance of scholastic standards, social relationships in schools, utilization of Negro teachers, and Negro-white community cooperation. It could also, as a conciliating agency, suggest the application of these lessons to local conditions. In carrying out its conciliation function, the Office could have available on a continuous basis the counsel and assistance of the Civil Rights Division of the Department of Justice. Senator Douglas' bill would also have authorized the Attorney General to go to court and enforce integration plans worked out by the Office of Education. But the President could send his law officers to court not as enforcement officials but as friends of the court, which was the way they did enter the original school cases, and later the Little Rock case.

The suggestion was made at a Conference on Civil Rights at Notre Dame University early in 1960 that the President could refuse to grant any federal aid to a college or university that discriminates in selecting its student body. The President would wish to give an opportunity for compliance rather than laying down a flat rule, and he would grant hearings (though not personally, of course) in cases where the facts were in dispute. But otherwise, as Father Hesburgh of Notre Dame indicated, the only thing lacking was the will.[4]

[3] 20 U.S.C. Sec. 1.
[4] H. Wofford, Jr., "Notre Dame Conference on Civil Rights: A Contribution to the Development of Public Law," 35 *Notre Dame Lawyer* 328, 360 (1960).

Housing. The President had—and in the course of the campaign promised to exercise—the power to follow another 1959 recommendation of the Civil Rights Commission[5] and establish a policy of nondiscrimination in federally aided housing. It could, no doubt, again not be a flat rule, for that might deprive Negroes as well as others of any new housing in areas where it was worst needed. But the authority to exert pressure was available, and it could be employed with most fruitful immediacy, perhaps, in the North. The Housing and Home Finance Agency, the Federal Housing Administration, the Veterans Administration, the Public Housing Administration, and the Urban Renewal Administration could work out policies to encourage the growth of racially integrated neighborhoods, or at least prevent the perpetuation of segregated ones. Consultation with local authorities was advisable, of course, but the federal policy would ultimately be enforced as a condition upon the receipt of federal funds and assistance.

Government building, employment, and contracts. It was common ground all around that the President could, if he wished, enforce the principle of equal protection in the employment practices of the government and its contractors, and thus incidentally cover a considerable segment of the economy. President Eisenhower indeed declared a policy of nondiscrimination by executive order, and delegated to a Committee on Government Contracts, headed by Vice-President Nixon, the authority to effectuate it. And that was all he did, except to complain to Congress that the Committee could do its job better if it was put on a statutory basis. The problem was—and remains—complex, involving as it does, for one example, labor union practices, and it is even larger than it is complex. If it was to yield, it needed less a statute and more the public attention and drive a President could give toward its solution.

That, to repeat, was the single most important generalization applying to everything that could be done on the President's unaided executive authority. The Assistant Attorney General in charge of the Civil Rights Division would have to have public evidence of the President's interest and trust. The same would hold

[5] U.S. Comm'n on Civil Rights, *With Liberty and Justice for All* 184–186 (1959).

for the head of the Office of Education. At lower levels, a great deal of staffing would have to be done within existing appropriations. Very often, therefore, the borrowing of personnel from within the government would be necessary, and if that was to work rapidly and result in the assignment of first-rate people, it would also have to receive the President's attention from time to time. Personnel would be needed not only for the litigating, technical assistance, and conciliation programs but for the others as well, since nondiscrimination policies could not just be decreed; they would have to be worked out to suit conditions, and they would have to be policed. Neither the mere appearance of discrimination nor of nondiscrimination would necessarily be true to the reality of things. It would often be necessary to investigate and to grant hearings. Finally, funds would have to be found within existing appropriations, and that also would require a form of personally conducted Presidential arbitrage.

But the returns could be high. The suggestions touched on here are far from being all that an imaginative rummager might have found in the back closet of Presidential powers.

REVIEW: THE KENNEDY RECORD
AT MID-TERM

The preceding section of this chapter canvassed the possibilities for action on civil rights that seemed open to President Kennedy at the beginning of his Administration. In view of these possibilities, how did the performance measure up? A good point in time on which to fix for an assessment of the record is November 20, 1962, when Kennedy signed an executive order barring future discrimination in federally supported housing.[6] Asked why he had waited till midway in his term of office to take this promised action, the late President replied: "Well, I said I would issue it at the time that I thought it was in the public interest, and now is the time." Now was the time also, although nobody quite knew it then, when the opening phase of the Kennedy performance was drawing to a close. There would soon be an end of the beginning. Within a very few months events in Birmingham, Alabama, would perma-

[6] Executive Order 11063, "Equal Opportunity in Housing," Nov. 20, 1962.

nently and radically alter conditions and launch John Kennedy on a second, quite new if foreshortened career as a champion of civil rights. There would be another record.

A portion of the first record, it may be said with no attempt at irony, was made in the Presidential campaign of 1960. In the course of this campaign, Kennedy and Nixon established a firm national consensus, and finally fixed the broad and pervasive principle of the *School Segregation* cases of 1954 as not only the judicial but also the political policy of the federal government. The campaign established a new mood of executive engagement in the civil rights struggle, and signaled an executive commitment to the morality of equal protection of the laws as a rule of independent, creative political action, rather than merely as an obligation to uphold the courts. As a direct consequence, some notable peaceful strides were made in school desegregation, and would continue to be made. The crisis at Ole Miss, although it was tragic, was rather an insignificant exception, as in their own context were the Montgomery Freedom Ride riots of the spring of 1961, which were followed by great progress in the peaceful integration of transportation facilities. The point is that after the campaign of 1960, forward movement in desegregation was—and was known to be—as ineluctable as the income tax or the social security system. This had not been the case before.

The Presidency, said Kennedy in 1960, quoting F.D.R., is "a place of moral leadership." So is a Presidential campaign, at least for the eventual winner, and Kennedy seized the opportunity in his campaign. Beyond this, he made one specific pledge—the famous "stroke of the pen" about housing—which he redeemed. But he promised also, more generally, vigorous executive action on all fronts. The performance must be judged against the expectations so raised, which came to seem natural, although they would have appeared strange and visionary during the previous decade.

A first and quite obvious generalization is that the performance through 1962 was wholly executive. The Administration broke no lances in Congress. As to this one need perhaps say no more than that President Kennedy was a realist, and that he had troubles enough in what was to all intents and purposes a three-party legislature, with a species of Free Democrats (à la West Germany's) holding the balance of power. A second and more interesting generalization, qualified by the housing order, is that the performance was heavily a litigating one. With this aspect of the performance I propose now to deal in some detail, before returning to the housing order and to other acts of commission and omission.

Transportation. Perhaps the most spectacular achievement was the apparently effective and almost universal desegregation of interstate transportation, including terminal facilities. It isn't very fruitful to debate whether the Administration's action was a consequence of the freedom rides in the spring of 1961 and of sit-ins before and after or was an independent initiative. The fact is that in a well-conceived and flawlessly executed move the Justice Department obtained from the Interstate Commerce Commission a self-enforcing order integrating not only interstate buses but also the terminals they use. The order evidently worked, although in some localities custom tended after a while to reassert itself, with the aid of unofficial white pressure. Where local officials tried to interfere, the department followed up by obtaining injunctions against them in the federal courts. Segregation on interstate trains had long since been abandoned, and it seems never to have been in effect on planes. But many terminals and airports remained segregated. Pursuing an altogether commendable and lawyerlike policy that it is worthwhile having a try at negotiation before filing suit, the Justice Department obtained the agreement of the chief Southern railroads, eighteen in number, to integrate their terminals; and this was done in hundreds of places. Again, where official state interference was attempted, court action followed. As to airports, the problem was somewhat different, being both easier, because federal funds often helped to build the facilities, and harder, because these are often—especially in their restaurants—more of a multipurpose local institution. Both the Civil Aeronautics Board and the Federal Aviation Agency exerted pressure, and the Justice Department negotiated and in a few instances litigated. Results here were perhaps a little slower in coming—and it is again possible that in some places the actual practice soon reverted to earlier custom—but the point was reached in the fall of 1962 where Attorney General Kennedy could report that "virtually every airport" as well as bus and railroad station in the South had been desegregated.

Voting. From Reconstruction to 1964, Congress legislated

twice and only twice on racial discrimination. It passed the Civil Rights Acts of 1957 and 1960. These closely connected statutes prescribed procedures for enforcing the Negro's right to vote, which is most explicitly guaranteed by the Fifteenth Amendment, and charged the Attorney General of the United States with the duty to prosecute the necessary lawsuits. The Eisenhower Administration, though it sponsored both bills, implemented them with about the vigor and imagination displayed by William McKinley in enforcing the Sherman Antitrust Act of 1890. The Kennedy Administration put life and purpose into these Civil Rights Acts.

The Eisenhower Administration filed six voting suits. It settled one and tried two. The other three had been filed too late to come to trial before Eisenhower left office. The Civil Rights Division in the Department of Justice, authorized by the 1957 act, was tardily organized and staffed by a handful of lawyers. Under Kennedy's Assistant Attorney General in charge of the division, Burke Marshall, a distinguished Washington lawyer, the legal staff was increased many times. By the end of 1962, it was nearing fifty and still growing. Collection, storage, and retrieval of evidence of discrimination—a massive task involving examination and classification of thousands of records of the registration of whites and the failure to register comparable Negroes—was systematized so that some of it could be performed by trained clerks. The FBI was heavily enlisted in gathering testimonial evidence, and its effectiveness was notable, owing, no doubt, to the fact that its agents had the confidence of the local whites. (Ironically—or sadly—enough, the FBI was less successful in interviewing Southern Negroes.) The number of suits that were brought stood at thirty-two after less than two years. When a suit was successfully concluded, the department collected compliance reports, and the FBI checked them.

This was and remains a magnificent effort—a tribute to Attorney General Kennedy who supported it and whose ultimate responsibility it was, and to Marshall and his First Assistant, John Doar, now himself the Assistant Attorney General, who directed and animated it. And it was bearing some fruit. The fact that Senator Lister Hill squeaked through to reelection in Alabama in

1962 by an incredibly narrow margin was generally taken to be a signal to Southern politicians that they had better abandon all support of the Administration and concentrate on trying to be more reactionary than their new Republican opponents. But Hill carried two counties in which the Justice Department had recently succeeded in registering substantial numbers of Negroes, while losing neighboring counties in which Negro registration was still negligible. Justice Department officials believed that, although there might be some panic to the right among Southerners in Congress, the more perceptive among them would realize that their future lay in an opening to the moderate left. For the reactionary position was being conclusively preempted by a new breed of Southern Republicans, while there would soon be many more counties like Bullock and Macon in Alabama, where the number of Negro voters was beginning to be counted in the thousands.

Yet other observers, admiring the moving of mountains, feared the production, in the end, of mice. It was not merely that litigation, no matter how formidably conducted, is a slow and piecemeal process. Nor was it merely that the law, legislative and judicial, was inadequate. To be sure, a statute making a sixth-grade education conclusive proof of literacy, such as the Administration had proposed but hardly pressed, would expedite litigation. But it could not avoid it. And it would not get at the root problem, which is that you can perhaps make sure a qualified Negro will be registered, but you can't qualify him, or make him want to register, or, once registered, to vote.

In some degree the trouble is affirmative acts of intimidation and discouragement—violence and the threat of it, economic reprisals, and the perverted use of state legal processes in frivolous, harassing prosecutions. The violence and the prosecutions are directed as often as not at members of such organizations as the Student Non-Violent Coordinating Committee, which conducts schools in registration procedures, and at leaders of the Negro community. In two instances as of the end of 1962, in Mississippi and in Georgia, the Department of Justice went to court for injunctions against intimidation by sheriffs and other officers, and against groundless prosecutions for vagrancy and breach of the peace, aimed at stopping registration drives. Workers of the Student Non-Violent Coordinating Committee and like organizations complained, however (and they still do), that the department was laggard in this aspect of its litigating activity. But such suits are nearly as difficult to prepare and frame as the suits that open registration books to begin with, and they are much harder to win. Perhaps the answer was that a concerted attempt to protect registration drives would have to await completion of the effort to make registration possible, though this was a hard answer for dedicated workers on the scene to swallow.

Intimidation and reprisals, in any event, may be the relatively minor obstacle. The heart of the matter may be apathy, born of poverty, ignorance, and consequent passive alienation. The right to vote, Attorney General Kennedy said, is basic, "and from it all other rights flow." This was the hope that informed the Justice Department's enormous effort, and this was, in part, the justification for slighting other possible initiatives open to executive power, which were, indeed, relatively slighted. But it may be—there is evidence in the North to support this hypothesis—that those who are deprived of other rights tend not to exercise the right from which the others flow, even when they are free to do so. It may be, in other words, that the cart was placed somewhat before the horse. No one of sound mind and worthy intentions would have wished to see the marvelous operation that was mounted in the Justice Department stopped short of full success in making the franchise at least available, whether or not availed of. But perhaps this operation should have been regarded less sanguinely. Perhaps it ought to have been seen more clearly that its success depended ultimately on simultaneous and equally important efforts in other directions.

Education and employment. One of the most dramatic results of the registration drive came in Macon County, Alabama, where registration shot up from a handful to some twenty-eight hundred. Macon County is the home of Tuskegee Institute. Other relatively high figures were also brought about in areas, mostly urban, where Negroes have reasonable employment and education. How were more such areas to be created, especially in the depressed hundred-county Black Belt? Economic and technical aid was needed, of course—some sort of Point IV or *Alianza para Progreso;* and it could not be allowed to bog down in seeking to abolish segregation, but would have to pursue its own prior objectives. Yet such aid would at least have to be administered so as not to perpetuate the existing social system, and it would have to aim first at elevating the poorest of the poor. Officials of the government's Distressed Area Redevelopment Program were said to have these ends in view. They were said to be aware of the special needs of the Black Belt, and to be consulting with Negro leaders and with the Justice Department's Civil Rights Division. Out of such consultations grew a program in Lafayette County, Tennessee, a sharecropping area where the Justice Department had to sue to prevent potent economic pressure against Negro registration. The cabinet committee studying a project for a domestic Peace Corps was significantly headed by the Attorney General, and it could be expected to have in mind the connection between economic development and political and social rights. But these were comparative bywaters of government activity. Programs of a different order of magnitude were needed, as was a major school-aid bill, which the Kennedy Administration was unable to put through.

There were a number of other existing programs, which were perhaps peripheral, though not in the aggregate, and which were not all being exploited with vigor and imagination. A committee, continued from the Eisenhower Administration and headed by then Vice-President Johnson, was attempting to persuade government contractors, including the large defense contractors, to hire Negroes. This was certainly a step in the direction of ensuring, in a phrase of a California court, that some democracy stuck to funds disbursed by the federal government. Yet other opportunities had too long been—and some were still being—missed. Thus the Department of Health, Education and Welfare conducts a program of vocational and technical education into which, of course, go federal funds. The following paragraphs appeared in a reply, dated April 19, 1962, by the department's Office of Education to an inquiry from Mr. Sanford Jay Rosen, then of the Yale Law School, concerning measures, if any, to foster integrated training for Negroes:

Vocational programs under the Federal-State cooperative program are administered by the State board for vocational education in each

State. Training is available for both Negroes and whites *according to the State and local patterns of school organization.*

The problem of the Negro insofar as vocational training is concerned has been primarily due to the fact that *in many Negro schools the training has been limited to a few trades in which there were employment opportunities.* With Negroes being denied employment in certain occupations it would have been an obvious waste of school money and disappointing to the Negro to take training and yet not be able to get a job for which he had been trained. With the job opportunities increasing as a result of non-discrimination clauses in defense and other Federal Government contracts and other factors schools are now offering vocational courses in a wider range of occupations for Negroes. [Italics supplied.]

The tone of such a letter spoke for itself—and not in the accents of the campaign of 1960. No doubt, lack of Negro skills had impeded the efforts of Vice-President Johnson's committee, for whose fruition the Office of Education appeared to be waiting. The policy of HEW in this matter was said to be undergoing change for the better. But there was no indication that making jobs available to Negroes was a concern of the U.S. Employment Service, which supports state employment services, some of which, in turn, surely were laboring hard to perpetuate existing job discrimination. Of course, these are problems that will not yield easily. And the exertion of federal money-pressure is necessarily a subtle and gradual process. But there was some evidence here of a failure of coordinated purpose. Unity of purpose over the full range of federal programs was—and remains—essential, for the plight of the Negro in our society is a complex social, economic, and political problem, and no single, isolated line of effort can attain truly significant results.

A degree of failure of coordinated purpose was further apparent with respect to the government's commitment to spur the desegregation, "with all deliberate speed," of public schools. As early as 1959, the Civil Rights Commission had reported that many school districts attempting to evolve desegregation plans suffered from having "no established source to which to turn for information and advice."[7] The gathering and active dissemination of such informa-

[7] U.S. Comm'n on Civil Rights, *With Liberty and Justice for All* 133 (1959).

tion was a function that could clearly be undertaken by HEW's Office of Education, which is empowered by its organic statute to "promote the cause of education throughout the country."[8] The phrase "throughout the country" could well be emphasized with salutary effect, for the office could do a great deal not only in teaching the lesson of the growing number of successful experiences in the South but also in helping to work out techniques for dealing with *de facto* segregated situations in the North, some of which were then just beginning to come into litigation. Given good faith, or a court order, or both, desegregation is, after all, a skill, a professional task. The federal professionals should be in it up to their necks. Moreover, the development of an accessible body of knowledge on the subject and of proved techniques would also help and speed the process of litigation itself, for judges will readily draw on the views of experts. The shelves are groaning with "how to . . ." books, and the federal government floods the country with them on everything from animal husbandry up and down. Only the educators were not educating.

The Office of Education could also, as its statute commands, "promote the cause of education" by engaging generally and systematically in conciliation and negotiation, with a view to easing and speeding the process of school integration. HEW did in fact cooperate on an *ad hoc* basis with Assistant Attorney General Marshall to bring pressure to bear in the so-called impacted areas surrounding defense installations, where local school systems are heavily supported by federal funds (to help them absorb the children of federal personnel), and where in too many places they nevertheless remained segregated. The federal government had available the alternative of building its own schools on the military reservations. It was obviously more desirable, however, to support and integrate the local schools. To this end, all else failing, litigation was necessary, and the Justice Department in the fall of 1962 filed the first such suit in Prince George County, Virginia, the site of Fort Lee. There was some legal question whether the Attorney General had, as the phrase goes, standing to bring such a suit. It might be that private persons would have to act as plaintiffs. This doubt accounted in part for the government's

[8] 20 U.S.C. Sec. 1.

relative tardiness in bringing the first action. In the judgment of many lawyers, however, the government's legal position was sound and its chances excellent.[9]

It should be added here that in the instances—from Montgomery through New Orleans and St. Helena Parish and Prince Edward County, Virginia, to Oxford—where the process of desegregation boiled up into crisis, the government intervened, vigorously and imaginatively, not only with force but with litigating help in court. It did so, for the most part, as a friend of the court, in suits initially commenced by private parties. This was an activity that was begun on a small scale by the Eisenhower Administration, but was much expanded under President Kennedy, and included appearances in major arguments in the Supreme Court. There is respectable opinion that the government was and still is overdoing this; pushing its friendship for the courts, as it were, to oppressive lengths. But in each crisis the President might have to discharge his obligation to take care that the laws be faithfully executed. Surely it is not unreasonable for his representatives to go in and assist—by expressing an opinion binding on no one—in the effort to prevent a crisis or to resolve it peaceably. Actually, quite often, the government's friendship was extended to the courts at the latter's invitation.

Federal grants-in-aid. It is a commonplace, illustrated by several of the government activities mentioned earlier, that the welfare state is here, and that it is substantially financed by federal money. There could be little doubt that the President had the power—perhaps the obligation, but in any event subject to his political discretion—to take care that federal moneys were expended in programs that conformed to the Constitution, as the Supreme Court had construed it and as he himself understood it. Before as after the Civil Rights Act of 1964, his ultimate sanction

[9] The suit mentioned in the text is U.S. v. County School Bd. of Prince George County, 221 F. Supp. 93 (E.D. Va. 1963). Other cases were brought, with indifferent effect: U.S. v. Biloxi Municipal School District, 219 F. Supp. 691 (S.D. Miss. 1963); U.S. v. Sumter Cty. School Dist., 232 F. Supp. 945 (E.D. S.C. 1964); U.S. v. Madison Cty. Bd. of Education, 326 F.2d 237 (5th Cir. 1964); U.S. v. Bossier Parish School Bd., 336 F.2d 197 (5th Cir. 1964). The problem has been rendered moot by Title VI of the Civil Rights Act of 1964.

—more expeditious than litigation, but not necessarily exclusive of the latter—was to withhold funds from programs that did not so conform. This is the power that was available with respect to government contractors, vocational training programs, the employment service, and impacted schools. And it is the power that was finally exercised in the Kennedy housing order. Of course, it is a power that could be effective prospectively only. If a little democracy was to stick to federal moneys expended in the past, the adhesion would have to be established by litigation. Prospectively, therefore, the housing order applied to housing built with federal money or with federally guaranteed loans. The order was well conceived, but much remained to be learned about it in the execution. It did not apply to private loans that are not guaranteed by the federal government, although made by banks that benefit from federal insurance of their funds; and it was going to be administered so as not to cover individually owned homes outside developments. These restrictions were wise initially, for it is in such circumstances that discrimination is most difficult to detect, and enforcement might have been more sham than genuine. It was reasonable, therefore, to concentrate federal energies first on what could be more easily achieved. In this fashion the more difficult problems would be rendered soluble. All measures in the civil rights field depend on each other for the effectiveness of each, but each also, within its own segment of the total problem, is habit-forming and has the sure tendency to snowball.

There were, however, a number of grant-in-aid programs—in addition to the few already mentioned—as to which neither the power exemplified by the housing order nor the threat of it had been employed. A highly selective list included the Hill-Burton Hospital Construction Act of 1946, the Library Services Act of 1956, and a rather remarkable variety of statutes providing aid to universities. The Hill-Burton Act carried a separate-but-equal clause which was as plainly unconstitutional as the state statutes segregating the schools of Mississippi. The clause had no legal effect on the President's powers. In May, 1962, the Justice Department intervened in a lawsuit in North Carolina to support, with ultimate success, the demand of Negro plaintiffs that two Greensboro hospitals, built in part with Hill-Burton funds, be enjoined from segregating or excluding Negro patients.[10] But in announcing his action, Attorney General Kennedy took pains to forswear any use of the executive power to cut off future funds to hospitals that insisted on discriminating. Library and—with one discrete exception—university funds also continued to go to institutions that segregated or excluded Negroes.

Justice Department officials argued that it is no simple matter to exert pressure through grants-in-aid, and that the federal government must be wary of cutting off its funds to spite its face. There is a hard-core area in the South, they maintained, where funds would be resolutely refused if the integration string were tied to them. To withhold funds there—where they are often most needed—would be counterproductive; it would hurt the Negro community ultimately, and sometimes hit it hardest immediately. And if funds continued to go to these areas, despite discrimination, how could the federal government threaten to withhold them in the upper South or on the border in order to force desegregation? That would be to put a premium on hard-core resistance. But there were those, not excluding the staff of the Civil Rights Commission, who thought—in the words President Kennedy used when deprecating alarms that his housing order would stop much new construction —that these "fears have been exaggerated." Moreover, would not another Presidential dictum, also delivered with reference to the housing order, be applicable: "In any case, it is sound public constitutional policy and we've done it"? It might be done again, many observers urged, in different contexts, as carefully and with as much restraint as in the housing order. Only the visionaries objected to a wise gradualism. But it was not visionary to wish to make a start.

Federal appointments. One of the Kennedy Administration's proudest boasts—and justly so—was that it had gone out of its way to employ Negroes in the government in other than the sadly customary menial positions. Negroes were also appointed to high office, including judicial office. All this was as it should be and, since things had scarcely been as they should in the past, was admirable. But it was perhaps more than offset by certain other

[10] Simkins v. Moses H. Cone Memorial Hospital, 323 F.2d 959 (4th Cir. 1963), *cert. denied,* 376 U.S. 938 (1964).

judicial appointments in the Fifth Judicial Circuit, which covers much of the Southern area where the racial problem was then and is now at its most acute. Lawyers representing private parties in racial cases in the South complained bitterly that a number of new Kennedy appointees, especially among the district judges, were totally out of sympathy with the Supreme Court cases on equal protection and that they showed it in their opinions and orders. This was a matter of the first importance, for district judges have life tenure, of course, they ordinarily sit alone, and they have much discretionary power which is not easily subject to review by the Court of Appeals, let alone the Supreme Court.

One device available to district judges, which may often defeat the purpose of a litigation and is almost totally beyond control, is simple delay. District Judge J. Robert Elliott, for example, a Kennedy appointee in Georgia, employed this device substantially to the disadvantage of a Negro protest movement in Albany, Georgia, despite an intervention by the Department of Justice on the side of the Negroes. Other Kennedy appointees exhibited a distinct tendency to exercise all available discretion against Negro plaintiffs or the federal government, to the point even of publishing rather transparently willful opinions. An example was *Anderson v. Martin.*[11] This was a suit attacking the constitutionality of a 1960 Louisiana statute which required the listing on the ballot of the race of all candidates in both primary and general elections. District Judges E. Gordon West of Baton Rouge and Frank B. Ellis of New Orleans, both Kennedy appointees, held, in the face of persuasive if not strictly binding precedent to the contrary from another Court of Appeals, that the statute was perfectly constitutional, because it merely informed the electorate, and because it was applicable, after all, to every candidate—white, colored, or Mongolian. This is the spirit of *Plessy v. Ferguson,* not of *Brown v. Board of Education.* Said Circuit Judge John Minor Wisdom, an Eisenhower appointee, dissenting: "In the eyes of the Constitution, a man is a man. He is not a white man. He is not an Indian. He is not a Negro. If private persons identify a candidate for public office as a Negro, they have a right to do so. But it is no part of the business of the State to put a racial stamp on the ballot."

[11] 206 F. Supp. 700 (D.C.D. La. 1962).

The *Anderson* case was appealed to the Supreme Court, which reversed in short order.[12] But the attitude displayed by Judges West and Ellis remained disturbing. Was it a fair charge against the Kennedy Administration that it appointed men to judicial office who rather plainly disagreed with current law on racial matters and who apparently stood ready to do what they could to give effect to their own contrary views? After all, these judges were acting within the limits of a power that is lawfully theirs, however much one might be convinced that they were acting wrongly and even abusing their discretion. Kennedy appointees went to no greater lengths than one or two others who were on the bench by appointment of prior Presidents. Moreover, judicial philosophies are notoriously unfathomable in advance.

But judgment, though fallible, is possible. There were instances —Judge Elliott was one of them, and so was Judge William Harold Cox of Mississippi—where an extraprofessional record of actions and associations made prediction more than possible. Justice Department officials maintained that, of course, President Kennedy would not have appointed a man who he had reason to believe would fail to do his duty; which one could cheerfully grant, whatever it might mean. And they said further that senators from the state concerned have a virtual veto over appointments, and that the choice was therefore not among various possible appointments but between a semipermanent vacancy and the one man who could be confirmed. Vacancies are serious, no doubt. However, the Chief Justice of the United States has ample and frequently exercised power to assign judges from other districts, including retired judges, to districts where there is a vacancy. It was such an assigned judge from one of the Dakotas who was sitting in Little Rock at the time of the trouble there. This was surely a usable counterpressure to the senatorial veto. And the South is not devoid of men who will do their judicial duty in an ampler sense than merely by not committing impeachable acts. President Eisenhower found a goodly number of them, as did even President Truman, whose judicial appointments are not his greatest claim to enduring renown. And so, to be sure, did

12 375 U.S. 399 (1964).

President Kennedy—with, however, what appeared to be some rather glaring exceptions.

Such were the salient features of the record at mid-term.

MORE ON THE KENNEDY JUDGES

Judge Clarence W. Allgood. At a crucial point during the demonstrations in Birmingham, Alabama, late in May, 1963, when the mass marching had stopped and the violence of the whites seemed under control, a segregationist group on the Birmingham Board of Education expelled or suspended over a thousand Negro children from the public schools for participating in mass marches earlier in the month. Dr. Martin Luther King, urged by his more militant adherents to resume marching, responded by opting first for the processes of law, and two days later he was rewarded with the back of the hand of District Judge Clarence W. Allgood, one of the earliest of President Kennedy's appointees to the federal bench in the South.

An undistinguished Birmingham lawyer whose experience ran heavily to service as a referee in bankruptcy ("That's about all there is," said a knowledgeable Southern source in Washington when asked for further information about the judge's career), Judge Allgood, as Claude Sitton reported in *The New York Times,* is "considered a segregationist by Birmingham Negroes," who it should be remembered possess the discrimination to distinguish on this score between "Bull" Connor and their present mayor, Albert Boutwell. Judge Allgood dismissed the suit for reinstatement of the Negro pupils out of hand, on the pleadings and without taking evidence, even though the school board's position was self-contradictory in several respects. The judge paused only long enough to give his gratuitous views on "experts in the field" (meaning Dr. King) who "exploit" the Negro children and cause them to run "loose and wild in all directions," and on "the patience and good judgment of the people of Birmingham and the police."

It so happened that there was an applicable precedent on public school expulsions in Judge Allgood's jurisdiction. In March, 1960, the Alabama Board of Education expelled some students from the

Alabama State College, a Negro school, for having taken part in sit-ins in Montgomery the previous month. The Court of Appeals for the Fifth Circuit, Judge Rives of Montgomery writing, held the expulsion invalid because the students had not been granted a hearing on the charges against them. (The case, for easy reference, is *Dixon v. Alabama State Board of Education*.[13]) There was no hearing in the Birmingham case either. It is not too much to say that a judge without prejudgment would have followed this precedent, or at least explored the facts before him with a view to determining its applicability.[14]

No doubt President Kennedy would not have appointed Allgood had he not believed that Allgood would, as a judge, do his constitutional duty. But that is much too porous a test. It is not good enough to appoint an Allgood because he is not all bad, is rated "qualified" by the American Bar Association, and has been identified with civic good works. There is a great deal of discretion open to a judge within the limits of his constitutional duty. It would have been well within the limits of Judge Allgood's duty to find the Birmingham situation distinguishable on its facts, and thus to hold the *Dixon* case precedent inapplicable. It was certainly well within Judge Allgood's power to decline to take the broader ground taken by Judge Tuttle of the Court of Appeals in ordering the Birmingham pupils readmitted. It is precisely because judges have discretion, because, as everyone should know by now, they make rather than find much of their law, that the appointing power must worry not only about whether prospective judges will do their duty but about how they are likely to see their duty. Senatorial pressure is no excuse. The matter is too important; it reaches too far into the future.

Judge E. Gordon West. The following passage is from the opinion of Judge E. Gordon West, a Kennedy appointee to the United States District Court for the Eastern District of Louisiana,

[13] 294 F.2d 150 (5th Cir. 1961).

[14] Judge Allgood's action was promptly cured by Chief Judge Tuttle of the U.S. Court of Appeals, who issued a temporary order reinstating the expelled and suspended pupils. Subsequently, a full panel of the Court of Appeals reversed Judge Allgood's decision. Woods v. Wright, 334 F.2d 369 (5th Cir. 1964).

in the case of *Davis v. East Baton Rouge Parish School Board,*
decided on March 1, 1963:

I could not, in good conscience, pass upon this matter today without
first making it clear, for the record, that I personally regard the 1954
holding of the United States Supreme Court in the now famous Brown
case as one of the truly regrettable decisions of all time. Its substitution
of so-called "sociological principles" for sound legal reasoning was
almost unbelievable. As far as I can determine, its only real accomplishment to date has been to bring discontent and chaos to many
previously peaceful communities, without bringing any real attendant
benefits to anyone.

And even more regrettable to me is the fact that almost without
exception the trouble that has directly resulted from this decision in
other communities has been brought about not by the citizens and
residents of the community involved, but by the agitation of outsiders,
from far distant states, who, after having created turmoil and strife in
one locality, are ready to move on to meddle in the affairs of others
elsewhere.[15]

The *Davis* case had originally been filed in February, 1956.
Now Judge West was acting under a binding mandate from the
Court of Appeals, dating from 1961. He ordered the school board
to present a desegregation plan to him no later than July, 1963.
But first he made the statement quoted above. Then he added that
he had "no choice, however distasteful it might be," but to follow
the mandate. Then he complimented "the local Negro leaders" for
not having pressed for more speed during the two years since the
mandate had been issued. And finally, "therefore, reluctantly" he
was "constrained" to act.

This is what the rare case may look like in which duty leaves a
man of Judge West's persuasion no recourse but to uphold Negro
claims. Or it may look like *McCain v. Davis,*[16] decided on May
15, 1963, in which a three-judge federal district court in New
Orleans struck down a Louisiana statute enforcing segregation in
hotels. The thing to wonder at in this case, of course, is not the
result but the fact that such a litigation was not initiated and

---

[15] 214 F. Supp. 624 (E.D. La. 1963). See also Davis v. East Baton Rouge
Parish School Bd., 219 F. Supp. 876 (E.D. La. 1963).

[16] 217 F. Supp. 661 (E.D. La. 1963).

brought to this result much earlier. Judge West was one of the three judges who acted in *McCain v. Davis*. He did not disagree with his colleagues in holding the Louisiana statute unconstitutional. Rather he fastened on an innocuous expression in the majority's opinion justifying the unusual procedure of convening a three- instead of the normal single-judge court (a procedure with which also he did not disagree) and used this as a pretext to deliver himself of an advisory opinion to the hotel owners of Louisiana, as follows:

Just as I believe that the federal government may not legally force the owner or operator of a private business to integrate [no such federal law existed as of then, nor was remotely before the court in this case], so do I believe that the state or local government may not compel the owner or operator of a private business to segregate [there is no record of Judge West's opposition, before his federal appointment, to Louisiana's many segregation laws]. Such continued and extended interference by state and federal government into the operations of purely private business will surely spell doom to our long cherished system of free enterprise. . . . Where, such as in the case of hotels, the business is not a state or federally franchised, monopolistic enterprise, the right of freedom to choose those with whom the owner or operator wishes to do business is just as fundamental as any of the so-called civil rights of which we lately hear so much. . . . In my opinion, the only right involved is the right of the hotel owner to conduct his business without undue governmental interference, rather than the right of the Negro to be admitted to the hotels in question. . . . After the discriminatory law in question is held unconstitutional, and therefore no longer effective, the same private persons may continue, with complete immunity, to voluntarily discriminate to their hearts' content in the conduct of their private affairs.

Perhaps Louisiana hotel owners needed no invitation to continue discriminating. But in another sense they certainly needed no such invitation from a federal judge. Judge West handed a weapon to those among them who wished to resist the pressure of national opinion. He also—by his wholly gratuitous remarks—strengthened the hands of opponents of the Administration's Civil Rights Bill, then in Congress. He had, of course, no business doing any of this. Judge West purposefully and quite improperly used his office to further the segregationist predilections he has elsewhere openly declared.

A case in which duty leaves Judge West no choice may also look like this: In the summer of 1964 Judge West had to be directly ordered by his superiors on the Court of Appeals for the Fifth Circuit to issue a decree in a school desegregation case. The Negro plaintiffs were forced to institute a mandamus proceeding against Judge West, which is about as rare a thing as is known to the law, and which can succeed only if the appellate court is convinced that the judge has been guilty of what in any other officer of government would be called, bluntly and simply, dereliction of duty. Against Judge West, it succeeded.[17] But at what cost! The case involved the school system of St. Helena Parish, Louisiana. Suit was begun over eleven years ago. By February, 1962, all possible issues of any substance had been litigated, and the Supreme Court had denied a second appeal. At this time, Judge West was asked to issue a decree. He did not even set the case down for a hearing. Plaintiffs went back to Judge West a year later. Now he set the case down for a hearing, but he never held one. A year later the plaintiffs were back again, and Judge West did hold a hearing, in March, 1964. But then he neither did anything nor expressed any intention to do anything, not even after the petition for mandamus had been filed. Pretty clearly, if the schools of this parish were going to be desegregated, Judge West was not going to be the one to do it, no matter what the Supreme Court might say.

Judge William Harold Cox. The Civil Rights Act of 1960 provides that the Attorney General may address a demand in writing for the production of federal voting records "to the person having custody, possession, or control" of them, so that they may be inspected for evidence of discrimination against Negro voters. If the demand is not voluntarily met, the appropriate federal district court is to issue an order for the production of the records.

In the case of *Kennedy v. Owen,* decided on July 3, 1963,[18] the Attorney General had addressed his demand in writing to the proper persons "having custody, possession, or control" in several

---

[17] Hall v. West, 335 F.2d 481 (5th Cir. 1964). And see Hall v. St. Helena Parish School Bd., 233 F. Supp. 136 (E.D. La. 1964).
[18] 321 F.2d 116 (5th Cir. 1963).

Mississippi counties. He had addressed his demand to them by name, and they had received it. But in his letter to them he had called them circuit clerks, which they are. He had omitted to address them also by the title of registrar, which is also part of their official designation. They refused to comply, and Judge William Harold Cox, a Kennedy appointee to the Federal District Court for the Southern District of Mississippi, upheld them with respect to records in their possession as registrars rather than as circuit clerks, meaning probably that he upheld them altogether, for it is very likely up to them to decide which records are in their possession under which hat. This is farcical. It is straight out of *Jarndyce v. Jarndyce,* or out of Kafka. It is also willful. Judge Cox got himself summarily reversed by the Court of Appeals for the Fifth Circuit. But time was lost. And, although there can be no further delay on this score, there is no law on the books that is not open to this kind of tactic.

LOUIS KOENIG

Social Justice

President Kennedy, in contrast [to President Eisenhower], became the first chief executive to place himself at the head of the Negro civil rights movement. He publicly asserted his support of the Supreme Court's rulings in the school segregation cases. He enforced the enrollment of James Meredith at the University of Mississippi and of Vivian Malone and James Hood at the University of Alabama, quelled the raging strife in Birmingham, Albany, Jackson, and other cities, North and South, and quietly encouraged or at least failed to discourage the march on Washington. Kennedy was faced with social revolution and had to act. That it was congenial to his own nature to act made his stand more consistent and more forceful. In meeting the civil rights issue, whether in its more subdued stage earlier in his Administration or in its later critical phase, Kennedy and his aides wielded, with skill and enterprise, a variety of executive tools.

Litigation. The 1957 Civil Rights Act authorizes the Justice Department to sue in federal courts or to seek injunctive relief where the right to vote is denied or threatened. In its first year, the Kennedy Administration initiated twice as many cases as the Eisenhower Administration did in three years. Although the latter Administration commenced the first exploratory cases under the

This selection is from Louis Koenig, *The Chief Executive*, pp. 322–329. © 1964 by Harcourt, Brace & World, Inc., and reprinted with their permission.

Civil Rights Acts of 1957 and 1960, the Kennedy Administration displayed greater litigious vigor and resourcefulness. Kennedy's Justice Department stepped up the tempo of school segregation cases and forged a major innovation by casting itself as plaintiff in the Prince Edward County, Virginia, case. The Kennedy Administration's law arm also struck in other urgent civil rights situations. When the city of Albany, Georgia, sought an injunction banning further Negro protest demonstrations in that city, the Justice Department filed a friend-of-the-court brief in opposition. Likewise, when Governor Ross Barnett of Mississippi interposed obstructions to the enrollment of James Meredith at the University of Mississippi, the Justice Department petitioned the Fifth Circuit Court of Appeals to levy a fine of $100,000 upon the governor.

The Presidential constabulary. The United States Code authorizes the President to suppress domestic violence stemming from unlawful assembly and a state's inability or unwillingness to protect a constitutional right. To keep order, the President is assisted by a tri-part constabulary: the Regular Army, the federalized National Guard, and the United States marshals. In the severe rioting in Birmingham in May 1963, Kennedy vowed before the nation, "This Government will do whatever must be done to preserve order, to protect the lives of its citizens and to uphold the law of the land." Even as the President spoke, units of the Armed Forces specially trained in riot control moved into military bases near Birmingham. The President simultaneously ordered the taking of all "necessary preliminary steps" to call the Alabama National Guard into federal service. James Meredith's presence and safety at the University of Mississippi depended, at least in its early season, upon units of the Regular Army and the federalized Mississippi National Guard. The busiest unit of the President's constabulary are the United States marshals, called upon to protect variously the freedom riders and demonstrators in Albany, Georgia. When a mob took over the bus station in Montgomery, six hundred marshals moved in to fill the law enforcement vacuum.

The government contract. Presidents since Franklin Roosevelt have employed the government contract as a weapon to clear pathways for civil rights progress. The one hundred largest defense contractors and their subcontractors employ approximately ten million persons. Countless other workers are employed under federal contracts or aid. From Franklin D. Roosevelt onward, interdepartmental committees composed of the departments contracting most heavily have existed to overcome job discrimination by private employers performing government contracts. Congress's disinclination to establish a Fair Employment Practices Commission has made reliance upon the interdepartmental committees all the heavier. Through the committees, Presidents have insisted upon antidiscrimination provisos in government contracts, heeding their implied duty as executors of the Constitution, with its affirmation of equal rights, to see that federal money is not tainted with racial prejudice.

In the Kennedy Administration Vice-President Johnson headed a Committee on Equal Employment Opportunity, whose enforcement powers were broadened by a March 6, 1961, executive order. Its impact was deepened by his persuasive talent and vigorous administration and Kennedy's strong support. Under the executive order employers must pledge, in taking on a government contract, to act against discrimination in hiring and on the job. The Johnson committee required employers to file regular reports, an innovation to prove their compliance with the executive order. More than a score of major contractors signed "Plans for Progress" agreements with the committee, pledging steps against employment discrimination. Militant civil rights groups pressed to cancel the contracts of gross violators, particularly in the textile industry, but the committee rejected this counsel.

The civil service. The United States government, as the nation's largest employer, has its own house to put in order. Legal authority to do so is abundant. The 1883 Pendelton Act established merit as the primary test for federal employment, and from 1940 onward various statutes prohibit discrimination "on account of race, creed, or color." The President's official oath and responsibility as chief administrator impart further authority. The Kennedy Administration's personnel policies put new stress upon the appointment and upgrading of qualified Negroes. Complaint procedures concerning discrimination were liberalized and the Committee on Equal Employment Opportunity investigated agency compliance.

The Kennedy Administration's emphasis upon Negro recruitment was reinforced symbolically by Kennedy's exercise of the Presidential appointment power. The selection of Robert Weaver as head of the Housing and Home Finance Agency, of Andrew Hatcher as White House associate press secretary, and of Carl Rowan (appointed USIA director by President Johnson), as Assistant Secretary of State for Public Affairs and later Ambassador to Finland, were indicative of the Administration's commitment. In 1961 Cecil Poole and Merle McCurdy became the first Negroes to serve as United States attorneys in the continental United States. Kennedy's judicial appointments stand as equally innovative. Wade McCree and James B. Parsons became, in 1961, the first Negroes ever to be appointed District Judges in the continental United States. Kennedy, wielding the appointment power, also reached up to the next judicial level, where Thurgood Marshall, former counsel of NAACP's Legal Defense and Educational Fund, was named to the United States Circuit Court.

Administrative regulation. The freedom riders' visitations in Southern territory spurred the Kennedy Administration to petition the Interstate Commerce Commission to desegregate facilities in terminals serving interstate bus travel. After months of delay and insistent Justice Department pressure, the desegregation order was issued. The Administration lacked power to move similarly upon airports under the Civil Aeronautics Act. To foster desegregation in various Southern airport facilities, the Justice Department relied upon court action and private persuasion.

Federal funds. The expenditure of federal funds is a Presidential weapon of vast potency in the civil rights struggle. Few aspects of American life are untouched by the incessant outpouring of federal money. In many states and localities, the federal wherewithal has, in actuality, supported rather than checked racial discrimination. Housing, education, job training, the National Guard, recreation facilities, hospitals, libraries, university research, agricultural extension, state employment services, vocational rehabilitation, school lunches, and highway and airport construction are objects of federal largess and occasional sources of racial discrimination.

In his 1960 campaign, Kennedy flayed the Eisenhower Administration for not blotting out racial discrimination in federally supported housing, holding it could be achieved merely by "a stroke of the pen." After long delay and much pressure by racial groups, the President finally issued an executive order of November 21, 1962, barring discrimination in the sale or rental of housing financed through federal assistance. The executive order's seeming breadth was badly sheared by administrative interpretation. "Conventional" or private financing, houses "already built," houses that are not in commercially developed neighborhoods, and FHA-insured loans for home improvements were ruled to be not covered.

President Kennedy was insistently pressed to issue a blanket order prohibiting discrimination in all federal programs. Indeed in Kennedy's encounters with Governor Barnett of Mississippi to enroll James Meredith in the state university, the Civil Rights Commission urged that Mississippi be barred from all federal funds. "I don't have the power to cut off the aid in a general way as was proposed by the Civil Rights Commission," Kennedy responded, adding that "I think it would probably be unwise" to grant the President that power.

Public appeals. In the major civil rights crises, Kennedy as a regular tactic made radio and television addresses, pleading and lecturing to the nation, stressing the moral aspects and local responsibilities. In the University of Alabama episode of 1963, Governor George C. Wallace stood in the doorway of a University of Alabama building to prevent the registration of two Negro students, Vivian Malone and James Hood. The governor, in his chosen stance, was both fulfilling a campaign pledge and violating a court order rendered to assure the students' registration at the university. The students eventually embarked upon their studies with the help of the National Guard. In his television address on the Alabama episode, Kennedy termed the rising tide of Negro discontent "a moral crisis," which "faces us all in every city of the North as well as the South." The problem of the Negro's place in American life, the President declared, "must be solved in the homes of every American across the country." In an address to the 1963 National Conference of Mayors, he urged increased local responsibility in coping with disturbances in Northern and Southern cities; the establishment of local biracial human relations committees to spot developing tensions and push for the revision of local segregation laws; and the adoption of equal opportunity ordinances for housing, public accommodations, and employment.

Kennedy's public appeals were also put to individuals and specific local communities. His most eloquent appeal in behalf of civil rights was his televised address to the nation in the crisis of James Meredith's enrollment in the University of Mississippi. Kennedy appealed to the students and people of Mississippi to comply with court rulings and therefore with federal law to bring the crisis to an end. "The eyes of the nation and all the world are upon you and upon all of us," he said, "and the honor of your university and state are in the balance." As rioting spread and Negro houses were bombed in Birmingham in 1963, the President implored that community to restore peace. Kennedy's public expressions included an appeal to Governor George C. Wallace of Alabama to stay away from the campus of the state university at Tuscaloosa. This rare proffer of advice from a President to a governor was sparked by Wallace's threat to bar physically the admission of two Negro students to the university. The governor's plan, the President stated candidly in a published telegram, was "the only announced threat to orderly compliance with the law." In addition, Kennedy pointed the finger of national opprobrium at local malfeasance. The burning of Negro churches near Albany, Georgia, in September 1963, he termed "cowardly as well as outrageous." When a general civil rights impasse seized that unhappy city, Kennedy declared in a news conference that he could not see why city officials could not sit down with Negro citizens to work out racial problems. In the New Orleans school integration crisis, he reminded segregationists that the Supreme Court's school desegregation decision was both constitutionally and morally unassailable.

Private persuasion. To head off brewing civil rights crises or to steady them at a low boiling point, President Kennedy, the Attorney General, and their aides counted heavily upon the arts of private persuasion. President Kennedy met at the White House with whole delegations of Southern businessmen, theater owners, and newspaper editors to put the case for voluntary desegregation and warn of the danger that Negro extremists might gain power should the moderates fail. Cabinet secretaries sometimes joined the effort. Secretary of Commerce Luther Hodges, a North Carolinian, wrote letters of encouragement to fellow Southerners; the Attorney General telephoned friendly and unfriendly local officials, encouraging, persuading, or scolding, as required. The Justice Department in private, unpublicized talks helped some Southern communities desegregate their schools without incident. The Justice Department quieted several violent intervals in Birmingham by negotiating agreements between the contending groups, and as tensions mounted in Jackson, Mississippi, in June 1963, a peace-building meeting transpired in the local Masonic Lodge between John Doar, Assistant Attorney General for Civil Rights, and Negro representatives. In its discussions with white Southern leaders, the Administration stiffened its language with appeals to party loyalty and used higher and lower forms of political inducement. The Administration also engaged in dialogue with Negro civil rights leaders, including an intensive discussion in New York at the peak of the 1963 crisis when Robert Kennedy reviewed with the leaders both what they were seeking and what the Administration could do.

President Kennedy and his aides invested many hours in White House discussions with Negro leaders to plumb their views and to convey the Administration's intentions and a sense of the political realities it faced. Soon after taking office, Kennedy invited the emissaries of several Negro groups to outline what they would consider a good Administration civil rights program. A sixty-one-page memorandum resulted, and, midway in discussing it with Roy Wilkins and Arnold Aronson, chairman and secretary, respectively, of the Leadership Conference on Civil Rights, Theodore Sorensen, the President's Special Counsel, let out the bitter news that the Administration would not push civil rights legislation, at least in its first year. This disclosure bathed the 1961 conference of the National Civil Liberties Clearing House in Washington in gloomy lamentation. Tempers were somewhat smoothed when

Harris L. Wofford, Jr., a special assistant to the President, candidly reviewed the pressures necessitating the Administration's course. Because of his own eminence in the Negro civil rights movement, Wofford's good faith could not be questioned, and his acceptance of the President's position lent it plausibility. Kennedy himself salved the feelings of Negro leaders when his Administration was politically unable to give them what they wanted. When Martin Luther King, after declaring to the National Baptist Convention that Negroes "cannot wait any longer" and that he would go to the President for a "new Emancipation Proclamation," called at the White House to make his request, Kennedy had a ready response. "Let me show you where the first one was signed," he said, leading the way to the Lincoln bedroom. The King-Kennedy talks proceeded by mutual consent not on the basis of a proclamation, but on specific areas of future concrete action.

Like other Presidents who, because of political restraints, could give social groups only a part of what they wanted, Kennedy sustained public criticism from Negro civil rights leaders. In the Administration's first years, when it held back civil rights legislation and shunned a futile fight to throttle the Senate filibuster, NAACP secretary Roy Wilkins sadly declared that an "atmosphere of super-caution" had "pervaded" all civil rights discussions with Kennedy and his staff since election day. In a television interview in June 1963, amid the demonstrations crisis, the Reverend Martin Luther King, viewing the cheerless scene, conceded that President Kennedy "may have done a little more" than President Eisenhower, "but the plight of the vast majority of Negroes remains the same." In the spirit of constructive criticism, Dr. King urged the President to forego a trip to Europe scheduled later in the month, and remain, instead, in Washington to push his civil rights program. The President, Dr. King said, in a further pointer, should revive "fireside chats" to explain civil rights to the nation.

The Negro civil rights revolution throws a sharp, unflattering glare upon the limitations of Presidential power as an instrument of social change. It is one thing for the President to issue executive orders and proclaim high policy; it is quite another to transmute policy into action and orders into compliance. In the acid test of performance, the President depends upon a vast federal bureaucracy and far-flung field organizations staffed heavily with local personnel. The President's housing order, for example, sweeping and well-intentioned on its face, was softened by administrative interpretation—the sweeping exemptions and the stress upon "persuasion" rather than enforcement. The unacknowledged motivation behind such choices is the fear that vigorous executive action will alienate Southern legislators situated on strategic committees.

Civil rights is also vulnerable to fluctuations in its capacity to command the President's attention. In June 1963, when Negro rights demonstrations gained their peak, the President could, for a time at least, give civil rights a maximum priority on his agenda, even above foreign affairs and the cold war. But as weeks passed, civil rights clung to its topmost position only fitfully, falling below the claims of foreign affairs at one time or another. Civil rights, like any other government business, must compete for the President's attention, priorities, and action. For all the heat of the street demonstrations and Dr. King's criticism, President Kennedy went off to Europe. Similarly, the Administration, dispatching its civil rights legislation to Capitol Hill, hailed the event by proclaiming that this bill would be given the "highest priority" in future political effort. Yet only a month later the Administration rather downgraded civil rights by declaring that its privileged priority would henceforth be "shared" with the tax cut bill. Still later President Kennedy, in one of his last major pronouncements on civil rights, gave his tax bill a higher priority than his rights bill, holding that a rising economy was indispensable for the betterment of Negro rights.

But Kennedy and his Administration continued to fight hard for civil rights legislation until his assassination. In few places did that tragedy evoke more grief than in the Negro community. On a Washington, D.C., street corner, a blind Negro woman plucked at the strings of her guitar, half singing and half weeping a dirge— "He promised never to leave me. . . ." In the Negro part of a Southern city, people rushed into the streets moaning, and one little girl, asked by a bystander what had happened, replied, "Jesus has died." Effort for civil rights legislation was lent a new urgency by a growing view of it as a kind of "memorial" for the late President. President Johnson accorded the bill the highest priority. In time it passed the House of Representatives, escaped the snare of the Senate filibuster, and, with strong bipartisan support, became law.

JEROME WIESNER

John F. Kennedy: A Remembrance

Never have I been given a more difficult task. To put into words the true spirit and charm and intelligence of John F. Kennedy would be impossible even for a writer far more gifted than I. It would take the telling of many tales, a description of his handling of problems large and small, a detailed history of his three brief years as a world leader, to show his true greatness.

I have just returned from Arlington National Cemetery where thousands of people from all over the world paid their last respects to the man who had given them so much hope. It was a beautiful, cold, sunshiny day, the kind he loved. One could almost call it a New England day. The day was like the President, radiant and crisp. He added something indescribable to every occasion; his smile brightened it, his humor livened it. He had a quick and often sardonic humor and a quick mind. To these he added an optimism about the future and a determination to bring out the maximum capabilities of our people, and, indeed, of all mankind. He was an intelligent, educated man. He was a kindly man. I never knew him to do a mean thing to any person. He was never too busy for a word of greeting. He had a strong temper but one that subsided quickly. Challenged, he responded firmly. Big problems were never allowed to submerge the small, today's problems to obscure tomorrow's. At the height of the great crises of his tenure—the Bay

"John F. Kennedy: A Remembrance" is from *Science* (Vol. 142), November 29, 1963, p. 1147, cols. 1–3, p. 1148, cols. 1–3, p. 1149, cols. 1–3, p. 1150, cols. 1–3. Copyright © 1963 by the American Association for the Advancement of Science.

of Pigs disaster, the resumption of nuclear testing by the Soviet Union, Mississippi, Birmingham, the confrontation with the Soviet Union over the missile installations in Cuba—he still talked about the future. He retained his monumental interest in the details of the ongoing business of government. He read an amazing amount, and seemingly remembered it all. He often asked about obscure stories concerning science buried in *The New York Times* or the *London Observer* or any one of the dozens of papers and periodicals he somehow found time to read.

VISION AND OUTLOOK

I met Jack Kennedy while he was a senator from my home state of Massachusetts. He needed advice on technical matters, particularly military technology and nuclear test ban, issues then occupying much of my time. I agreed to help largely because friends asked me to and because he was my senator. I heard from him only infrequently at first and saw him even less. But even those brief contacts caused me to admire him, so that I readily agreed to join up and provide what little help I could when he became the Democratic candidate for the Presidency. Many things impressed me then and drew me to him. There was, of course, his charm but there was much more. I was most impressed by his quick, almost instinctive understanding of problems once he was given the facts. His background ill prepared him for an interest in scientific matters, yet his interest was lively. He was, in fact, then a member of the Harvard University visiting committee. Obviously unprepared to understand the theory of scientific subjects, he tried to get a physical feel of the matter. For example, he was forever trying to get someone to explain electromagnetic propagation comprehensibly. He didn't call it that. He wanted to know how radio worked. But when one tried to answer, one learned that the question was not about electron tubes or transistors or coils—these were man-made things which he could believe—but why and how did nature really allow energy to be sent through space.

Someone called him a truly modern man, the first American President to be born in the twentieth century. And he was that. He had confidence in and used the modern tools. In a real sense technological marvels gave him his chance to be President. Without the airplane and television, he would not have been able to wage his successful campaign in 1960. And he never forgot this. His vision and outlook made it easy for him to understand other products of technology. President Kennedy, better than any political figure I have known, understood the social significance of modern science and technology.

As I try to remember the things that impressed me most about the President, four qualities stand out: his intelligence, his hopefulness, his sense of history, his striving for excellence. All of us who worked with him were proud of him. His very appearance, his composure, his sensitivity for every situation led us to an ever-growing admiration. He was the President from the very beginning, and as he was tested in his terrible job, he grew.

His vision and perfectionism may best be seen in his speeches. He had a vision of what he thought the world could be, and he projected this in his poetic prose. His Inaugural Address set the plan for his administration, and he strove consistently to reach the goals he set then. He said, "To those peoples in the huts and villages of half the globe struggling to break the bonds of mass misery, we pledge our best efforts to help them help themselves, for whatever period is required—not because the Communists may be doing it, not because we seek their votes, but because it is right. If a free society cannot help the many who are poor, it cannot save the few who are rich."

And about the arms race, "Finally, to those nations who would make themselves our adversary, we offer not a pledge but a request: that both sides begin anew the quest for peace, before the dark powers of destruction unleashed by science engulf all humanity in planned or accidental self-destruction. . . . Let both sides explore what problems unite us instead of belaboring those problems which divide us. Let both sides, for the first time, formulate serious and precise proposals for the inspection and control of arms—and bring the absolute power to destroy other nations under the absolute control of all nations."

Much of President Kennedy's hopefulness was derived from his conviction that science provided our nation with vast powers for good. In the Inaugural speech, he summed this up with, "Let both sides seek to invoke the wonders of science instead of its terrors. Together let us explore the stars, conquer the deserts, eradicate disease, tap the ocean depths and encourage the arts and commerce." He was ever pressing to put technology to work. In foreign affairs, for helping other nations, for insuring our security, in seeking solutions to our domestic problems, he looked to science for the clues.

NATIONAL ACADEMY SPEECHES

Twice he responded to invitations to speak before the National Academy of Sciences, and, as far as I know, set a precedent for Presidential attendance at Academy functions.

On April 25, 1961, the President, in dedicating the new wing of the Academy, disregarded his prepared text and in an eloquent extemporaneous talk revealed his sensitive understanding of the necessary cooperation between the government and the scientific community. In calling upon the Academy and the scientific community, the President remarked:

"This country must move forward, and most of the areas where we must move forward involve most sophisticated problems which your experience and training can help us to solve. One of the problems, it seems to me, of a free society is the fact that all of the questions which we must decide now are extremely sophisticated questions. It is difficult enough for those who hold office, either in the Administration or in the Congress, to attempt to make a determination between alternate courses of action—fiscal policy, monetary policy, agricultural policy, international policy, disarmament, arms control, all the rest, all of these involve questions to confound the experts. For those of us who are not expert and yet must be called upon to make decisions which involve the security of our country, which involve the expenditures of hundreds of millions of billions of dollars, we must turn, in the last resort, to objective, disinterested scientists who bring a strong sense of public responsibility and public obligation. So this Academy is most important."

Again, on October 22, 1963, a month to the day before the

tragic events in Texas, the President appeared before the Academy on the occasion of its Anniversary Convocation and he emphasized the importance of basic scientific investigations, the contributions that science can make to international objectives, and the interdisciplinary and intercultural aspects of science in playing its role in modern society. He also dwelt on a theme that he many times expressed, the need for applying the results of scientific and technological advances to the conservation and development of natural resources. During his relatively brief stay in office he gave physical meaning to these objectives.

On the subject of basic scientific research, the President said in his last Academy speech:

"But if basic research is to be properly regarded, it must be better understood. I ask you to reflect on this problem and on the means by which, in the years to come, our society can assure continuing backing to fundamental research in the life sciences, the physical sciences, the social sciences, on natural resources, on agriculture, on protection against pollution and erosion. Together, the scientific community, the government, industry, and education must work out the way to nourish American science in all its power and vitality."

President Kennedy regarded international scientific cooperative activities and scientific exchanges as one of the strongest bridges to other nations, and at the Academy celebration he expanded on this view. "I would suggest that science is already moving to enlarge its influence in three general ways: in the interdisciplinary area, in the international area, and in the intercultural area. For science is the most powerful means we have for the unification of knowledge, and a main obligation of its future must be to deal with problems which cut across boundaries, whether boundaries between the sciences, boundaries between nations, or boundaries between man's scientific and his humane concerns."

He closed his talk with an anecdote that revealed the strength of his conviction about the importance of basic research to the country's future when he remarked, "the great French Marshal Lyautey once said to his gardener: 'Plant a tree tomorrow.' And the gardener said, 'It won't bear fruit for a hundred years.' 'In that case,' said Lyautey to the gardener, 'plant it this afternoon.' That is how I feel about your work," said the President.

BASIC RESEARCH AND MANPOWER

Under the President's leadership there has been a substantial strengthening of the basic research grants of the National Science Foundation in recognition not only of the need for the results of such research, but also of the essential role of basic research in the training of new scientists. In a news conference on January 15, 1962, the President expressed his concern about the future adequacy of our scientific and technical manpower in referring to a study of Soviet technical manpower that had just been published by the National Science Foundation. He said, "This has been a matter of some concern to me for some time because one of the most critical problems facing this Nation is the inadequacy of the supply of scientific and technical manpower, to satisfy the expanding requirements of this country's research and development efforts in the near future." He called upon the President's Science Advisory Committee, in cooperation with the Federal Council for Science and Technology, to report as quickly as possible on the specific measures that could be taken to develop the necessary, well-qualified scientists and engineers, and he reinforced his personal concern with the words, "To all those who may be within the sound of my voice or who may follow your stories in the papers, I want to emphasize the great new and exciting field of the sciences. . . ." Following submission of the Science Advisory Committee report of December 1962 on needs for graduate training in engineering, mathematics, and physical sciences, the President's 1964 budget for the National Science Foundation reflected his acceptance of the PSAC judgment of the importance of increased support for graduate education. This is also reflected in his proposed legislation to increase the number of fellowships under the National Defense Education Act, and in his extemporaneous remarks at the National Academy celebration he expressed his deep disappointment in the failure of the Congress to support this program.

SPACE PROGRAM

During his Administration he made persistent efforts to strengthen the U.S. space program. He saw in it the opportunity to serve many national needs. He was firmly convinced that Soviet space supremacy had greatly weakened the United States in its foreign affairs. He saw military hazards in a lagging space capability. He saw the exploration of space as one of the great human adventures of this century, and he appreciated the important scientific possibilities of space exploration. He dedicated this nation to a massive space program with a firm target of a manned lunar landing in this decade. This is a costly program and his decision to undertake it was not made lightly. He talked to hundreds of people in the process of making his decision and he weighed the costs with real concern. In the end he became convinced that the U.S. could not remain second in this important field. Despite continual review, he remained convinced of the correctness of this course.

Yet with the closing of the gap between U.S. and U.S.S.R. outer space capabilities, he followed through his Inaugural theme with the proposal to the U.S.S.R. for a joint moon venture.

He also followed through on his Inaugural hopes of conquering the deserts, and the national efforts at desalinization were greatly reinforced, along with a stepped-up program of underlying basic and applied research to overcome the barriers to economic desalinization.

NATURAL RESOURCES

In the field of natural resources, the President early in his Administration took steps to accelerate the pace of the national program in oceanography, and at the same time provided leadership and backing both for congressional support and for a coordinated, balanced, and imaginative interagency approach to oceanographic research. An old sailor, he had a special interest in this research. He got a particular pleasure when the Presidential yacht *Williamsburg* was converted into an oceanographic research vessel. For a film on oceanographic research just completed, the

President provided the opening and closing lines. Recently, after I had recovered from the consequences of a sailing accident, inaccurately reported, he offered to give me lessons in sailing and press relations. He called upon both the National Academy of Sciences and the Federal Council for Science and Technology to study and make recommendations for strengthening the federal efforts across the broad horizons of natural resources in the land, sea, and air so that they can better serve the needs of the American people.

Early in his Administration, too, the President lent substance to his desire to encourage commerce through science and technology by initiating a national program to strengthen civilian technology, including the appointment of an Assistant Secretary of Commerce for Science and Technology. In remarks prepared for delivery in Dallas, never given, the President pointed out that communities possessing the best in research and graduate facilities tend to attract the new and growing industries. He congratulated those who recognized the relationship between leadership and learning and the need for community support for the advancement of learning underlying the creation of the forward-looking Graduate Research Center of the Southwest.

President Kennedy's interest in international aspects of science was again highlighted in his September 20, 1963, address to the United Nations, where he urged a world center for health communications to warn of epidemics and the adverse effects of certain drugs; regional research centers to advance common medical knowledge and train new scientists and doctors for new nations; and a cooperative system of satellites to provide communication and weather information on a world-wide basis. As a result of his initiative, work has already begun in the World Meteorological Organization to develop the outlines of a world weather system and to strengthen basic research in atmospheric sciences on an international basis.

In connection with technical assistance to newly developing countries, the President was instrumental in bringing about closer attention to the need for research underlying the planning and execution of the AID program. This was reflected in the formulation of his Alliance for Progress program with its emphasis on science education, and in the establishment of the Office of Human

Resources and Social Development in the Agency for International Development.

There are numerous other examples of President Kennedy's interest in promoting the development and application of science on an international basis, ranging from his initiative in establishing the U.S.–Japan Science Committee and his encouragement of the scientists' Pugwash movement, to his request for specific studies from his Science Advisory Committee, including a study of the problem of hoof and mouth disease in Argentina, the problem of water logging in Pakistan, and most recently his initiation of a study of the boll weevil problem in cotton production, a matter of international as well as national concern.

ARMS CONTROL

I have already referred to the President's strong conviction about the need for bringing about adequately safeguarded international arms control, a matter that occupied a very substantial part of his time from the very first days of his Administration. The whole world can be thankful for two major accomplishments that flowed from his efforts, two monuments to his labors on the road to peace—the Arms Control and Disarmament Agency and the nuclear test-ban treaty—which can inspire us to persist in the efforts to avoid the nuclear holocaust that so haunted him. One of his first acts was to propose to Congress the creation of the Arms Control and Disarmament Agency, the world's first governmental activity dedicated solely to the study of disarmament problems. As a result, the United States government now has a small cadre of professionals in this extremely complicated and important field.

The signing of the nuclear test-ban treaty gave the President enormous satisfaction. For him it proved that meaningful disarmament steps were possible, and it justified the hundreds of hours of debate and study, the deep disappointments along the way. His striving for this treaty, begun in the first days of his Administration, weathered many bitter disappointments and was the subject of much unjust criticism. He could hardly have been blamed had he abandoned hope after the Russians resumed nuclear testing in the summer of 1961. Characteristically, though, he continued his attempts to work out an acceptable agreement. The question of the need for further nuclear tests in order to enhance our national security involved highly technical issues and extremely controversial ones as well. So did the capabilities of nuclear test detection systems. The President made himself an expert on these subjects. He listened to many briefings and more debates. He talked to experts with every possible view and finally formed his own conclusions.

In the process he also achieved an understanding of the role of scientific advice in policy matters. In his last National Academy address he said, "As the country had reason to note in recent weeks during the debate on the test-ban treaty, scientists do not always unite themselves on their recommendations to makers of policy. This is only partly because of scientific disagreements. It is even more because the big issues so often go beyond the possibilities of exact scientific determination.

"I know few significant questions of public policy which can safely be confided to computers. In the end, the hard decisions inescapably involve imponderables of intuition, prudence, and judgment."

The President called the nuclear test-ban treaty a small first step. Since its signing the nations of the world have also responded to his call for a pledge to prohibit the placing of nuclear weapons in orbit. He hoped that these agreements would be followed by many more.

President Kennedy not only understood the need to invest resources for extending our understanding of science and its applications but also saw the need for institutional change to guide and assist the mounting governmental involvement in science and technology to serve national objectives. He shared the view that the federal scientific enterprise would be best served by strengthening the individual agencies whose missions required the exploitation of science, rather than by the creation of an all-encompassing department of science. Toward this end he sought the inclusion of a technically educated individual at the policy level in each department which is heavily dependent upon science for the accomplishment of its mission. The evolution of the Office of Science and Technology also reflects this policy of building strength in the individual agencies. On March 29, 1962, after much discussion, he sent a message to the Congress providing for reorganization in the field of science and technology. He pointed out that the ever-growing significance and complexity of federal programs had earlier necessitated several steps for improving the organizational arrangements of the Executive Branch. The President believed that the creation of the Office of Science and Technology would facilitate communication between the Executive Branch and the Congress. The wisdom of the President in making this proposal is being increasingly realized through the activities of its director, in its close collaboration with the Bureau of the Budget, its presentations to congressional committees, and through its leadership in initiating long-range planning of research and development within the federal agencies. To assist this work, the National Science Foundation has created an Office of Resources Planning, and closer ties with the National Academy of Sciences have been established through its newly created Committee on Science and Public Affairs.

These are only the highlights of President Kennedy's broad interest in science and technology and the tangible forms they have taken. Although much progress has been made, much more needs to be done. But because of his interest and support we have a stronger base upon which to extend the already impressive contributions of American science and technology.

Part III

—

THE KENNEDY PRESIDENCY

WILLIAM G. CARLETON

Kennedy in History: An Early Appraisal

Although John F. Kennedy has been dead less than a year, it is not too early to assess his place in history. Judgments about historical figures never come finally to rest. Reputations fluctuate through the centuries, for they must constantly do battle with oblivion and compete with the shifting interests and values of subsequent generations. Even so, contemporary estimates are sometimes not markedly changed by later ones.

The career of a public man, the key events of his life, most of his record, the questions he confronted, the problems he tackled, the social forces at work in his time are largely open to scrutiny when he leaves public life. The archives and subsequently revealed letters, memoirs, and diaries will yield important new material, but usually these merely fill out and embellish the already known public record.

What more frequently alters an early historical appraisal than later revealed material is the course of events after the hero has left the stage. For instance, should President Johnson, during the next few years, succeed in breaking the legislative log jam and driving through Congress a major legislative program, then President Kennedy's failure to do this will be judged harshly. But should the congressional stalemate continue, then the Kennedy difficulties likely will be chalked up not so much against him

"Kennedy in History: An Early Appraisal" is from the Fall 1964 issue of *The Antioch Review* (Vol. XXIV, No. 3). Copyright © 1964 by The Antioch Press. Reprinted by permission.

personally but against the intricacies of the American system of separation of powers and pluralized, divided parties. Even so, it will not be easy to defend the meager Kennedy legislative performance.

If popular passion is running high at the time an historical personage makes his exit, then it is difficult for a contemporary to be relatively objective in his evaluation. (At no time is there absolute objectivity in history.) For instance, Woodrow Wilson left office amidst such violent misunderstanding that few contemporaries could do him justice, and only now, four decades later, is he being appraised with relative fairness. With Kennedy, one collides with adoration. The uncritical bias in favor of Kennedy derives from his winsome personality, his style and élan, the emotional euphoria arising from his tragic death, and the sympathetic spiritual kinship with him felt by historians, political scientists, intellectuals, and writers. There is, to be sure, considerable hate-Kennedy literature, most of it written before his death and reflecting ultra right-wing biases, but few will be fooled into taking diatribes for serious history.

II

Although as President he clearly belongs to the liberal tradition of the Democratic party's twentieth-century Presidents, Kennedy's pre-Presidential career can scarcely be said to have been liberal. During his congressional service he refused to hew to an ideological or even a party line. Kennedy often asked: "Just what is a liberal?" He confessed that his glands did not operate like Hubert Humphrey's.

Reviewing Kennedy's votes in House and Senate from 1947 to 1958, the AFL–CIO's Committee on Political Education gave him a pro-labor score of twenty-five out of twenty-six, which in considerable part may be explained by the large number of low-income wage-earners in his district. Kennedy usually followed the views and interests of his constituents, and this gave his congressional career its greatest measure of consistency. With respect to welfare programs which did not much concern his constituents—

farm price supports, flood control, TVA, the Rural Electrification Administration—Kennedy sometimes joined the Byrd economy bloc. On occasion, Kennedy could fly in the face of New England sentiment, as when he supported reciprocal tariff laws and the St. Lawrence Seaway, and again when he publicly stated that he thought President Eisenhower, in an attempt to salvage the Paris summit conference, should apologize to Khrushchev for the U-2 incident. At such times, Kennedy displayed a disarming candor.

In foreign policy, Kennedy's early pronouncements had a right-wing flavor, especially with respect to China, but he soon developed a greater interest in foreign affairs than in domestic ones, and he moved away from right-wing attitudes to favor foreign economic aid, to rebuff the Committee of One Million devoted to keeping Red China out of the United Nations, to speak up for abandoning Quemoy and Matsu, to fight for economic help to Communist Poland, to advocate Algerian independence, and to encourage international arms-control negotiations.

In general, through the years, in both domestic and foreign policy, Kennedy moved from positions right of center or at center to positions left of center.

Since Negro rights played so important and dramatic a part in his Presidency, historians will always be interested in Kennedy's earlier stand on civil rights. Until the Presidential campaign of 1960, Kennedy was not an aggressive fighter for the Negro. During his quest for the Vice-Presidential nomination in 1956, he wooed the Southern delegations and stressed his moderation. After 1956, he sought to keep alive the South's benevolent feeling for him, and his speeches in that region, sprinkled with unflattering references to carpetbaggers like Mississippi Governor Alcorn* and praise for L. Q. C. Lamar and other Bourbon "redeemers," had a faint ring of Claude Bowers' *Tragic Era*.[1] In 1957, during the fight in the Senate over the civil rights bill, Kennedy lined up for the O'Mahoney amendment to give jury trials to those held in criminal contempt of court. Civil rights militants regarded this as emasculating,

---

* Editor's note: Alcorn was a "scalawag," not a "carpetbagger."

[1] Kennedy made a number of speeches in the South in 1957. Illustrative of their tone is the commencement address at the University of Georgia and the address at the Democratic state dinner at Jackson, Mississippi.

since those accused of impeding Negro voting would find more leniency in Southern juries than in federal judges.

What will disturb historians most about Kennedy's pre-Presidential career was his evasion of the McCarthy challenge. In his early congressional days, Kennedy himself often gave expression to the mood of frustration, especially with reference to the loss of China, out of which McCarthyism came. In a talk at Harvard in 1950, Kennedy said that "McCarthy may have something," and he declared that not enough had been done about Communists in government.[2]

By the time McCarthyism had emerged full blown, Kennedy was caught in a maze of entanglements. His Irish-Catholic constituents were ecstatically for McCarthy, and Kennedy's own family was enmeshed. Westbrook Pegler, McCarthy's foremost journalistic supporter, was close to father Joseph P. Kennedy; the elder Kennedy entertained McCarthy at Hyannis Port and contributed to his political fund; brother Robert Kennedy became a member of McCarthy's investigating staff. John Kennedy himself not only kept mum on the McCarthy issue but actually benefited from it. During Kennedy's senatorial campaign against Lodge, the latter was portrayed as soft on Communism, leading McCarthyite politicians and newspapers in Massachusetts backed Kennedy, and McCarthy was persuaded to stay out of Massachusetts and do nothing for Lodge there.

When McCarthyism finally climaxed in the debate and vote in the Senate over censuring the Great Inquisitor, Kennedy was absent because of an illness which nearly cost him his life. At no time did Kennedy ever announce how he would have voted on censure. He did not exercise his right to pair his vote with another absent colleague who held an opposite view. It may be that Kennedy was too ill for even that. Kennedy's subsequent private explanations—that to have opposed McCarthy would have been to commit political harakiri and that he was caught in a web of family entanglements—were lame and unworthy.[3]

Nevertheless, there can be no doubt that McCarthyism was a

[2] See John P. Mallan, "Massachusetts: Liberal and Corrupt," *The New Republic,* October 13, 1952.

[3] See an interview granted by Senator Kennedy to Irwin Ross, the *New York Post,* July 30, 1956.

searing experience for John Kennedy. During his convalescence, as a sort of personal catharsis, he wrote his book *Profiles in Courage,* which dealt with famous senators of the past who had to choose between personal conscience and violent mass execration and political extinction. Kennedy seems to be saying: "This is the kind of cruel dilemma I would have faced had I been present in the Senate when the vote was taken on the McCarthy censure." *Profiles in Courage* is Kennedy's examination of his own Procrustean anguish. Such soul-searching may have helped him psychologically, but it added not a whit to the fight against McCarthy's monstrous threat to the free and open society.

Some years later, when even then Eleanor Roosevelt sought to prod Kennedy into making an *ex post facto* condemnation of McCarthyism, he wisely refused. He observed, with that candor which was his most engaging hallmark, that since he had not been in opposition during the controversy, to take a decided stand after Senator McCarthy was politically dead would make him (Kennedy) a political prostitute and poltroon.[4]

In the future, historians sympathetic to President Kennedy are likely to seriously underestimate the right-wing influences that played upon him and his brother Robert during their formative years and early life in politics. The influence of Joseph P. Kennedy was strong, and in the pre–Pearl Harbor years the Kennedy household was the center of "America First" leaders, journalists, and ideas, and in the early 1950's of McCarthy leaders, journalists, and ideas. It is not remarkable that John and Robert reflected some right-wing attitudes in their early political careers; what is remarkable is that first John and then Robert, who is less flexible, emancipated themselves from these attitudes.

III

In all likelihood, John Kennedy would never have become President had his brother Joe lived; or had he (John) been nominated

[4] For the Kennedy–Eleanor Roosevelt byplays over McCarthy, including the incident here mentioned, see Ralph G. Martin and Edward Plaut, *Front Runner, Dark Horse* (Doubleday, 1960) pp. 74–75; J. M. Burns, *John Kennedy—A Political Profile* (Harcourt, Brace, 1960) p. 153; Eleanor Roosevelt, *On My Own* (Harper, 1958) pp. 163–164; Alfred Steinberg, *Mrs. R.: The Life of Eleanor Roosevelt* (Putnam, 1958) p. 343.

for Vice-President in 1956; or had the Paris summit of May 1960 not blown up.

All of those who have followed the Kennedy story know well that it was the eldest son of the family, Joe, Jr., and not John, who was slated for politics. If Joe, Jr., had lived, John would not have gone into politics at all. This is not to say that Joe, Jr., would have "made the grade" in high politics, as believers in the Kennedy magic now assume. Joe, Jr., was an extrovert; he was obviously the political "type." John's mind was more penetrating and dispassionate, and he did not fit the stereotype of the politician, particularly the Irish politician. What endeared John to the status-seeking minorities was that he appeared more the scion of an old aristocratic Yankee family than the authentic scions themselves. Had Joe, Jr., lived, the Kennedy family in all probability would never have had a President at all.[5]

Had John Kennedy been nominated for Vice-President in 1956, he would have gone down to disastrous defeat along with Stevenson. That year Eisenhower carried even more of the South than he had in 1952. Both the elder Kennedy and John are reported to have felt that this poorer showing by the Democratic national ticket in 1956 would have been attributed to the continued vitality of anti-Catholic sentiment, thus rendering Kennedy unavailable for the 1960 nomination. It seems that this is a sound judgment.

Despite the fact that more Americans were registered as Democrats than as Republicans, the chances for Republican success in 1960 looked rosy indeed until after the dramatic U-2 incident and

[5] In part, this evaluation of Joe, Jr., and John is derived from personal observation. I recall vividly an evening, April 4, 1941, when I was a guest at the Kennedy home in Palm Beach. Following dinner, the entire family, including the younger children, assembled in the drawing room for a discussion of public affairs. Ambassador Kennedy was particularly interested in canvassing our views about the content of commencement addresses he was to deliver later that spring at Oglethorpe University and at Notre Dame University, but the discussion ranged widely over world politics and foreign policy. Mr. Kennedy, John, and I were the chief participants, although Mrs. Kennedy and Joe, Jr., often broke in with comments. It was clear to me that John had a far better historical and political mind than his father or his elder brother; indeed, that John's capacity for seeing current events in historical perspective and for projecting historical trends into the future was unusual. After the family conclave broke up, John and I continued an animated conversation into the early morning hours.

the collapse of the Paris summit conference. Had the summit accomplished anything at all, the result would have been hailed as the crowning achievement of Eisenhower, the man of peace, and Nixon would have been effectively portrayed as Eisenhower's experienced heir, one who could be both resolute and conciliatory. The explosion of the summit paved the way for Republican defeat and gave plausibility to the kind of "view-with-alarm" campaign waged by Kennedy. In any general climate favoring Republican victory, even Kennedy's ability to win the Catholic vote would not have elected him.

Will historians be hard on Kennedy for his extravagant charges during the 1960 campaign that the Eisenhower Administration had been remiss about America's missiles and space programs? (The fact is that the "gap" in intercontinental missiles was decidedly in favor of the United States.) No, for Presidents are rated in history by the records they make in office, not by how they wage their campaigns. In his first campaign for the Presidency, Lincoln assured voters that the South would not secede; Wilson promised his New Freedom but in office wound up closer to Theodore Roosevelt's New Nationalism; and Franklin Roosevelt pledged economy and a balanced budget but became the founder of the New Deal. Kennedy's zeal will likely be put down as no more than excessive "campaign oratory." Oddly enough, it may be Eisenhower who will be blamed for failing to "nail" Kennedy and to tell the nation bluntly the true state of its defenses, for missing the opportunity to add credibility to America's nuclear deterrent. Liberal historians, impressed by Kennedy's domestic promises and, except for Cuba, his more liberal program than Nixon's in foreign policy—Quemoy and Matsu, emphasis on foreign economic aid, stress on international arms control—will not be prone to hold Kennedy accountable for the alarmist flavor of his campaign.

Of 1960's "issues," only the religious one will loom large in history. It was the religious implication which gave Kennedy the victory. Democratic gains in the pivotal Catholic cities in the states with the largest electoral votes were greater than Democratic losses in the Protestant rural areas. It was the Democrats, not the Republicans, who actively exploited the religious aspect. In the

Protestant areas, citizens were made to feel they were bigots if they voted against Kennedy. But Catholics were appealed to on the grounds of their Catholicism. Any evidence of Protestant intolerance was widely publicized to stimulate Catholics and Jews to go to the polls to rebuke the bigots. But history will treat these Democratic tactics—a kind of bigotry in reverse—with kindness. The means may have been objectionable, but the good achieved was enormous. For the first time in American history a non-Protestant was elected President. The old barriers were downed. Now that an Irish-Catholic had been elected President, the way was opened for the election of an Italian Catholic, a Polish Catholic, a Jew, eventually a Negro. A basic American ideal had at last been implemented at the very pinnacle of American society.[6]

The second permanent contribution of the 1960 election lies in its underscoring the large degree to which Presidential pre-convention campaigns and election campaigns have been geared to democratic mass behavior. Kennedy and his team wisely recognized that a mere pursuit of the politicians and delegates was not enough, that beginning with 1928, conventions had nominated the outstanding national favorite as indicated by the primaries and the polls. In Kennedy's case, winning the primaries and the polls was especially necessary to convince the doubters that a young man

[6] In emphasizing the religious issue as affecting the outcome of the campaign, I incline to the conclusions reached by Elmo Roper in "Polling Post-Mortem," *Saturday Review,* November 26, 1960; the Gallup figures in "Catholics' Vote Analyzed, a 62% Switch to Kennedy," *New York Herald Tribune,* December 6, 1960; Richard M. Scammon, "Foreign Policy, Prestige Not a Big Election Factor," *Washington Post,* December 15, 1960; Louis Bean's comment in Anti-Defamation League of B'nai B'rith press release, January 14, 1961. These coincide with my own findings as the result of interviews with voters in certain sensitive election districts during the campaign of 1960. However, behavioral statisticians differ about this, and doubtless a number of more definitive studies will be forthcoming. Whatever the reasons for the election of Kennedy, the fact that for the first time a Catholic was elected President is what has made the large and permanent impact on history. Even so, every Kennedy biographer must of necessity be concerned with the old question of means and ends, the moral implications of using a religious prejudice in reverse to break the old Protestant monopoly on the Presidency. A striking example of appealing to religious emotion in the guise of opposing it is found in Robert Kennedy's Cincinnati address of September 13, 1960, which was climaxed by this: "Did they ask my brother Joe whether he was a Catholic before he was shot down?"

and a Catholic could be elected President. Hence Kennedy organization, money, and high-level experts were directed not merely to
bagging delegates but even more to winning mass support, primaries, and high ratings in the polls. In this they succeeded
marvelously well. In effect, the Democratic convention merely
ratified the choice already made by the primaries, the polls, and
the mass media. The revolution in the Presidential nominating
process had been in the making for over three decades, but it took
the Kennedy campaign to make the public and even the pundits
aware of it.

During the election campaign itself, Kennedy kept alive his
personal organization; brother Bob, his personal manager, was
more important than the chairman of the Democratic National
Committee; the nominee himself made all the meaningful decisions
and virtually monopolized the limelight; other party leaders were
dwarfed as never before. The TV debates further spotlighted the
nominees. Again, as in the pre-convention campaign, the Kennedy
team did not create the trend to a personalized campaign, to
glamourous celebrity politics. The trend and the techniques to
make it work had been on the way for decades. Basically these
emerged from the increasingly mass nature of American society.
But Kennedy exploited the trend and the techniques in conspicu-
ously successful fashion; he widened, intensified, and accelerated
them; he made the nation aware of them; he did much to institutionalize them.

Thus the Kennedy campaigns will always be remembered for the
dramatic way they contributed to the personalized and plebiscitic
Presidency.

IV

No administration in history staffed the executive departments and
the White House offices with as many competent, dedicated, and
brilliant men as did Kennedy's. Kennedy paid little attention to
party qualifications at top level; the emphasis was on ability, drive,
imagination, creativity. Politicians made way for specialists and
technicians; but Kennedy was on the lookout for specialists *plus,*
for men who had not only technical competence but intellectual

verve. Kennedy himself was a generalist with a critical intelligence, and many of the most prized of his staff were men of like caliber—Sorensen, Goodwin, Bundy. After the brilliance of the Kennedy team, and with the ever-growing complexity of government problems, no administration is ever likely to want to go back to the pedestrian personnel of earlier administrations, although few Presidents are apt to have the Kennedy sensitivity and magnetism capable of gathering together so scintillating an administration as his. F.D.R. will be known as the founder of the Presidential brain trust, but Kennedy will be known as the President who widened and institutionalized it.

In contrast to his performance in the executive departments, Kennedy's relations with Congress can scarcely be said to have been successful. The dream of enacting a legislative program comparable to that of Wilson and F.D.R. soon vanished. The one outstanding legislative achievement of Kennedy was the Trade Expansion Act of 1962. All of Kennedy's other major goals—farm legislation, tax reform, a civil rights law, Medicare, federal aid to schools—bogged down in Congress.

Since 1938, major welfare legislation had repeatedly been smothered in Congress at the hands of a Republican–conservative-Southern Democratic coalition. During the bobtail, post-conventions session of 1960, both Kennedy and Johnson, the Democratic party's new standard bearers, had met humiliating legislative failure when they found themselves unable to budge the Democratic Congress. Kennedy had explained that once the powers of the Presidency were in his hands, things would be different. But when he achieved the Presidency and still failed with a Democratic Congress, Kennedy apologists contended that after Kennedy's reelection in 1964 he would be in a position to press more boldly for legislation. This argument stood experience on its head, for most Presidents have secured much more legislation during their honeymoon first years than during their lame-duck second terms.

Kennedy will not escape all blame for his legislative failures, for despite his awareness of the stalemate since 1938, he had promised a "strong" legislative leadership like that of Wilson and the second Roosevelt. Moreover, in various ways Kennedy contributed to the personalized and plebiscitic Presidency: by the manner in which he waged his 1960 campaign, by his assigning to key posts not party leaders but men personally chosen for their expertise and creative intelligence, and by his monopolizing of the limelight. Kennedy and his family naturally made exciting publicity, but the President seemed to go out of his way to get even more—holding televised press conferences, for example, and permitting TV cameras to capture the intimacies of decision-making in the executive offices and of private life in the White House. All of this further exalted the Presidency, further dwarfed politicians, party, and Congress, and added to Congress' growing inferiority complex.

Now, Kennedy was not unaware of the susceptibilities of Congress. He carefully cultivated individual congressmen and senators, frequently called them on the phone, had them up for chats, extended them an unusual number of social courtesies and parties in the White House. His legislative liaison team, headed by Kenneth O'Donnell and Lawrence O'Brien, was diplomatic and astute, pumped and twisted congressional arms, applied both the carrot and the stick. But Kennedy left too many of the congressional chores to his liaison team. He simply did not give this aspect of the Presidency enough attention. Foreign affairs interested him intellectually much more than domestic measures. Despite his years in Congress and his love of politics, Kennedy did not really like or feel at home with small-bore politicians and congressional "types," and he was not skillful in his personal bargaining with them.

Moreover, Kennedy made no attempt to initiate and institutionalize new devices for easing Presidential-congressional relations, nor did he even explore this problem intellectually. The breath of life to politicians is publicity, but no effort was made to share the Presidential glory, of which there was a superabundance. What could be done to enhance the publicity and prestige of congressional leaders and committee chairmen who consented to carry the Administration ball in Congress? How give them credit for "creating" and "initiating" the Administration's legislative measures? How let them become spokesmen before the nation of the Administration's legislative goals? True, other Presidents had made no such probings, but in recent years, with a legislative log jam piling up, the Presidential-congressional deadlock had reached crisis-like proportions. The President did not give this question, inherently baffling at best, his full creative effort.

Kennedy's Presidency will be known as the time of the Negro

revolution, when Negro aspirations widened to include desegregation in the private sector and were spectacularly supported by sit-
ins and street demonstrations. As President, Kennedy not only
gave full executive backing to the enforcement of court decisions
but personally identified himself with the goals of the Negro
revolution and gave them the full moral support of the Presidency.

By 1960, Kennedy had become an aggressive fighter for Negro
rights. With the South lined up behind the Lyndon Johnson
candidacy, Kennedy's nomination depended on the support of the
Northern liberals and the metropolitan areas outside of the South.
During the election campaign, Kennedy's strategy was geared to
winning the Negro vote in the big cities of the states with large
electoral votes. Kennedy's new militancy carried over to his Presidency.

But by 1963, it appeared that what had been a political
advantage might turn into something of a political liability. "The
Kennedys" were denounced in the South, and the President faced
the loss of much of that section in 1964. More serious, there were
indications that the civil rights issue would cost Kennedy many
votes in the North, where considerable opposition to the Negro
drive had developed. However, by this time Kennedy had chosen
his course, and while there might be temporary shifts in tactics,
there could be no turning back. Robert Kennedy has stated that at
this point the Administration really did not have any choice and
that, besides, the Administration's course was the correct one. He
reports the President as saying: "If we're going to lose, let's lose
on principle."

There seems little question that Kennedy would have been
reelected in 1964, but the civil rights issue would have been his
biggest worry. In sizing up Kennedy as a politician, it is significant
that he appears not to have anticipated the extent to which his
position on civil rights might become politically hazardous. Otherwise it is difficult to explain the appointment of his brother as
Attorney General, upon whom the brunt of enforcing the civil
rights court decisions would necessarily fall. Astute rulers take
care to divert the political lightning of an offended public from
themselves to subordinates. But in appointing his brother Attorney
General, the President left himself no "out." Those hostile to the

Negro revolution could not say: "President Kennedy is all right; it is that Attorney General of his." Instead, they blamed "the Kennedys." With another Attorney General, President Kennedy might well have escaped some of the venom of the opposition. And incidentally, Robert Kennedy, in some other important job, would have been made better available for high politics in the future.

V

In foreign policy, the first two years of Kennedy were ambiguous. In the third year, there was a clearer sense of direction, one which promised to harmonize American policy with emerging new realities in the world.

At the time of the Kennedy accession, the postwar world was disintegrating. Bipolarization was giving way to depolarization. The Sino-Soviet rift was widening. With the single exception of little Vietminh, all the old European colonies that had recently gained their independence had escaped Communism, although there were Communist guerrilla activities in some of them. The trend was to a new pluralism, a new diversity. The nuclear revolution in war and the American-Soviet nuclear deterrents had rendered an ultimate military showdown unthinkable. The United States was ahead in the nuclear arms race.

In Europe, despite Khrushchev's bluster about West Berlin, the existing arrangements in East and Central Europe were ripening into a more overt *modus vivendi,* by way of tacit understanding rather than formal political agreements. Trade and intercourse between East and West Europe were increasing, the satellites were operating more independently of Moscow, and an all-European economic and cultural cooperation seemed slowly to be replacing the postwar's clear-cut division between the "two Europes." West Europeans were becoming less interested in NATO because they were more and more convinced that there would be no Soviet military aggression in Europe, due to the nuclear deterrent and other reasons. The drive to West European political integration was slackening, owing to the decline of external pressures and to de Gaulle's opposition to the supranational approach. Forces within the Six, composing the Common Market, were honestly divided over whether they wanted an inward-looking European community or an outward-looking Atlantic one.

In short, Kennedy was confronted with a new fluidity, a necessity and an opportunity for a reappraisal of American foreign policy. How much of the old foreign policy was still applicable? What aspects required a new orientation? To what degree was it safe, realistic, and advantageous to strike out in new directions? In some ways this ambiguous situation was more agonizing to decision makers than the obvious crisis situation with which Truman and Acheson had had to deal in the late 1940's and early 1950's. It is no wonder that some aspects of the Kennedy record in foreign affairs seem somewhat confused, even contradictory.

The chief stumbling block to an American-Soviet *détente* continued to be Berlin, the two Germanies, and the territorial arrangements in East and Central Europe. Kennedy rejected explorations of a definitive settlement, and if in the future a genuine American-Soviet *rapprochement* develops, this rejection is likely to be held against him. However, he did move informally in the direction of a more openly tacit recognition of the existing arrangements in East and Central Europe. He deferred less to Adenauer's views than previous administrations had done. In his interview in *Izvestia,* remarkable for its clarity and candor, he agreed that it would not be advisable to let West Germany have its own nuclear weapons. After the Communists built the Berlin Wall, Kennedy resisted all pressures to use force to tear it down.

Nevertheless, during his first two years in office, Kennedy seems needlessly to have fanned the tensions of the dying cold war. (It may be that "needlessly" is too strong a word; perhaps Kennedy thought he needed to arouse the country to obtain a more balanced military program, more foreign economic aid, the Alliance for Progress; perhaps he thought, too, that a truculent tone was necessary to convince Khrushchev that America would stand firm under duress for its rights in Berlin.) His Inaugural Address was alarmist, already historically off key, more suited to the Stalinist era than to 1961. His first State of the Union Message was even more alarmist. The nation was told that the world tide was unfavorable, that each day we were drawing near the maximum danger. His backing of the Cuban invasion in April, 1961, further fanned the cold war. His statement to newspaper publishers and editors gathered at the White House in May—that the United States was in the most critical period of its history—increased the popular anxieties. He overreacted to Khrushchev's Vienna ultimatum in June, for in recent years Khrushchev's repeated deadlines and backdowns over West Berlin had become a kind of pattern. But for Kennedy, Vienna seems to have been a traumatic experience. On his return home he appealed to Americans to build do-it-yourself bomb shelters, and this produced a war psychology in the country and all manner of frenetic behavior, caused rightwingism to soar (1961 was the year the membership and financial "take" of the right-wing organizations reached their peak[7]), and weakened confidence abroad in Kennedy's judgment.

There are no defenders of the Cuban fiasco of April, 1961. Even had the expedition of the Cuban exiles been given American naval and air support and forced a landing, there is scant evidence that the Cubans, at that time devoted to Castro, would have revolted en masse and welcomed the invaders as deliverers. More likely a nasty civil war would have followed, with the Americans, giving increasing support to the invaders, cast in the role of subjugators. The CIA had already rejected the social-revolutionary leadership of the anti-Castro Manuel Rey for a nonleftist leadership, and this would have made the task of overthrowing Castro even more difficult. The world would have looked on with dismay, and outside the United States the whole affair would have come to be regarded as "another Hungary." It is ironical that Kennedy, the generalist with a critical intelligence, the politician with a feel for popular moods, should on this occasion have been taken in by the bureaucrats and the "experts." Prodded by his own anti-Castro stand during the election campaign, Kennedy must have wanted desperately to believe in the reliability of those dossiers of the intelligence agents.

With respect to Western Europe, the Kennedy Administration underestimated those forces within the Common Market that wanted a European community rather than an Atlantic community, at first regarded de Gaulle as a kind of maverick without

[7] Donald Janson and Bernard Eismann, *The Far Right* (McGraw-Hill, 1963) pp. 56 and 127.

group support for his position, and framed the Trade Expansion Act of 1962 in such a way that the most decisive tariff cuts between the United States and the Common Market would depend upon Britain's inclusion in the Market. Nevertheless, the Act as written still allowed for much liberalization of trade, even with Britain outside the Market, and the responsibility for failure to take advantage of this opportunity must be borne by parochial-minded groups and interests inside the Market.

The Kennedy Administration's contributions to national defense were notable. It emphasized a balanced and diversified establishment—both strategic and tactical nuclear weapons, conventional arms, and guerrilla forces—so the nation would never have to make the choice between the ultimate weapons and no other adequate defense. It was realistic in its shift from bombers to missiles as the chief nuclear carriers of the future, and in its dismantling of the intermediate missiles bases in Britain, Italy, and Turkey as the Polaris submarines and intercontinental missiles became increasingly operational. Its attempt to find a formula for a NATO multilateral nuclear force was a way of countering de Gaulle's blandishments to the West Germans and of balancing the possibility of a *détente* with Russia with reassurances to Bonn. Its experiments with massive airlifts of ground troops was in part a response to the desires of many of America's NATO allies for less rigidity, less insistence on fixed ground quotas, and more flexibility. However, NATO was plainly in transition, and while the Polaris submarines and intercontinental missiles were making the United States less dependent on European bases, ways were not yet actually implemented to share America's nuclear weapons with European allies on a genuine multilateral basis and satisfy their desires for less centralized direction from the United States.

There was an honest facing up to the terrible responsibilities inherent in the nuclear deterrent. That deterrent was put under tighter control to guard against accident and mistake, and the "hot line" between Washington and Moscow was set up. A much more determined effort was made to get arms-control agreements and a treaty banning nuclear-weapons testing than had ever been made by Kennedy's predecessors. Negotiations with the Soviet Union had been going on for years, but the Americans now so yielded in their former demands for strict international inspection as to put the Russians on the defensive, making world opinion for the first time believe that it was the Russians and not the Americans who were the obstructionists. Kennedy's Administration believed that the United States and Russia had an enormous common interest in preventing the spread of nuclear weapons to other countries, that the Sino-Soviet rift gave Khrushchev a new freedom and a new urge to make agreements, and that the increasing accuracy of national detection systems made the possibility of cheating on a test-ban treaty, even one without international inspection, "vanishingly small."

Kennedy's regime also showed its international-mindedness in its firm support of the United Nations. It defended the Secretariat, the executive, from Soviet attacks, and in practice the activities of the Secretariat were widened. The organization was saved from bankruptcy by American financial aid. The operation of the United Nations military force in the Congo, backed by the United States, showed that the American government had no sympathy for "neocolonialism" as practiced by the Katanga secession, and it added another successful precedent for international enforcement of international decisions.

With respect to the underdeveloped nations, the Kennedy policies paralleled the trend of history. Anticolonialism and self-determination were more valiantly espoused than in the preceding administrations. The Dulles doctrine that neutralism is "immoral" was abandoned, and neutralism was cordially accepted for nations which wanted it. Neutralism was positively encouraged in Laos and in the Congo. Help to South Vietnam was so hedged as to prevent the guerrilla war there from escalating into another Indo-China war, another Korea. Foreign economic aid was increased. The Food for Peace program was expanded. The Peace Corps was launched. The Alliance for Progress, an ambitious economic-aid program in Latin America coupled with domestic reforms, an experiment in "controlled revolution," was undertaken.

However, Kennedy, like his predecessors, did little to make the average American understand foreign economic aid—that it is not only an attempt to raise living standards, prevent Communism, and contribute to the world's economic well-being and stability, but is also a substitute for those obsolete ways in which the old colonialism supplied capital to the underdeveloped areas. Until an American President takes to television and in a series of fireside chats explains to Americans in simple terms the real meaning of the foreign-aid program, that program will be in jeopardy.

The Cuban crisis of October, 1962, provoked by the discovery of secret Soviet intermediate missiles in Cuba, was the high point, the turning point, in the Kennedy Administration. Could this crisis have been avoided? This will be debated by future historians. True, Khrushchev could not have declined giving Castro economic aid, technical assistance, and some military help, even had he desired to do so, for to have refused this would have been tantamount to surrendering Communist leadership to the Chinese. But why did he go to the length of planting intermediate-missile bases in Cuba? As an appeasement to the Stalinist and Chinese opposition? As a countermeasure to American missile bases in Turkey (which were soon to be dismantled)? As a means of blackmailing Americans into making a compromise on Berlin? To extract a promise from the Americans not to invade Cuba? Whatever the causes, some future historians will have nagging questions: Might this terrible gamble in nuclear brinkmanship have been prevented had Kennedy previously shown more disposition to come to a *détente* with the Soviet Union by a somewhat clearer recognition of the two Germanies and other *de facto* boundaries and arrangements in East and Central Europe; and if so, did this Kennedy reluctance, coming in part out of regard for West German opinion, represent a realistic appraisal of the world situation?

Anyway, when the crisis came, even neutralist opinion seemed to feel that Khrushchev's attempt to compensate for his own intercontinental-missiles lag and the open and avowed American intermediate missiles in Turkey did not justify the sneaky Soviet operation in Cuba. America's quiet, deliberate planning of countermeasures, both military and diplomatic, was masterly. America's prudent use of force, enough but not more than enough to achieve its objective, won world-wide acclaim. Khrushchev and Castro lost face. The Chinese denounced the Soviet backdown, and Chinese-Russian relations worsened. Most important, the peak of the crisis, a spectacular nuclear brinkmanship, cleared the atmosphere like a bolt of lightning. The lunacy of an ultimate nuclear showdown was traumatically revealed. Khrushchev's personal correspondence to Kennedy, reputedly revealing a highly emotional state and a genuine horror of nuclear war, the President had the grace, sportsmanship, and wisdom to keep secret.

Thereafter Khrushchev spoke even more insistently about the need to avoid nuclear war and pursue a policy of peaceful but competitive coexistence. From then on Kennedy gave more public recognition to emerging new international realities, the world's escape from monolithic threats, the trend to pluralism and diversity. In his address at American University in June, 1963, Kennedy spoke as if the cold war scarcely existed and emphasized the common stake both the United States and the Soviet Union had in world peace and stability. This address, one of the noblest and most realistic state papers of our time, will be remembered long after Kennedy's Inaugural Address is forgotten.

The new spirit in world affairs expressed itself concretely in the consummation of the limited nuclear test-ban treaty in the summer of 1963, the first real break in the American-Soviet deadlock. After this, Kennedy proposed a joint American-Soviet effort to explore the moon, and he agreed to permit the Soviet Union to purchase American wheat.

By 1963, then, Kennedy had come to much awareness that the postwar world was ending and to a determination to attempt more shifts in American foreign policy in harmony with the emerging fluidity. By this time, too, he had developed close personal relations with a large number of premiers and heads of state the world over. It was felt that after his reelection in 1964 he would be in an unusually strong position to give American foreign policy a new direction, that the test-ban treaty was but a foretaste of more significant measures yet to come, measures which might lead to an American-Soviet *détente,* eventually even to a *rapprochement.* Thus the President's life ended in a tragic sense of incompleteness and unfulfillment.

Every twentieth-century American President with a flair for world politics and in power in time of momentous international decision has been felled by sickness or death before his term was over, before his work was completed. First Wilson. Then Roose-velt. Then Kennedy. For sheer bad luck, this is a record unique among nations.

VI

Because of the vividness of his personality and the shortness of his tenure, Kennedy will be known more for the intangibles—a tastemaker, a symbolic embodiment of the values of his time, a romantic folk hero—than for his achievements in statesmanship.

Government requires pageantry, and rulers are expected to put on a show. The Kennedys put on a superb one. Never before, not even under Dolly Madison, was the White House the scene of such a dazzling social life, one which combined beauty and intelligence, radiance and creativity. There were, to be sure, crabbed Mrs. Grundys who derided "peacock opulence" and looked back long-ingly to the decorous days of Lucy Webb Hayes. But most Americans were fascinated, pleased as punch that even Elizabeth and Philip appeared a bit dowdy in contrast to those two young American thoroughbreds in the White House. They figuratively crowned Jacqueline Queen of Hearts. This aspect of the Kennedy reign has been inimitably described by Katherine Anne Porter, and no historian will ever record it with more grace, insight, and tenderness.[8]

Kennedy's contributions to the cultural life of the nation also belong to the intangible, and they are difficult to measure. Now of course President Kennedy did not engage in as wide-ranging an intellectual life as President Jefferson or President Theodore Roosevelt. He did not carry on a voluminous and polemical correspondence with American and foreign intellectuals as these men had done, even when they were in the White House. And Kennedy himself realized that his "little promotions" did not help young and struggling artists and writers in the direct and material way the New Deal works projects had done.

But never before Kennedy's time had the White House paid so

[8] Katherine Anne Porter, "Her Legend Will Live," *Ladies' Home Journal*, March 1964.

much personal and social attention to the nation's writers, artists, musicians, scientists, and scholars. At first some of the public was inclined to take a snidely skeptical view of all this. Was not this celebrity-hunting, highbrow name-dropping, a further drive to Presidential glamour? The recipients of these attentions did not think so. Only William Faulkner, in bad-tempered petulance, rebuffed the President. For the rest, a chat with the President or an invitation to an event in the White House was an occasion of a lifetime, and these felt that Kennedy was not merely honoring them but the creative work they represented. As Richard Rovere has pointed out, Kennedy was tremendously concerned that the American society become a good, even a brilliant, civilization. He thought of himself as a promoter, an impresario, of excellence in every phase of American life, and he hoped that future Presidents would emulate him in this.[9]

To latter twentieth-century Americans, Kennedy will be a kind of beau ideal reflecting what they consider admirable in the politician—a shunning of corniness and hokum, an accent on youth and wealth, the glamorous videographic personality favored by Hollywood and TV, a contrived casualness in dress and manner, the sophistication and urbanity of the ivy league, direct and clear speech sprinkled with wit, an avoidance of doctrine and dogma, a pragmatism just emotionally enough involved to be effective, the capacity for using expertise and Madison Avenue techniques, the ability to create and sustain an "image." In these, most of them externals, Kennedy will have many imitators.

The Kennedy élan will not be easy to imitate. Even more difficult of imitation will be the Kennedy mind—rational and balanced thinking, objectivity, the ability to see all around a question, resilience, elusiveness, the capacity for keeping judgment in suspense, a detachment reaching to one's self and one's own image, an avoidance of absolute commitment combined with genuine intellectual involvement, a general critical intelligence brought to bear on the findings of the specialists. The Kennedy

[9] See Richard Rovere, "Letter from Washington," *The New Yorker,* November 30, 1963. [Editor's note: Rovere's "letter" is reprinted in Part III of this volume.]

magic lies in its combination of the various elements: the externals, the verve with which the externals were carried off, and the cast of mind.

There is still another Kennedy intangible, perhaps the most important, one which belongs to the nonrational. Kennedy is becoming a folk hero, a subject of myth and legend, one of those few in history who capture the poetic imagination and affection of the masses. Solid achievement may have something to do with arriving at such a place in history, but very often it has little or nothing to do with it. Indeed, the titans who have wrought most mightily and in the end been felled by tragedy inspire awe and reverence more frequently than they do folk affection. They are too mature, their lives too devoid of colorful gallantries and foibles, their achievements too overwhelming for the average man to identify himself with such figures. To this class belong Caesar, William the Silent, Lincoln. Increasingly Lincoln has become a father image and "the martyred Christ of the democratic passion play."

The folk hero in the affectionate, indulgent sense is one who leaves behind him an overall impression of élan, style, beauty, grace, gaiety, gallantry, bold and light-hearted adventure, valor—mingled in one way or another with the frail, the fey, the heedless, the mystic, the tragic. This is the romantic tradition, the tradition of Achilles, David, Alcibiades (despite his damaged soul), Arthur, Roland, Abélard, Richard the Lion Hearted, St. Francis, Bayard, Raleigh, Henry of Navarre, Gustavus Adolphus, Byron. Alexander the Great is often put in this tradition, but his exploits were so dazzling, so epoch-making, that he became more a god than a hero.

Kennedy's death has in it the touch of religious epic, of man pitted against fate. Here surely was one favored by the gods, one possessed of power, wealth, youth, the aura of manly war heroism, zest for living, personal charm and beauty, glamour, imagination, keen insight, intelligence, immense popularity, the adoring love of family and friends. Great achievements were to his credit, and even greater ones seemed in store. Then in the fullness of his strength, he was cut down in a flash. History has no more dramatic demonstration of the everlasting insecurity of the human condition.[10]

Was Kennedy himself a romantic? In some ways, mostly in appearance and manner. There are photographs of him, for instance several public ones taken in Tampa five days before his assassination, which reveal him in a kind of narcissistic euphoria. (Those who understand how wondrously flexibly human nature can be will see nothing damaging in this.) James Reston once observed that the effect Kennedy had on women voters was "almost naughty." In his personal relations—and this is a matter not of appearance but of substance—Kennedy had an outgoing freshness and (there is no other term for it) a sweetness of temper. But basically Kennedy was not a romantic. He was a rationalist with a critical intelligence, a realist who knew the hard and subtle uses of power.

However, one need not be a romantic to become a romantic hero of history. Many romantics miss it—sometimes for a variety of reasons just barely miss it: Bolívar, Garibaldi, Gambetta, Jaurès, Michael Collins. In modern times romantic heroes have become rare. Kennedy is the first in this tradition in a long time, and he is the only American in its top echelon. Strange that he should have come out of the America of the machine and mass production. Or is it? People in our prosaic age, particularly young Americans, were yearning for a romantic hero, as the James Dean cult among our youth revealed. Now they have an authentic one.

[10] Although the folk think of Kennedy as a child of fortune, actually he suffered much physically. He seems never to have been robust; the state of his health often concerned his father; in my own brief Kennedy files are letters from the elder Kennedy which speak of Jack's poor health in periods prior to World War II. Following his service in the war, Jack was plagued with malaria and his serious back injury. Even after the successful operation on his back, it would appear that he was rarely free from pain. When this comes to be realized, Kennedy's pace as President will appear even more gallant.

DOUGLASS CATER

The Do-It-Yourself Nature of
Presidential Power

President Kennedy's early career offered few indications of
that zestful love of power which Roosevelt exhibited. The eldest
son, Joseph Kennedy, Jr., was slated to be the politician in the
family. Only after Joe, Jr.'s death in World War II did the second
son, as his father has noted, feel obliged to take over the legacy.
Kennedy's record in both the House of Representatives and the
Senate showed him to be a tough campaigner, but not one of the
power-conscious elite of those two bodies. He neither sought nor
was invited to join the so-called inner clubs. Until near the end of
his career in Congress, he did not exhibit much concern for legislative achievement.

Close friends differ about the origins of Kennedy's Presidential
ambition. As late as 1956, he was remarkably indifferent to the
efforts of his associates to promote him for Vice-President on the
Democratic ticket. He took stoically his narrow defeat at the
Chicago Convention in 1956. Three years later, when he had
already commenced the sustained drive for first place, he still
managed to convey a certain dispassion about his high ambition.
Asked bluntly by reporters why he *ought* to be President, he

This selection is from Douglass Cater, *Power in Washington,* pp. 78–88.
© 1964 by Douglass Cater. Reprinted by permission of Random House, Inc.

answered simply that he thought he could do as good a job as anyone else available. To the question of why he should *want* to be President, he quoted an ancient Greek proverb he had learned from Dean Acheson: "Happiness lies in the exercise of vital powers along lines of excellence in a life affording them scope." Kennedy admitted he found in politics, as in no other pursuit, a purely personal happiness. This seemed hardly a driving motivation for seeking power.

Kennedy's writings provide a few clues to his notions about leadership. His first book, *Why England Slept,* an expansion of his college thesis written in 1940, gave an impressive analysis of the British government's failure to keep pace with German rearmament. The chief villains were not the politicians but the unthinking British public which, he felt, refused to support forthright leadership and then sought "to make scapegoats for its own weaknesses."

Fifteen years later, while recuperating from an operation, Kennedy drafted his *Profiles in Courage* which took quite a different approach to the problem of leadership. This time he paid glowing tribute to the politician who, in time of crisis, stood staunchly against the prevailing sentiment of colleagues and public. The book was a testament to a leadership prepared to sacrifice power for the keeping of conscience.

There were to be further shifts in Kennedy's perspective. Almost a year before his inauguration, he delivered a speech to the National Press Club which drew heavily on the charismatic school of Presidential interpretation. (A short time before the speech, one of his aides had borrowed Sidney Hyman's book.) "In the decade that lies ahead," Kennedy declared, "the challenging, revolutionary Sixties, the American Presidency will demand more than ringing manifestos issued from the rear of the battle. It will demand that the President place himself in the very thick of the fight, that he care passionately about the fate of the people he leads, that he be willing to serve them at the risk of incurring their momentary displeasure." Referring to Woodrow Wilson's assertion that a President is at liberty to be as big a man as he can, Kennedy argued, "But President Wilson discovered that to be a big man in the White House inevitably brings cries of dictatorship. So did

Lincoln and Jackson and the two Roosevelts. And so may the next occupant of that office, if he is the man the times demand."

During the spring or summer of 1960, Kennedy read Neustadt's book.* That it struck a responsive chord is evident from the thinly veiled account of its author's experience as reported by Richard Rovere in *The New Yorker* a month after the election:

About a month ago, the President-elect asked a man from an eastern university to advise him on a wide but clearly defined range of current problems and to give him the name of people competent to deal with them in the new administration. A day or two earlier, the newspapers had reported that Mr. Kennedy had asked another man—one whose background was more practical than theoretical—to do a job that sounded to the new recruit very much like, if not identical with, the one he was being asked to undertake. The scholar, who has a fluent command of the local patois, asked Mr. Kennedy how he should "relate" to the other appointee. The answer was crisp and categorical: "Don't." The President-elect went on to say that it would suit him down to the ground if the two men never saw each other; he supposed, though, that they would have to confer, and he only hoped that they would do as little conferring as possible before they reported, as he wished each of them to do, directly to him. With his eyes on the ceiling and the merest hint of apology in the voice that is noted for its rather narrow emotional range, he said, "I simply cannot afford to have just one set of advisers." Far from being offended, the scholar left with a spring in his step and a firmer conviction than he had had up to then that the republic was in good hands. . . .

Mr. Kennedy, he felt, had already mastered the beginning of Presidential wisdom. "If he had not made that remark," he said, "I should have gone directly to my hotel room and got to work on a memorandum pointing out the weaknesses of the command system and urging him not to be afraid of a little administrative untidiness. If a President has only one set of advisers, the advisers take over the Presidency."

The attempt to measure Kennedy leadership presents a number of bafflements. At times there appeared to be a conflict between the "passionate" President of the Press Club speech and the power-conscious President of Neustadtian analysis. Or, using Kennedy's earlier writing, there was a tension between the politician of con-

* Editor's note: Richard E. Neustadt, *Presidential Power*.

science depicted in his second book and the politician constrained by an apathetic public of his first.

Critics have found evidence of this conflict on all sides. The politics of foreign aid provides a clear example. In the first Inaugural Address, the Alliance for Progress proposals, and numerous other pronouncements, the President promised eloquently to assist the underdeveloped countries along the road to progress. Foreign aid was to be rescued from its former stereotype as simply a way of supporting the defense effort. Impact programs to stimulate basis growth in Latin America, Africa, and Asia were to be given the highest priority.

The results were hardly in accord with all these high hopes. The progress of the new AID agency was frustrated by frequent delays as well as a rapid succession of three directors during its first three years. The President's legislative proposal to finance development aid on a long-term basis finished with a hastily negotiated compromise which left power intact in the hands of the obstinate lords of the congressional appropriation subcommittees. With foreign aid subjected to ever increasing reexamination, its political future looked increasingly dark. Members of Congress who have sought to fight for the program complained bitterly of being abandoned by the White House.

On other foreign fronts, critics have also pointed to a dualism between "vigorous" and "realistic" Presidential leadership:

Laos: The President held a televised press conference to emphasize, with use of maps, the threat to Southeast Asia of a Communist takeover of this little country. The settlement in Laos, negotiated not long afterward, promised at best that if the Communists kept their word the country would remain neutral;

Berlin: Kennedy voiced repeated determination not to yield Allied rights. Yet he did not make a passionate protest when the Soviets erected a wall dividing that beleaguered city, and lesser officials tried to characterize "the Wall" as a psychological defeat for the Soviets;

Cuba: Kennedy accepted the "tunnel vision" of his CIA advisers by agreeing to the ill-fated invasion in the Bay of Pigs. Yet a cautious concept of power caused him to eliminate plans for U.S. air "cover" of the refugee invasion force which was sadly under strength for such a mission. Only a year and a half later, with Soviet missile sites under construction in Cuba, did he pick up the challenge.

On the domestic front, there were similar contrasts between courageous expectations and cautious operations. In Congress, President Kennedy offered quiet support to Speaker Sam Rayburn in the fight to enlarge the House Rules Committee. But enlargement was a timid and, in retrospect, not wholly effectual way of trying to tame that recalcitrant group, and when Rayburn died, Kennedy remained fastidiously aloof from any show of preference in the short-lived struggle for leadership in the House. There was little evidence that the President was willing to take risks to obtain congressional reforms that might lessen the legislative stalemate. The very narrowness of the margins of defeat—on Medicare, on the Administration farm bill, on the Urban Affairs Department— revealed a discouraging inability to supply the necessary inducement to shift the balance.

The legislative struggle took on a quite different character from the trail blazing of the New Deal era. It is more reminiscent of the dogged trench warfare of the First World War than of the swift panzer movements of the Second. The item-by-item fight on Kennedy's tax reform proposals was more typical of the massed confrontation of forces that frustrated spectacular gains.

In a number of major battles Kennedy appeared to make a display more for the record than for anticipated results. There was the frantic and futile effort to push the Urban Affairs plan through the Senate before it received an inevitable veto in the House. Similarly, Medicare was hurried before the senators in hopes of diverting attention from the slow strangulation it was receiving in the House Ways and Means Committee. Bills for federal aid to lower and higher education went down to defeat in a way that obscured party responsibility.

Despite his campaign promises to "get America moving," Kennedy's actions in the economic field created the image of a President whose primary role was to adjust and balance the delicate mechanisms of the economy instead of stoutly exhorting it to new furies of movement. The effort to stem the gold flow, to correct the adverse balance of payments, and to spur industry through sizeable tax concessions gave evidence of this cautious preoccupation with balance and adjustment. As he declared somewhat impatiently to criticism, "What we need is 'not more labels and more clichés' but more basic discussion of the sophisticated and technical questions involved in keeping our mighty economic machine moving steadily ahead."[1]

The President was equally impatient with criticisms that his policies in the foreign field appeared to lack a "grand design." After one background session, *The New York Times* reported that "President Kennedy believes that the grand design of his Administration's foreign policies derives from what he thinks has been a generally consistent United States course since 1945. As he sees it, the long-range purpose of himself and the nation is to work toward a world in which free states can develop sufficient internal resources to maintain their independence."[2] Of course, the critic could respond that this was a concept so grand that it was entirely lacking in design.

It must be admitted that the vantage point of a Washington reporter is not the best for gauging leadership. Trevelyan wrote of the first Queen Elizabeth, "Her bold decisions were few and can be numbered, but each of them began an epoch." Yet a scribe attending Elizabeth's court might well have had difficulty perceiving which ones were epochal. The press corps in Lincoln's capital did not discern greatness in the President's often irresolute behavior. Hindsight tends to etch deeply the sharp lines of leadership that appeared blurry close at hand.

Unlike Queen Elizabeth, a modern President must feel content not to begin any epoch if only he can maintain prosperity and avoid a war. Conceding his many difficulties, Kennedy enthusiasts found promising portent in three decisive acts during his early years in office: the challenge and rebuff to the steel industry's attempt to raise prices; the dispatch of federal deputies and troops to enforce the court-ordered enrollment of a Negro, James Mere-

---

[1] President Kennedy's Address at Yale University, June 11, 1962. Text from the *Wall Street Journal,* Tuesday, June 12, 1962, p. 20.

[2] Tom Wicker, "President Feels West Gained in '61 But Sees Danger," *The New York Times,* Sunday, December 31, 1961, p. 1.

dith, in the University of Mississippi; and the confrontation of Khrushchev with the "quarantine" of Cuba. All three were successful in accomplishing short-term objectives. Steel reduced its prices; Meredith was enrolled; Khrushchev withdrew his missiles and bombers from Cuba.

In staging the showdowns, the President displayed a capacity to mobilize the strength of his office speedily and efficiently. Particularly in the second Cuban crisis, he acted in such a way that sustaining strength was drawn from other holders of power, at home and abroad. By Neustadtian analysis, he showed keen awareness of the stakes and came through these crises with his personal power not only intact but enhanced.

Yet, it must be pointed out that the three episodes had other factors in common. None started as acts of the President's own volition, but were forced upon him—by U.S. Steel President Roger Blough, by Mississippi Governor Ross Barnett, and by Soviet Premier Nikita Khrushchev. All three had been attempts to call the President's bluff; he had to respond or be counted a coward. In each case, his opponents grossly overplayed their strength. Blough lacked the economic conditions to sustain a price rise; Barnett had no troops to back him up once the President federalized the National Guard; and Khrushchev was without conventional military capacity to break a blockade.

Those who participated most intimately with the President during the Cuban crisis—dramatically described as the prototype war of the thermonuclear age—are cautious about drawing lessons from it. One White House participant has pointed out privately that certain conditions made the situation unique. First, for nearly a week the government had possession of documented intelligence —evidence of the missile sites—about which no one in the press knew, or knew that the government knew. This permitted remarkable facility in planning the response, catching the enemy by surprise, and forewarning friendly allies. In marked contrast, for example, the building of the Berlin Wall was known simultaneously to government and press and was accomplished before government officials could confer with one another or consult the Allied powers in Berlin.

Secondly, the military phase of the Cuban quarantine was

directed, quite literally, from a telephone on Secretary McNamara's desk, providing tight control against the accidental or the unexpected. The chief anxiety in Washington was whether Soviet communications were as foolproof as those of the U.S. Doubt on this matter prompted the decision to allow the first Soviet ship, the tanker *Bucharest,* to pass through the blockade uninspected.

A third condition set the course of the Cuban crisis. In responses to questions at his press conference the previous month, the President had flatly committed himself to act in the event of aggressive build-up in Cuba. Would he have acted had he not made that public commitment? Having experienced the awful loneliness of the decision to risk cataclysmic war, the White House assistant was unwilling to make that assumption lightly. He reported that not a single member of the inner council really believed that the quarantine alone would accomplish Soviet withdrawal. The terror of total war was a living reality.

Success in Cuba clearly resulted as much from the flaws in Khrushchev's strategy as from Kennedy's counter strategy. Once the quarantine had been evoked, the only options left to the Soviet leader were to launch a thermonuclear attack against the U.S., or to back down. Evidently he had not even made plans for staging a diversionary aggression elsewhere in the event of being challenged in Cuba. Kennedy, on the other hand, guarded his options by preparing for a swift escalation of force if the Soviets failed to withdraw the missiles. But he left the terrible choice of nuclear retaliation entirely up to Khrushchev.

After more than two years in office, the President's Special Counsel, Theodore C. Sorensen, a long-time aide, gave two lectures at Columbia University soberly reassessing the business of decision-making in the White House; both his words and mood were a far cry from Kennedy's exuberant Press Club speech of 1960 which Sorensen had helped draft. Now the deputy chose to stress the perplexities of leadership: ". . . too often a President finds that events or the decisions of others have limited his freedom of maneuver—that, as he makes a choice, that door closes behind him. And he knows that, once that door is closed, it may never open again—and he may then find himself in a one-way tunnel, or in a baffling maze, or descending a slippery slope. He cannot count on turning back—yet he cannot see his way ahead. He knows that if he is to act, some eggs must be broken to make the omelet, as the old saying goes. But he also knows that an omelet cannot lay any more eggs." Sorensen also underlined five limitations that encumber a President. "He is free to choose only within the limits of permissibility, within the limits of available resources, within the limits of available time, within the limits of previous commitments, and within the limits of available information."

As President Johnson suddenly took over the reins, the toting up of success and failure made judgment difficult. Successful negotiation of a nuclear test ban had marked an easing of tension, even if momentary, with the Soviets. On the other hand, the Western Alliance, so carefully woven together since the war, had begun to show signs of unraveling. Despite the successful passage of the President's mutual trade bill in Congress, U.S. negotiations with the Common Market had reached a state of mutual recriminations. Domestically, the economic indicators were showing advancing prosperity while the political indicators continued to reveal deep pockets of poverty. On the racial front, the late President had been making a try with tardy haste to provide equal citizenship and opportunity for Negroes before pent-up frustrations boiled over. Yet the very effort was threatening to rouse bitter opposition from powerful sectors of the white community.

Amid such perplexities, it is hard to decide on a yardstick for measuring a President, much less on how to apply it. Even while pondering Neustadt's brilliant analysis of Presidential muscle structure, one instinctively comes to feel certain reservations. Like Machiavelli's earlier anatomy of power, it is susceptible to misreading. A President preoccupied with his personal stakes can make all the wrong choices—for the nation if not for himself. Taken too literally, preoccupation with power could result in a "what's-in-it-for-me?" attitude compounding caution with caution. Or, contrarily, preoccupation with power can produce a cynicism about its usage. Presidential leadership has other ingredients, including some as difficult to define as "intuition," "vision," "conviction," and—to borrow from Kennedy—"courage." In any diagnosis, these ingredients contribute much to the health or ills of the body politic. There is danger that by overly concentrating on the muscle the body culturist ignores what moves the muscle.

This is merely to conclude, contrary to Lord Bryce, that Presidents *ought* to be great men and that a prime characteristic of greatness is the ability to employ power consciously but never too self-consciously. History reveals that great Presidents must show a capacity not only to conserve power but to risk squandering it when the occasion demands. The nation has profited from such philanthropy.

JAMES RESTON

What Was Killed Was Not Only the President But the Promise

Time seems to be trying to make amends to John Fitzgerald Kennedy. Robbed of his years, he is being rewarded and honored in death as he never was in life. Deprived of the place he sought in history, he has been given in compensation a place in legend. What was a monstrous personal and historic crime a year ago is now something even more elemental and enduring: It is a symbol of the tragedy and caprice of life, and it is likely to be remembered by the novelists and the dramatists long after the historians have gone on to other things.

Will he seem different to the historians from the way the dramatists will see him? What are they likely to say of his conduct of foreign affairs, domestic affairs, the Presidency itself? Are we already confusing myth with reality, as he was always telling us we should not do?

Probably we are, but this is only fair and maybe even natural. For there was always something vaguely legendary about him. He was a storybook President, younger and more handsome than mortal politicians, remote even from his friends, graceful, almost elegant, with poetry on his tongue and a radiant young woman at his side.

He was a sudden and surprising person. He never did things when other men were doing them. He went to Congress and the White House earlier than most. He married much later than his contemporaries. His war record, his political record and his personal life were marked by flashes of crisis and even by a vague premonition of tragedy. He always seemed to be striding through doors into the center of some startling triumph or disaster. He never reached his meridian: we saw him only as a rising sun.

Accordingly, it is not easy to make an estimate of his one thousand days in the White House. He didn't have a fair chance and he didn't even give himself a fair chance. He often made his decisions alone after a series of private talks with several individuals, none of whom shared the whole process of his thought.

Oddly in one who had such an acute sense of history, he was disorderly about keeping records of what led up to his decisions, and though he had a great gift for conversation, he seems to have spent little time talking to his closest associates about how he had decided things in the past.

All this complicates the task of placing him in the catalogue of the Presidents. We do not have the record. We do not have the full story of the two Cuban crises, or his meeting with Khrushchev in Vienna, or the reasoning behind his gambles in Vietnam, or the communications that led up to the atomic test-ban treaty with the Soviets. We have only our clippings, memories, and impressions, and these can be uncertain guides.

FOREIGN POLICY

Historians—and here we are in the realm of opinion—will probably rate President Kennedy's handling of foreign policy higher than his contemporaries did. It is a spotty record. He dreamed occasionally of an interdependent Atlantic world and this has become part of the legend, but the reality is that the alliance was in poor shape during most of his Administration. He courted Latin America like a thoughtful lover, but, again, the Alliance for Progress was more dream than reality.

Even so, he had a feeling for the way the world was going. He understood the challenge of change. He was fascinated by the political revolution produced by the liberation of the colonial peoples: sometimes too fascinated with it, and too inclined to give it a higher priority than it deserved. He studied and understood the intricate problems of the atomic revolution and the scientific revolution, probably better than any of his predecessors.

Yet this keen, analytical intelligence was not always a help. It enabled him to see the problems, but it often depressed him about finding the answers. I always thought—perhaps wrongly—that his intelligence made him pessimistic. The evidence that science was transforming the world seemed so clear and overwhelming to him that he was irritated by the failure of men and institutions to adapt and keep up.

In his very first State of the Union Message, ten days after he had been sworn in, he told the Congress and the nation: "Before my term has ended, we shall have to test anew whether a nation organized and governed such as ours can endure. The outcome is by no means certain. The answers are by no means clear."

His bungling of his first foreign-policy gamble, when he tried to help the Cuban refugees overthrow the Castro government, made him all the more conscious, not only of the complexities of political decision, but of the possible consequences of failure.

The events at the Bay of Pigs contributed to his natural caution, and added to his problems with the Communists for most of the rest of his days in the White House. It is impossible to be sure about this, but I was in Vienna when he met Khrushchev shortly after the fiasco of the Bay of Pigs, and saw him ten minutes after his meeting with the Soviet leader. He came into a dim room in the American Embassy shaken and angry. He had tried, as always, to be calm and rational with Khrushchev, to get him to define what the Soviet Union could and would not do, and Khrushchev had bullied him and threatened him with war over Berlin.

We will have to know much more about that confrontation between Kennedy and Khrushchev, one now deprived of life and the other of power, before we can be sure, but Kennedy said just enough in that room in the embassy to convince me of the following: Khrushchev had studied the events of the Bay of Pigs; he would have understood if Kennedy had left Castro alone or destroyed him; but when Kennedy was rash enough to strike at

Cuba but not bold enough to finish the job, Khrushchev decided he was dealing with an inexperienced young leader who could be intimidated and blackmailed. The Communist decision to put offensive missiles into Cuba was the final gamble of this assumption.

The missile crisis brought out what always seemed to me to be Kennedy's finest quality and produced the events on which Kennedy's place in history probably depends. There is a single fact that repeats itself in the Kennedy story like the major theme in a symphony: He was always at his best in the highest moment of crisis.

He could be ambiguous and even indecisive on secondary questions. He obviously trifled with the first Cuban crisis. He also temporized with the Vietnamese crisis, partly supporting those who wanted to intervene "to win," partly going along with those who reminded him that the French had suffered 175,000 casualties against the same Communist army, but never really defining his aims or reconciling his power with his objectives.

Yet always in his political life he acted decisively when faced with total defeat. He was supremely confident, almost presumptuous, in going for the Presidency in the first place against the opposition of the most powerful elements in his party. He was bold and effective when first Hubert Humphrey, then Harry Truman and finally Lyndon Johnson challenged him publicly during the campaign for the nomination. He probably won the Presidency in the critical debates with Richard Nixon. And this same quality came out in the missile crisis in Cuba.

Then he was, as Robert Frost had urged him to be, "more Irish than Harvard" but with a dash of Harvard intelligence, too. If the first Cuban crisis was the worst example of the uses of American power and diplomacy in this generation, the second Cuban crisis was the best. And the significance of this fact can be understood only in relation to the longer perspective of war in this century.

Twice in this century, the leaders of the free world have been confronted by the menacing power of a totalitarian state. From 1912 until 1914, and again from 1935 until 1939, Germany made a series of moves that clearly threatened the peace and order of the world, and during those critical testing periods, Britain, France and the United States failed either to raise enough military power or to show enough will power to avoid the holocaust. The resulting tragedies of the two great wars transformed the history of the world.

The Soviet decision to place long-range missiles in Cuba, capable of firing atomic rockets into almost any part of the United States, was a similar and in some ways even more ominous test. This lunge into the Western Hemisphere was clearly an effort to change the world balance of power in Moscow's favor, and Kennedy faced it at the risk of war and turned it back.

It is ironic that he went to his grave with many of his fellow countrymen condemning him for failing to get rid of all the Communists and all the defensive missiles in Cuba as well as all the offensive missiles. Yet this view has not been shared by most of the political leaders and historians of the world.

I saw Prime Minister Macmillan of Britain just before he resigned and before President Kennedy was murdered. "If Kennedy never did another thing," Macmillan remarked, "he assured his place in history by that single act. He did what we failed to do in the critical years before the two German wars."

Within a year of Kennedy's death, Khrushchev was removed from power, partly as a result of his humiliating defeat in the Cuban missile crisis, but something important and maybe even historic remained: The Communist world was relieved of the illusion that the United States would not risk atomic war to defend its vital interests. This new awareness greatly reduced the danger of miscalculating American intentions and led almost at once to the first really serious steps to bring atomic weapons under control.

THE HOME FRONT

Mr. Kennedy was more at ease in the larger world of diplomacy and the struggle between nations than he was in the world of congressional politics and the struggle between contending national forces. He had more freedom of action in foreign than in domestic policy. He did not seem to mind the small talk of ceremonial meetings with heads of state or foreign students at the White House, and he had a rare combination of informality and dignity that made him very effective in this role. But blarneying with pompous congressmen bored him and he simply would not take time to do it, as his successor, President Johnson, has with such marked success.

This was odd, in a way. He was a superb politician in planning and running a Presidential campaign, but he didn't really know the deck on Capitol Hill and he did not really like to play the political game there. Even though he spent most of his political life in the House and the Senate, he was always sort of a nonresident member of those peculiar clubs, always a backbencher with a high truancy record and an excessive respect for the chairmen of the committees and the other elders of the Congress.

The very qualities of appearance, style and cast of mind that won him the admiration of the intellectual and diplomatic worlds somehow marked him as an outsider in his dealings with the Congress. He had little patience for the tiresome loquacity and endless details of legislation, and he never cared much for the boisterous bantering and backslapping of the cloakrooms.

He had a kind of gay magic as a political speaker, most of it as carefully contrived as it seemed spontaneous. He was good at the arts of Hollywood and Madison Avenue, and this delighted his fellow politicians, but he was a little too polished, ambitious and out of the ordinary to escape the envy and criticism of the Hill.

Congress likes typical Americans and Kennedy was not one. In his mature life, he probably crossed the Atlantic more often than he crossed the Allegheny range. He never seemed at home in the West. The America he understood best was bounded by Harvard Yard, the State Department, Park Avenue and Palm Beach. His political style and humor were not based on the exaggerated language and gymnastics of the American hustings but on the gentler models of the House of Commons.

Maybe these things had nothing to do with his troubles in getting a legislative program through the Congress; maybe it was just the old stubborn resistance of the Congress to change—"the government of the living by the dead"—but the fact remains that his domestic program was in deep trouble when he was killed, and some of us despaired that Capitol Hill would ever be his field of triumph.

Part of the Kennedy legend is connected with his introduction of the most radical legislation on behalf of Negro equality in this century. But again the reality is less romantic. He did not normally like to take on anything more than he had to tackle, no matter how worthy. Oddly for a man who wrote a book celebrating the heroes of lost causes (*Profiles in Courage*), he was always saying: "Why fight if you are not sure to win?" The Negro demonstrations in the summer of 1963, however, forced his hand, and he went along when some Republican leaders and his brother Robert urged that action was necessary.

Yet, on the home front, as in the foreign field, he did start one major innovation of transcending importance. At the urging of Walter Heller, the chairman of the Council of Economic Advisers, he broke with the traditional economic concepts of Capitol Hill and plunged for a large tax cut and a planned budget deficit. Liberal economists in Europe and in the American universities had been arguing for years that it was no longer necessary to redistribute the wealth of the rich in order to elevate the poor, but that the total production of wealth could be increased to the benefit of everybody if modern technology and fiscal measures were applied.

Kennedy was not by temper a fiscal reformer. He came to the White House as a rather timid liberal, but the longer he was in office the more he cried out against the restraining economic and fiscal traditions of the past and the more he appealed to the country to deal with the world as it is. He never saw his tax bill go through; he died before it was passed. But he was largely responsible for heading the country into the most prolonged period of peacetime prosperity since the last World War. There was a recession when he took over in 1961. Unemployment was up to almost 7 per cent of the work force. There was a balance-of-payments deficit of nearly $4 billion. The outflow of gold to other countries in 1960 totaled $1.7 billion. But by the time he died, this trend had been reversed, at least in part as a result of his initiatives.

THE IMPONDERABLES

Yet even if he turned the tide of the cold war toward the control of nuclear arms, and started the trend toward acceptance of the new economics of increased production and general prosperity, this is not the Kennedy story that is likely to be remembered.

These things were only dramatic symbols of his critical mind. He was a critic of his age. He did not think we could deal with the menace of nuclear weapons unless we searched constantly for means of accommodation with the Communists. He did not think we could employ our people in the midst of a revolution in labor-saving machinery unless we changed our attitude toward federal budgets and federal deficits.

He did not think we could deal with the pressures of Communism, rising population, or galloping automation, or that we could contain the rising expectations of the nonwhite races and the new nations unless we moved faster to integrate the races at home and the nations of the free world abroad. In short, he did not believe we could deal effectively with a transformed world unless we transformed ourselves—our attitudes of mind and our institutions.

This was a youthful mind asking the big questions. He was not one for big plans and grand designs, though contemporary writers often professed to see such things in some of the speeches of Ted Sorensen. Incidentally, it was always difficult to tell when the soaring rhetoric of Sorensen's bolder and more liberal mind left off and the more cautious Kennedy mind picked up, but Kennedy was not a great planner.

I once asked him in a long private talk at Hyannis Port what he wanted to have achieved by the time he rode down Pennsylvania Avenue with his successor. He looked at me as if I were a dreaming child. I tried again: Did he not feel the need of some goal to help guide his day-to-day decisions and priorities? Again a ghastly pause. It was only when I turned the question to immediate, tangible problems that he seized the point and rolled off a torrent of statistics about the difficulty of organizing nations at different levels of economic development.

Yet there is a puzzle in all this. For while he wanted to transform the thought and institutions of the nation, and regarded the machinery of the Congress as almost an anachronism, he concentrated on working—not, on the whole, very successfully—with the Congress, and he never really exploited his considerable gifts as a public educator.

"Give me the right word and the right accent," said Joseph Conrad, "and I will move the world." This was Churchill's way, and nobody admired it more than Kennedy. But while he made a few glorious trial flights, something held him back, some fear of appealing to the people over the heads of the Congress, some fear of too much talk (he hated verbosity), some modesty, maybe—always so apparent in his embarrassment before applauding crowds.

The essence of the tragedy, however, is perfectly clear. What was killed in Dallas was not only the President but the promise. The death of youth and the hope of youth, of the beauty and grace and the touch of magic.

The heart of the Kennedy legend is what might have been. His intelligence made people think that the coming generation might make the world more rational. It even made it hard for the intellectuals of Europe to be anti-American. His good looks and eloquence put a brighter shine on politics, and made his world relevant and attractive to young people all over the world.

All this is apparent in the faces of the people who come to his grave daily on the Arlington hill. In the world of their dreams, Presidents would be young and heroic, with beautiful wives, and the ugly world would be transformed by their examples.

John Finley, the master of Eliot House at Harvard, sent me a letter which sums up this sense of loss better than anything else:

"No doubt, like innumerable people, I feel suddenly old without Mr. and Mrs. Kennedy in the White House. On reflection, ours seems a society of older people; it takes a while to reach the top in science, law, business and most other things. Yet, paradoxically, only the young have the freshness to enjoy and not be wearied by the profusion and vitality of present American life.

"Not only by ability, but by sheer verve and joy, the Kennedys imparted their youth to everyone and put a sheen on our life that made it more youthful than it is. Mr. Johnson now seems Gary Cooper as President—'High Noon,' the poker game, the easy walk and masculine smile. But even Gary Cooper was growing older, and the companions and adversaries around the poker table reflect a less fresh, if no doubt practical and effective, mood. All will be well, I feel sure . . . but it is August, not June. . . ."

Always we come back to the same point. The tragedy of John Fitzgerald Kennedy was greater than the accomplishment, but in the end the tragedy enhances the accomplishment and revives the hope.

Thus the law of compensation operates. "The dice of God are always loaded," wrote Emerson. "For everything you have missed you have gained something else. . . . The world looks like a multiplication table, or a mathematical equation, which, turn it how you will, balances itself. . . . Every secret is told, every crime is punished, every virtue rewarded, every wrong redressed, in silence and certainty."

RICHARD E. NEUSTADT

Kennedy in the Presidency:
A Premature Appraisal

There are many ways to look at the performance of a President of the United States. One way—not the only one—is to assess his operational effectiveness as man in office, a single individual amidst a vast machine. This has been my own approach in previous writings on past Presidents. Regarding our most recent President, John F. Kennedy, it is foolhardy to attempt appraisal in these terms. He died too soon and it is too soon after his death. Still, the *Political Science Quarterly* has asked me to attempt it. And assuming that my readers will indulge the folly, I shall try.

I

In appraising the personal performance of a President it is useful to ask four questions. First, what were his purposes and did these run with or against the grain of history; how relevant were they to what would happen in his time? Second, what was his "feel," his human understanding, for the nature of his power in the circumstances of his time, and how close did he come in this respect to

"Kennedy in the Presidency: A Premature Appraisal" is reprinted with the permission of the *Political Science Quarterly* (Vol. LXXIX, No. 3), September 1964, pp. 321–334.

the realities around him (a matter again of relevance)? Third, what was his stance under pressure in office, what sustained him as a person against the frustrations native to the place, and how did his peace-making with himself affect the style and content of his own decision-making? This becomes especially important now that nuclear technology has equipped both Americans and Russians with an intercontinental capability; stresses on the Presidency grow apace. Fourth, what was his legacy? What imprint did he leave upon the office, its character and public standing; where did he leave his party and the other party nationally; what remained by way of public policies adopted or in controversy; what remained as issues in American society, insofar as his own stance may have affected them; and what was the American position in the world insofar as his diplomacy may have affected it?

With respect to each of these four questions, the outside observer looks for certain clues in seeking answers.

First, regarding purpose, clues are found in irreversible commitments to defined courses of action. By "commitment" I mean nothing so particular as an endorsement for, say, "Medicare," or anything so general as a pledge to "peace." (All Presidents desire peace.) By "course of action" I mean something broader than the one but more definable than the other: Harry S. Truman's commitment to "containment," so called, or Dwight D. Eisenhower's to what he called "fiscal responsibility." By "commitment" I mean personal involvement, in terms of what the man himself is seen to say and do, so plain and so direct that politics—and history—will not let him turn back: Truman on civil rights, or Eisenhower on the Army budget.

Second, regarding feel for office, sensitivity to power, clues are drawn from signs of pattern in the man's own operating style as he encounters concrete cases, cases of decision and of following through in every sphere of action, legislative and executive, public and partisan, foreign and domestic—Truman seeking above all to be decisive; Eisenhower reaching for a place above the struggle.

Third, regarding pressure and its consequences, clues are to be drawn again from cases; here one examines crisis situations, seeking signs of pattern in the man's response—Truman at the time of the Korean outbreak, or of Chinese intervention; Eisenhower at the time of Hungary and Suez, or of Little Rock—times like these compared with others just as tough in terms of stress.

And fourth, regarding the man's legacy, one seeks clues in the conduct of the *next* administration. Roosevelt's first New Deal in 1933 tells us a lot about the Hoover Presidency. Truman's troubled turnabout in postwar foreign policy casts shadows on the later Roosevelt Presidency. And Kennedy's complaint at Yale two years ago about the "myths" retarding economic management is testimony to one part of Eisenhower's legacy, that part identified with the redoubtable George Humphrey.

To list these sources of the wherewithal for answers is to indicate the folly of pursuing my four questions when the object of the exercise is Kennedy-in-office. He was President for two years and ten months. Were one to assess Franklin Roosevelt on the basis of performance before January 1936, or Harry Truman on his accomplishments before enactment of the Marshall Plan, or Eisenhower had he not survived his heart attack—or Lincoln, for that matter, had he been assassinated six months after Gettysburg—one would be most unlikely to reach judgments about any of these men resembling current judgments drawn from the full record of their terms. We cannot know what Kennedy's full record would have been had he escaped assassination. Still more important, we can never know precisely how to weigh events in his truncated term.

Truman's seven years and Eisenhower's eight suggest a certain rhythm in the modern Presidency. The first twelve to eighteen months become a learning time for the new President who has to learn—or unlearn—many things about his job. No matter what his prior training, nothing he has done will have prepared him for all facets of that job. Some aspects of the learning process will persist beyond the first year-and-a-half. Most Presidents will go on making new discoveries as long as they hold office (until at last they learn the bitterness of leaving office). But the intensive learning time comes at the start and dominates the first two years. A President's behavior in those years is an uncertain source of clues to what will follow after, unreliable in indicating what will be the patterns of performance "on the job" once learning has been done. Yet the fourth year is also unreliable; traditionally it brings a period of pause, dominated by a special test requiring special effort—the test of reelection. The way that test is taken tells us much about a President, but less about his conduct on the job in other years. The seventh year is the beginning of the end—now guaranteed by constitutional amendment—as all eyes turn toward the coming nominations and the *next* administration.

So in the search for signs of pattern, clues to conduct, the key years are the third, the fifth, the sixth. Kennedy had only one of these.

Moreover, in this Presidential cycle, retrospect is an essential aid for sorting evidence. What a man does in his later years sheds light on the significance of what he did in early years, distinguishing the actions which conform to lasting patterns from the aspects of behavior which were transient. The man's early performance will include a host of clues to what is typical throughout his term of office. But it also will include assorted actions which turn out to be unrepresentative. Looking back from later years these become easy to distinguish. But in the second or the third year it is hard indeed to say, "This action, this behavior will be dominant throughout." That is the sort of statement best reserved for retrospect. Kennedy's case leaves no room for retrospect; he was cut off too early in the cycle. (And when it comes to sorting out the legacy he left, Lyndon Johnson has not yet been long enough in office.)

No scholar, therefore, should have the temerity to undertake what follows.

II

Turning to appraise this President in office, I come to my first question, the question of purpose. This is not a matter of initial "ideology," fixed intent; far from it. Franklin Roosevelt did not enter office bent upon becoming "traitor to his class." Truman did not swear the oath with any notion that he was to take this country into the cold war. Lincoln certainly did not assume the Presidency to gain the title of "Great Emancipator." The purposes of Presidents are not to be confused with their intentions at the start; they are a matter, rather, of responses to events. Nor should they be confused with signs of temperament, with "passion." Whether Kennedy was "passionate" or not is scarcely relevant. Truman certainly deserves to have the cause of civil rights cited among his purposes, but were he to be judged in temperamental terms according to the standards of, say, Eastern liberals, he scarcely could be called a man of passion on the point. And F.D.R. goes down historically as "Labor's friend," although his coolness toward the greatest show of that friendship in his time, the Wagner Act, remained until he sensed that it was sure to be enacted. What counts here is not "passion," but the words and acts that lead to irreversible *commitment*.

In his three years of office, what were Kennedy's commitments? Never mind his private thoughts at twenty, or at forty; never mind his preferences for one thing or another; never mind his distaste for a passionate display—taking the real world as he found it, what attracted his commitment in the sense that he identified himself beyond recall?

The record will, I think, disclose at least three purposes so understood: First, above all others, most compelling, most intense, was a commitment to reduce the risk of holocaust by *mutual* miscalculation, to "get the nuclear genie back in the bottle," to render statecraft manageable by statesmen, tolerable for the rest of us. He did not aim at anything so trite (or unachievable) as "victory" in the cold war. His aim, apparently, was to outlast it with American society intact and nuclear risks in check. Nothing, I think, mattered more to Kennedy than bottling that genie. This, I know, was deeply in his mind. It also was made manifest in words, among them his address at American University on June 10, 1963. That speech is seal and symbol of this purpose. But other signs are found in acts, as well, and in more private words accompanying action: from his Vienna interview with Khrushchev, through the Berlin crisis during 1961, to the Cuban missile crisis and thereafter—this commitment evidently deepened with experience as Kennedy responded to events.

Another speech in June of 1963 stands for a second purpose: the speech on civil rights, June 11, and the message to Congress eight days later launched Kennedy's campaign for what became the Civil Rights Act of 1964. Thereby he undertook an irreversible commitment to Negro integration in American society, aiming once again to get us through the effort with society intact. He evidently came to see the risks of social alienation as plainly as he saw the risks of nuclear escalation, and he sought to steer a course toward integration which could hold inside our social order both impatient Negroes and reactive whites—as tough a task of politics as any we have known, and one he faced no sooner than he had to. But he faced it. What Vienna, Berlin, Cuba were to his first purpose, Oxford and then Birmingham were to this second purpose: events which shaped his personal commitment.

A third speech is indicative of still another purpose, a speech less known and a commitment less apparent, though as definite, I think, as both of the others: Kennedy's commencement speech at Yale on June 11, 1962, soon after his short war with Roger Blough. He spoke of making our complex economy, our somewhat *sui generis* economy, function effectively for meaningful growth, and as the means he urged an end-of-ideology in problem-solving. His speech affirmed the notion that the key problems of economic growth are technical, not ideological, to be met not by passion but by intellect, and that the greatest barriers to growth are the ideas in people's heads—"myths" as he called them—standing in the way of reasoned diagnosis and response. Kennedy, I think, was well aware (indeed he was made painfully aware) that only on our one-time Left is ideology defunct. Elsewhere it flourishes, clamping a lid upon applied intelligence, withholding brainpower from rational engagement in the novel problems of our economic management. He evidently wanted most of all to lift that lid.

Failing a response to his Yale lecture, Kennedy retreated to the easier task of teaching one simple economic lesson, the lesson of the recent tax reduction: well-timed budget deficits can lead to balanced budgets. This, evidently, was the most that he thought he could manage in contesting "myths," at least before election. But his ambition, I believe, was to assault a lot more myths than this, when and as he could. That ambition measures his commitment to effective growth in the economy.

Stemming from this third commitment (and the second) one discerns a corollary which perhaps would have become a fourth: what Kennedy's successor now has named "the war against poverty." During the course of 1963, Kennedy became active in promoting plans for an attack on chronic poverty. His prospective timing no doubt had political utility, but it also had social utility which evidently mattered quite as much. Historically, the "war" is Lyndon Johnson's. All we know of Kennedy is that he meant to make one. Still, for either of these men the effort, if sustained, would lead to irreversible commitment.

Each purpose I have outlined meant commitment to a course of action which engaged the man—his reputation, *amour propre,* and sense of self in history—beyond recall. The question then becomes: how relevant were these, historically? How relevant to Kennedy's own years of actual (and of prospective) office? Here I can only make a judgment, tentative of course, devoid of long perspective. These purposes seem to me entirely relevant. In short perspective, they seem precisely right as the pre-eminent concerns for the first half of this decade.

III

So much for Kennedy as man-of-purpose. What about the man-of-power?

He strikes me as a senator who learned very fast from his confrontation with the executive establishment, particularly after the abortive Cuban invasion which taught him a great deal. On action-issues of particular concern to him he rapidly evolved an operating style whch he maintained consistently (and sharpened at the edges) through his years of office. If one looks at Berlin, or Oxford, Mississippi, or the Cuban missile crisis, or at half a dozen other issues of the sort, one finds a pattern: the personal command post, deliberate reaching down for the details, hard questioning of the alternatives, a drive to protect options from foreclosure by sheer urgency or by *ex parte* advocacy, finally a close watch on follow-through. Even on the issues which were secondary to the President and left, perforce, primarily to others, Kennedy was constantly in search of means and men to duplicate at one remove this personalized pattern with its stress on open options and on close control. Numbers of outsiders—Hans Morgenthau and Joseph Alsop for two—sometimes viewed the pattern with alarm and saw this man as "indecisive." But that was to consult *their* preferences, not his performance. Kennedy seemed always keen to single out the necessary from the merely possible. He then decided with alacrity.

Not everything was always done effectively, of course, and even the successes produced side effects of bureaucratic bafflement, frustration, irritation which were not without their costs. Even so, the pattern testifies to an extraordinary feel for the distinction between President and Presidency, an extraordinary urge to master the machine. This took him quite a way toward mastery in two years and ten months. We shall not know how far he might have got.

Kennedy's feel for his own executive position carried over into that of fellow rulers everywhere. He evidently had great curiosity and real concern about the politics of rulership wherever he encountered it. His feel for fine distinctions among fellow "kings" was rare, comparable to the feel of Senate Leader Johnson for the fine distinctions among fellow senators. And with this Kennedy apparently absorbed in his short time a lesson Franklin Roosevelt never learned about the Russians (or de Gaulle): that in another country an *effective* politician can have motives very *different* from his own. What an advantageous lesson to have learned in two years' time! It would have served him well. Indeed, while he still lived I think it did.

The cardinal test of Kennedy as an executive in his own right and also as a student of executives abroad was certainly the confrontation of October 1962, the Cuban missile crisis with Khrushchev. For almost the first time in our foreign relations, the President displayed on that occasion both concern for the psychology of his opponent and insistence on a limited objective. Contrast the Korean War, where we positively courted Chinese intervention by relying on Douglas MacArthur as psychologist and by enlarging our objective after each success. "There is no substitute for victory," MacArthur wrote, but at that time we virtually had a nuclear monopoly and even then our government hastened to find a substitute. Now, with mutual capability, the whole traditional meaning has been taken out of "victory." In nuclear confrontations there is room for no such thing. Kennedy quite evidently knew it. He also knew, as his performance demonstrates, that risks of escalation lurk in high-level misjudgments *and* in low-level momentum. Washington assuredly was capable of both; so, probably, was Moscow. Accordingly, the President outstripped all previous efforts to guard options and assure control. His operating style was tested then as not before or after. It got him what he wanted.

In confrontations with Congress, quite another world than the executive, the key to Kennedy's congressional relations lay outside his feel for power, beyond reach of technique; he won the Presidency by a hair, while in the House of Representatives his party lost some twenty of the seats gained two years earlier. The Democrats *retained* a sizeable majority as they had done in earlier years, no thanks to him. With this beginning, Kennedy's own record of accomplishment in Congress looks enormous, indeterminate, or small, depending on one's willingness to give him credit for enactment of the most divisive, innovative bills he espoused: the tax and civil rights bills passed in Johnson's Presidency. Certainly it can be said that Kennedy prepared the way, negotiating a bipartisan approach, and also that he took the heat, stalling his whole program in the process. Equally, it can be said that with his death—or by it—the White House gained advantages which he could not have mustered. Johnson made the most of these. How well would Kennedy have done without them? My own guess is that in the end, with rancor and delay, both bills would have been passed. But it is a moot point. Accordingly, so is the Kennedy record.

Whatever his accomplishment, does it appear the most he could have managed in his years? Granting the limits set by his election, granting the divisiveness injected after Birmingham with his decisive move on civil rights, did he use to the fullest his advantages of office? The answer may well be "not quite." Perhaps a better answer is, "This man could do no more." For Kennedy, it seems, was not a man enamored of the legislative way of life and legislators knew it. He was wry about it. He had spent fourteen years in Congress and he understood its business, but he never was a "member of the family" on the Hill. "Downtown" had always seemed his native habitat; he was a natural executive. They knew that, too. Besides, he was a young man, very young by Senate standards, and his presence in the White House with still younger men around him was a constant irritant to seniors. Moreover, he was not a "mixer" socially, not, anyway, with most members of Congress and their wives. His manners were impeccable, his charm impelling, but he kept his social life distinct from his official life and congressmen were rarely in his social circle. To know how Congress works but to disdain its joys is an acquired taste for most ex-congressmen downtown, produced by hard experience. Kennedy, however, brought it with him. Many of the difficulties he was to encounter in his day-by-day congressional relations stemmed from that.

But even had he been a man who dearly loved the Congress, even had that feeling been reciprocated, nothing could have rendered their relationship sweetness-and-light in his last year, so long as he persisted with his legislative program. As an innovative President confronting a reluctant Congress, he was heir to Truman, and to Roosevelt after 1936. Kennedy's own manner may have hurt him on the Hill, but these were scratches. Deeper scars had more substantial sources and he knew it.

In confrontations with the larger public outside Washington (again a different world), Kennedy made a brilliant beginning, matched only by the start in different circumstances of his own successor. The "public relations" of transition into office were superb. In three months after his election, Kennedy transformed himself from "pushy," "young," "Catholic," into President-of-all-the-people, widening and deepening acceptance of his Presidency out of all proportion to the election returns. The Bay of Pigs was a severe check, but his handling of the aftermath displayed again superb feel for the imagery befitting an incumbent of the White House, heir to F.D.R. *and* Eisenhower. That feel he always had. I think it never failed him.

What he also had was a distaste for preaching, really for the preachiness of politics, backed by genuine mistrust of mass emotion as a tool in politics. These attitudes are rare among American politicians; with Kennedy their roots ran deep into recesses of experience and character where I, as an outsider, cannot follow. But they assuredly were rooted in this man and they had visible effects upon his public style. He delighted in the play of minds, not of emotions. He doted on press conferences, not set performances. He feared "overexposure"; he dreaded overreaction. Obviously he enjoyed responsive crowds, and was himself responsive to a sea of cheering faces, but I think he rarely looked at their reaction—or his own—without a twinge of apprehension. He never seems to have displayed much fondness for the "fireside chat," a form of crowd appeal without the crowd; television talks in evening hours evidently struck him more as duty than as opportunity, and dangerous at that; some words on air-raid shelters in a talk about Berlin could set off mass hysteria—and did. At the moment when he had his largest, most attentive audience, on the climactic Sunday of the Cuban missile crisis, he turned it away (and turned attention off) with a two-minute announcement, spare and dry.

Yet we know now, after his death, what none of us knew before: that with a minimum of preaching, of emotional appeal, or of self-justification, even explanation, he had managed to touch millions in their private lives, not only at home but emphatically abroad. Perhaps his very coolness helped him do it. Perhaps his very vigor, family, fortune, sense of fun, his manners, taste, and sportsmanship, his evident enjoyment of his life and of the job made him the heart's desire of all sorts of people everywhere, not least among the young. At any rate, we know now that he managed in his years to make enormous impact on a world-wide audience, building an extraordinary base of public interest and affection (interspersed, of course, with doubters and detractors). What he might have made of this or done with it in later years, nobody knows.

IV

So much for power; what of pressure? What sustained this man in his decisions, his frustrations, and with what effect on his approach to being President? For an answer one turns to the evidence of crises, those already mentioned among others, and the *surface* signs are clear. In all such situations it appears that Kennedy was cool, collected, courteous, and terse. This does not mean that he was unemotional. By temperament I think he was a man of mood and passion. But he had schooled his temperament. He kept his own emotions under tight control. He did not lose his temper inadvertently, and never lost it long. He was observer and participant combined; he saw himself as coolly as all others—and with humor. He always was a witty man, dry with a bit of bite and a touch of self-deprecation. He could laugh at himself, and did. Often he used humor to break tension. And in tight places he displayed a keen awareness of the human situation, human limits, his included, but it did not slow his work.

Readers over forty may recognize this portrait as "the stance of junior officers in the Second World War"; Elspeth Rostow coined that phrase and, superficially at least, she is quite right. This was the Kennedy stance and his self-confidence, his shield against frustration, must have owed a lot to his young manhood in that war.

This tells us a good deal but not nearly enough. At his very first encounter with a crisis in the Presidency, Kennedy's self-confidence seems to have been severely strained. The Bay of Pigs fiasco shook him deeply, shook his confidence in methods and associates. Yet he went on governing without a break, no change in manner, or in temper, or in humor. What sustained him? Surely much that went beyond experience of war.

What else? I cannot answer. I can only conjecture. His family life and rearing have some part to play, no doubt. His political successes also: in 1952 he bucked the Eisenhower tide to reach the Senate; in 1960 he broke barriers of youth and of religion which had always held before; on each occasion the Conventional Wisdom was against him: "can't be done." Beyond these things, this man had been exceptionally close to death, not only in the war but ten years after. And in his Presidential years his back was almost constantly a source of pain; he never talked about it but he lived with it. All this is of a piece with his behavior in a crisis. His control, his objectivity, his humor, and his sense of human limits, these were but expressions of his confidence; its sources must lie somewhere in this ground.

Whatever the sources, the results were rewarding for this President's performance on the job. In the most critical, nerve-straining aspects of the office, coping with its terrible responsibility for use of force, Kennedy's own image of himself impelled him neither to lash out nor run for cover. Rather, it released him for engagement and decision as a reasonable man. In some of the less awesome aspects of the Presidency, his own values restrained him, kept him off the pulpit, trimmed his guest list, made him shy away from the hyperbole of politics. But as a chief *executive,* confronting action-issues for decision and control, his duty and his confidence in doing it were nicely matched. So the world discovered in October 1962.

V

Now for my last question. What did John Kennedy leave behind him? What was the legacy of his short years? At the very least he left a myth: the vibrant, youthful leader cut down senselessly before his time. What this may come to signify as the years pass, I cannot tell. He left a glamorous moment, an engaging, youthful time, but how we shall remember it depends on what becomes of Lyndon Johnson. He left a broken promise, that "the torch has been passed to a new generation," and the youngsters who identified with him felt cheated as the promise, like the glamor, disappeared. What do their feelings matter? We shall have to wait and see.

May this be all that history is likely to record? Perhaps, but I doubt it. My guess is that when the observers can appraise the work of Kennedy's successors, they will find some things of substance in his legacy. Rashly, let me record what I think these are.

To begin with, our first Catholic President chose and paved the way for our first Southern President since the Civil War. (Woodrow Wilson was no Southerner *politically;* he came to the White House from the State House of New Jersey.) While Texas may be suspect now in Southern eyes, it certainly is of the South in Northern eyes, as Johnson found so painfully in 1960. Kennedy made him President. How free the choice of Johnson as Vice-Presidential candidate is subject to some argument. But what appears beyond dispute is that once chosen, Johnson was so treated by his rival for the White House as to ease his way enormously when he took over there. Johnson may have suffered great frustration as Vice-President, but his public standing and his knowledge of affairs were nurtured in those years. From this he gained a running start. The credit goes in no small part to Kennedy.

Moreover, Kennedy bequeathed to Johnson widened options in the sphere of foreign relations: a military posture far more flexible and usable than he himself inherited; a diplomatic posture more sophisticated in its whole approach to neutralists and leftists, markedly more mindful of distinctions in the world, even among allies.

On the domestic side, Kennedy left a large inheritance of controversies, opened by a youthful, Catholic urbanite from the Northeast, which his Southwestern, Protestant successor might have had more trouble stirring at the start, but now can ride and maybe even "heal." This may turn out to have been a productive division of labor. However it turns out, Kennedy lived long enough to keep at least one promise. He got the country "moving again." For in our politics, the *sine qua non* of innovative policy is controversy. By 1963 we were engaged in controversy with an openness which would have been unthinkable, or at least "un-American," during the later Eisenhower years.

Events, of course, have more to do with stirring controversy than a President. No man can make an issue on his own. But Presidents will help to shape the meaning of events, the terms of discourse, the attention paid, the noise-level. Eisenhower's years were marked by a pervasive fog of self-congratulation, muffling noise. The fog-machine was centered in the White House. Perhaps there had been need for this after the divisive Truman years. By the late nineteen-fifties, though, it fuzzed our chance to innovate in time. Kennedy broke out of it.

Finally, this President set a new standard of performance on the job, suitable to a new state of Presidential being, a state he was the first to face throughout his term of office: the state of substantial, deliverable, nuclear capability in other hands than ours. Whatever else historians may make of Kennedy, I think them likely to begin with this. There can be little doubt that his successors have a lighter task because *he* pioneered in handling nuclear confrontations. During the Cuban missile crisis and thereafter, he did something which had not been done before, did it well, and got it publicly accepted. His innovation happened to be timely, since the need for innovation was upon us; technology had put it there. But also, in his reach for information and control, his balancing of firmness with caution, his sense of limits, he displayed and dramatized what Presidents must do to minimize the risk of war through mutual miscalculation. This may well be the cardinal risk confronting his successors. If so, he made a major contribution to the Presidency.

RICHARD H. ROVERE

From "Letter from Washington" by Richard H. Rovere in *The New Yorker*

The familiar measures of political effectiveness, diplomatic skill, and the ability to preserve national unity are quite inadequate for appraising the Republic's loss. As a chief magistrate, performing the functions required of him by his oath, John Kennedy was, as they say in the Senate, able and distinguished. He was also subtle, imaginative, daring, and—to use a word he liked—prudent. He had, then, most of the qualities that are called for in a statesman if the statesman is to do the single most important thing required of him, which is, specifically, to keep the ship of state from being blown out of the water—to keep everything from going to hell and gone. Lincoln and Roosevelt were great because they performed prodigies of rescue and salvage, because they kept the worst from happening. Kennedy had two superb moments as a statesman. In the first, during the Cuban crisis in October of last year, he did what was essentially a job of high-class fire prevention. In the second, when he proclaimed a state of "moral crisis" in June of this year, he did something a bit more creative. He used words to shame his countrymen, to make them look at the squalor about them. To be sure, it took only normal vision to see that there was a "moral crisis" in the United States in the summer of 1963. It was no less apparent than the earlier "missile crisis." What

---

"Letter from Washington" is from *The New Yorker*, November 30, 1963. Reprinted by permission; © 1963 The New Yorker Magazine, Inc.

Kennedy undertook was a rescue job, begun close to the point of despair.

Again, this is what a statesman does, or what a good statesman does. Many statesmen do less. The opportunity to do more is rarely given to anyone—and, as often as not, when it is given, and grasped, disaster ensues, and the fire department must be called. In doing the things that simply had to be done, Kennedy had, as a rule, uncommon skill and finesse and very sharp eyes. It was not, however, his primary gift for politics that created—especially in the first days but also whenever, in the days that followed, history allowed him a few easy breaths and a bit of time for speculation— the air of excitement and immense possibility that could be felt in Washington, whether or not it was felt much outside. What made for excitement was that Kennedy and those who were closest to him—those whom he had freely chosen to associate himself with—had large, bold aims and a large, expansive view of life. There was not a reformer among them, as far as anyone could tell. Pragmatism—often of the grubbiest kind—was rampant. "Facts" were often valued beyond their worth. "Ideology" was held in contempt—too much so, perhaps—and was described as a prime source of mischief in the world. But if there were no do-gooders around, and no planners, and not even, really, very much in the way of plans, there were large thoughts and large intentions and very long looks into the future. Under Kennedy, for the first time in American history, a foreign policy was being fashioned that looked several administrations ahead, several decades ahead, several adversaries ahead. The unitary, jihad view of foreign affairs that had dominated American thinking for so long was scrapped— and without anyone's saying much about it. There was more to the world that Kennedy saw than the cold war. The aim of his disarmament policy was not merely to relax tensions in the years in which he thought he would be responsible for American diplomacy but to de-fuse conflict in a world that can thus far only be imagined, and even now can hardly be mentioned—one in which there could be higher tensions than any the cold war ever generated. Kennedy was never concerned with "winning" the cold war. He saw that it wasn't going to be won or lost, and that one real danger was that unless the United States composed its differences with the Soviet Union, its power to influence events would decline in those parts of the world where the cold war would be regarded, properly, as an irrelevancy.

There were many such enterprises, some of them less abstract and inherently more interesting. Kennedy's mind was not a philosophical tool but a critical one. He had, above all, a critical intelligence and a critical temper—these, and a curiosity as broad as Montaigne's. He was interested in and amused by and critical of everything in American life. His zest for simply watching the show was as great as H. L. Mencken's. His curiosity seemed at times not only astonishing in itself but almost frivolous, almost perverse; he would spend time (government time) talking and bothering about things in a way that somehow seemed idle and improper for a man who should have been thinking about Khrushchev, de Gaulle, and the tax bill—the typography of a newspaper, for example, and how much it offended him, and how it might be improved. This critical bent, though, was the important, stimulating thing. He could not, with his sort of mind, look at American life and think that everything would be jim-dandy if we just had Medicare and stepped up production in our engineer factories and got Negroes into nice, clean motels. As he was the first Abolitionist President (in the sense that he was the first to take office with the conviction, not passionate but sturdy, that no form of segregation or discrimination was morally defensible), so he was the first modern President who gave one a sense of caring—and of believing that a President ought to care—about the whole quality and tone of American life. (Theodore Roosevelt and Woodrow Wilson had some of this, but not so much. The others either have not cared or have been hobbyists of a sort—like Franklin Roosevelt, with his dabbling in architecture.) Kennedy's concern with motels was not only with whether Negroes should get into them but with the *idea* of motels—with their function, with the way they looked, with the strange names they bore, and with what they revealed about us. His concern with urban rot and the urban sprawl was not simply that of the criminologist or the social worker or the transit engineer but that of the man who recoils at ugliness and vulgarity and intellectual impoverishment whether or not they are associated with juvenile delinquency, unemployment, and so on. His concern with education ran far deeper than his publicly expressed concern over whether there was, quantitatively, enough of it and whether it should have federal aid and on what basis; he was interested in its character and in the direction it was taking—in whether it was any good or not.

His interests far outran his mandate; some of them, indeed, may have been unconstitutional. He proposed to have, in time, an impact on American taste. He proposed to impress upon the country—to make it, if he could, share—his own respect for excellence of various kinds. His respect for excellence was, he knew, greater than his capacity for identifying it and appreciating it. He himself did not respond much to painting or music, or even to literature—though as a rule he found his attention riveted by almost anything in print—but he looked at paintings he didn't enjoy, and listened to music he didn't much care for, because people who he thought were excellent people had told him they were excellent things, and he wished his own patronage (the picture of him alertly pursuing self-improvement) to win from others the appreciation of those things that their excellence merited. In any man but a President—and perhaps even in a President —this sort of thing might be the opposite of admirable; the father who lays down Mickey Spillane long enough to tell his bored son that every American boy should have a fine time reading "Il Penseroso" is a sinner of some kind. But Kennedy did believe— and did act upon the belief—that a President of the United States could do more than help insure domestic tranquility, secure the blessings of liberty, and the rest. He thought that a President might help a fundamentally good society to become a good, even a brilliant, civilization. And it pleased him to think of himself as a promoter, an impresario. He was a shrewd enough observer to know that there are always a number of Americans who look in the mirror and see reflected there the President of the United States—or who make certain alterations that will enable them to see that reflection. (This didn't take much shrewdness when new trends in male and female hair styles began to develop a few years back, or when the Casals White House record began to sell—he kept checking the sales figures as though he had been cut in on the royalties—or when the mail began to come in from people who

were taking up calisthenics and hiking.) What Truman did for
sports shirts, what Eisenhower did for golf, Kennedy planned—
with the most deliberate kind of intent—to do for the things and
the people and the institutions he thought excellent, and thus
deserving. Perhaps in death he will gain more immediate success
than he would have gained if he had lived on. It will hardly be fair
to him, though, if it happens that way. He wished to do it by sneak
plays of his own devising.

It was not Kennedy's little promotions—Casals, Robert Frost,
the Mona Lisa, French cooking, Ian Fleming, Harvard College,
Stravinsky, Whig history, the *London Observer*—that were stimulating but, rather, the idea that he might do something to advance
American civilization. And if this idea has, as it must have, a
fatuous sound, that was somehow part of it; it was moving and
exciting in its fatuousness. What was also moving, and not at all
fatuous, was the admiration for excellence that led Kennedy to
surround himself, as much as he could, with the best people our
present civilization has to offer, and to give them, as much as he
could, their heads. If he had to rely on the judgment of others for
the identification of excellence in the arts and the sciences, his
instinct for excellence in people was, if not unerring, fine—itself
excellent. (It was pretty close to unerring if one counts only those
with whom he surrounded himself in government, and leaves out
of account some of those he had about him at such times as he
wearied of cerebration and high policy.) He had simply enormous
confidence in broad, general, generalizing human intelligence.
Mere expertise seemed to bother him, possibly because he had
little of it himself, in anything. He was an educated man, not a
trained one. At any rate, he felt that any adequately educated man
with a really good head on his shoulders could get on top of just
about any problem that a President was likely to face. When he
found a brilliant young man like Theodore Sorensen, he commis-
sioned him to function as an expert on anything that came along.
McGeorge Bundy became his principal adviser on foreign policy
with qualifications that no other recent President would have given
two cents for. Bundy had worked on a couple of books about
Henry Stimson and Dean Acheson, but his experience in the field
of his responsibilities was almost nonexistent; he had done a good

job of pulling things together on the Harvard faculty, and Kennedy took him on to pull things together in the world. Adam Yarmolinsky, a lawyer who had served a hitch as an editor in a publishing house, was put in the Pentagon to see if mere reason and common sense could be applied to its staggering problems of organization and finance. The impact he has had on the military establishment—as one of the chief Whiz Kids, the computerized intellectual task force that so enrages Senator McClellan—has probably been as great as that of most civilian secretaries or most members of the Joint Chiefs of Staff. Perhaps the most striking case of this kind, though surely the least known, is that of Richard N. Goodwin, a lawyer who hadn't turned thirty when Kennedy engaged him, and who has spent the last three years jumping all over the government. Goodwin became Mr. Justice Frankfurter's law clerk in 1958. Upon finishing that apprenticeship, he went as an investigator to the House committee that was looking into the rigging of television quiz shows. He then came to the attention of Robert Kennedy, who brought him to the attention of his brother, who took him on, late in 1959, as a speech writer. He could, it turned out, write about anything—briskly, and by the yard—because, it turned out, he knew about everything, or knew something about everything. One thing he did not know very much about was Latin America. Before the President took office, it was announced that Goodwin would be one of the new Administration's experts on that difficult region. He studied hard and became an authority; he is today acknowledged as one both here and in Latin America. Goodwin went into the White House, and worked on Latin America and much else. He was the principal architect of the Alliance for Progress. He went from the White House to the State Department, where he got the treatment that amateurs generally get from professionals; he was thereupon taken out and put in the Peace Corps, where he put together and headed an International Secretariat; and this coming week he was scheduled to go back into the White House, as, of all things, the President's Consultant on the Arts. The most revealing part of this story is that whatever his title happened to be at the moment, his relationship to John F. Kennedy was the same and his functions were pretty much the same. He wrote speeches on everything, he continued to be an important expert on Latin America, and he was an adviser on the arts long before it was decided to give him such a title. He decided one day early in 1961 that this country should really do something about saving the Nile monuments, and he worked out a plan, which was followed. More recently, he addressed himself to a scheme for getting around the congressional resistance to foreign aid by finding congenial projects in this field that state governments could undertake. He kicked this off last year by persuading the state of California to undertake a program of aid to Chile, on goodness knows what theory—perhaps just that Chile is also long and narrow and washed by the Pacific.

It is unlikely that any other President in our time will operate in such a fashion. But Kennedy's reliance on general excellence received one great vindication, more or less in reverse. Only once, on a really crucial matter, did he close his ears to his generalists and rely wholly on expertise. That was, of course, the Bay of Pigs, when the people who knew the most were shown to know the least, and those who used nothing much more than the brains God gave them were proved mostly right. Among the generalists he stood first, for he was the one who had felt the gravest skepticism. He cursed himself for suppressing it. No mistake of a similar nature or of comparable magnitude was subsequently made. The things he can now be said to have accomplished are few in number, but he was prepared—indeed, he found the prospect far from dismaying—to go through two terms and face just such a judgment on his accomplishments. Once, early in 1962, his artist friend William Walton brought to the President's office a scale model of the projected remodelling of Lafayette Square. The President spent an inordinate amount of time talking about it and moving little pieces around. Walton was embarrassed. He apologized for detaining the President so long over a matter that was so far from earth-shaking —so far, even, from nation-shaking. "No, let's stay with it," the President said. "Hell, this may be the only thing I'll ever really get done." Kennedy wished very much to be known and written about as a great President, and he took a chance on having history judge him not for the things he actually completed in his time but for the things he set in motion, the energies he released, the people and ideas he encouraged, the style he brought to the Presidency. Even now it is possible to say that he set a great deal in motion, that he organized a generation of public servants who will be serving Presidents (and perhaps being Presidents) into the next century, that he made thinking respectable in Washington, and that he brought to the Presidency a genuinely distinctive style, which is bound, in time, to be emulated.

THEODORE C. SORENSEN

Epilogue

On November 22 [John F. Kennedy's] future merged with his past, and we will never know what might have been. His own inner drive, as well as the swift pace of our times, had enabled him to do more in the White House in three years than many had done in eight—to live a fuller life in forty-six years than most men do in eighty. But that only makes all the greater our loss of the years he was denied.

How, then, will history judge him? It is too early to say. I am too close to say. But history will surely record that his achievements exceeded his years. In an eloquent letter to President Kennedy on nuclear testing, Prime Minister Macmillan once wrote: "It is not the things one did in one's life that one regrets, but rather the opportunities missed." It can be said of John Kennedy that he missed very few opportunities.

In less than three years he presided over a new era in American race relations, a new era in American-Soviet relations, a new era in our Latin-American relations, a new era in fiscal and economic policy and a new era in space exploration. His Presidency helped launch the longest and strongest period of economic expansion in our peacetime history, the largest and swiftest build-up of our defensive strength in peacetime history, and new and enlarged roles for the federal government in higher education, mental

This selection is from Theodore C. Sorensen's *Kennedy*, pp. 756–758. Copyright © 1965 by Theodore C. Sorensen. Reprinted by permission of Harper & Row, Publishers.

affliction, civil rights and the conservation of human and natural resources.

Some moves were dramatic, such as the Cuban missile crisis and the test-ban treaty and the Peace Corps and the Alliance for Progress. Some were small day-by-day efforts on Berlin or Southeast Asia, where no real progress could be claimed, or on school dropouts or National Parks. Some were simply holding our own— no nation slipped into the Communist orbit, no nuclear war raised havoc on our planet, no new recession set back our economy. But generally Kennedy was not content to hold his own. His efforts were devoted to turning the country around, starting it in new directions, getting it moving again. "He believed," said his wife, "that one man can make a difference and that every man should try." He left the nation a whole new set of basic premises—on freedom now instead of someday for the American Negro—on dampening down instead of "winning" the cold war—on the unthinkability instead of the inevitability of nuclear war—on cutting taxes in times of deficit—on battling poverty in times of prosperity—on trade, transportation and a host of other subjects.

For the most part, on November 22, these problems had not been solved and these projects had not been completed. Even most of those completed will impress historians a generation from now only if this generation makes the most of them.

But I suspect that history will remember John Kennedy for what he started as well as for what he completed. The forces he released in this world will be felt for generations to come. The standards he set, the goals he outlined and the talented men he attracted to politics and public service will influence his country's course for at least a decade.

People will remember not only what he did but what he stood for—and this, too, may help the historians assess his Presidency. He stood for excellence in an era of indifference—for hope in an era of doubt—for placing public service ahead of private interests—for reconciliation between East and West, black and white, labor and management. He had confidence in man and gave men confidence in the future.

The public complacency plaguing his efforts was partly due to a sense of hopelessness—that wars and recessions and poverty and political mediocrity could not be avoided, and that all the problems of the modern world were too complex to be understood, let alone unraveled. I believe that John Kennedy believed that his role as President was to initiate an era of hope—hope for a life of decency and equality, hope for a world of reason and peace, hope for the American destiny.

It will not be easy for historians to compare John Kennedy with his predecessors and successors, for he was unique in his imprint upon the office: the first to be elected at so young an age, the first from the Catholic faith, the first to take office in an age of mutual nuclear capabilities, the first to reach literally for the moon and beyond, the first to prevent a new recession or inflation in modern peacetime, the first to pronounce that all racial segregation and discrimination must be abolished as a matter of right, the first to meet our adversaries in a potentially nuclear confrontation, the first to take a solid step toward nuclear arms control—and the first to die at so young an age.

He was not the first President to take on Big Steel, nor was he the first to send a controversial treaty to the Senate, nor was he the first to meet state defiance with federal forces, nor was he the first to seek reform in a coordinate branch of government. But he may well have been the first to win all those encounters. Indeed, all his life he was a winner until November, 1963. In battle he became a hero. In literature he won a Pulitzer Prize. In politics he reached the Presidency. His Inaugural, his wife, his children, his policies, his conduct of crises, all reflected his pursuit of excellence.

History and posterity must decide. Customarily they reserve the mantle of greatness for those who win great wars, not those who prevent them. But in my unobjective view I think it will be difficult to measure John Kennedy by any ordinary historical yardstick. For he was an extraordinary man, an extraordinary politician and an extraordinary President. Just as no chart on the history of weapons could accurately reflect the advent of the atom, so it is my belief that no scale of good and bad Presidents can rate John Fitzgerald Kennedy. A mind so free of fear and myth and prejudice, so opposed to cant and clichés, so unwilling to feign or be fooled, to accept or reflect mediocrity, is rare in our world—and even rarer in American politics. Without demeaning any of the great men who have held the Presidency in this century, I do not see how John Kennedy could be ranked below any one of them.

His untimely and violent death will affect the judgment of historians, and the danger is that it will relegate his greatness to legend. Even though he was himself almost a legendary figure in life, Kennedy was a constant critic of the myth. It would be an ironic twist of fate if his martyrdom should now make a myth of the mortal man.

In my view, the man was greater than the legend. His life, not his death, created his greatness. In November, 1963, some saw it for the first time. Others realized that they had too casually accepted it. Others mourned that they had not previously admitted it to themselves. But the greatness was there, and it may well loom even larger as the passage of years lends perspective.

One of the doctors at the Parkland Hospital in Dallas, observing John Kennedy's six-foot frame on the operating table, was later heard to remark: "I had never seen the President before. He was a big man, bigger than I thought."

He was a big man—much bigger than anyone thought—and all of us are better for having lived in the days of Kennedy.

Contributors

ALEXANDER M. BICKEL, a lawyer and former clerk to Justice Felix Frankfurter, is now professor in the Yale Law School. His writings include *The Unpublished Opinions of Mr. Justice Brandeis* and *The Least Dangerous Branch*.

MCGEORGE BUNDY was Dean of the Faculty of Arts and Sciences at Harvard before becoming special assistant to President Kennedy for national security affairs. Co-author of *On Active Service,* he is now President of the Ford Foundation.

WILLIAM G. CARLETON, a political scientist at the University of Florida, was an occasional speech adviser to Ambassador Joseph P. Kennedy in the early 1940's. He is the author of *The Revolution in American Foreign Policy.*

DOUGLASS CATER was the Washington editor of *Reporter* magazine from 1950 to 1963 and national affairs editor until 1964 when he became special assistant to President Johnson. He has written *The Fourth Branch of Government* and is co-author of *Ethics in a Business Society.*

SEYMOUR E. HARRIS was a member of the Harvard economics department for many years and is now chairman of the department of economics at the University of California at San Diego. He is a trustee of the John F. Kennedy Library. Two of his numerous books are *Foreign Economic Relations of the United States* and *The Economics of the Political Parties*.

DAVID HOROWITZ holds a master's degree from the University of California, Berkeley, and is now a doctoral candidate at the London School of Economics. He has taught at the University of Maryland in England and is the author of *The Free World Colossus* and *Shakespeare: An Existential View*.

CARROLL KILPATRICK has been a Washington correspondent for over a generation and has been a staff writer for *The Washington Post* since 1952. He is co-author of *The Kennedy Circle* and editor of *Roosevelt and Daniels: A Friendship in Politics*.

LOUIS KOENIG is professor of government at New York University. One of his many books is *The Invisible Presidency;* he is co-author of *The Presidency Today* and *Public Administration*.

WILLIAM E. LEUCHTENBURG is professor of history at Columbia University and the author of many books on twentieth-century America, including *The Perils of Prosperity* and the Bancroft Prize-winning *Franklin D. Roosevelt and the New Deal*.

RICHARD E. NEUSTADT, White House assistant to President Truman and consultant to President Kennedy, is professor of government at Harvard and associate dean of the School of Public Administration. He is the author of *Presidential Power*.

JAMES RESTON has been with *The New York Times* since 1939 and is now an associate editor. He was awarded the Pulitzer Prize for national correspondence in 1945.

RICHARD H. ROVERE has been a staff writer for *The New Yorker* since 1944. He is the author of several books, including *Affairs of State: The Eisenhower Years* and *Senator Joe McCarthy*.

ARTHUR M. SCHLESINGER, JR., was professor of history at Harvard before joining the Kennedy Administration as a special assistant. He is the author of many books and won his second Pulitzer Prize for *A Thousand Days*. He is now Regents Professor and Albert

Schweitzer Professor in the Humanities in the City University of New York.

THEODORE C. SORENSEN was associated with John F. Kennedy since 1953 and was appointed special counsel to the President in 1961. His books include *Decision Making in the White House*.

JEROME WIESNER, special assistant to President Kennedy on science and technology, is now Provost of the Massachusetts Institute of Technology. He is the author of *Where Science and Politics Meet*.

A Bibliographical Note

For some years to come the two indispensable books on the Kennedy years will be Theodore C. Sorensen, *Kennedy,* New York: Harper & Row, Publishers, 1965, and Arthur M. Schlesinger, Jr., *A Thousand Days,* Boston: Houghton Mifflin Company, 1965. Sorensen's volume is an impressive, informative piece of work because the author was not only the closest Presidential aide, but also a principal adviser. Since *Kennedy* is a closely textured narrative, with Sorensen's judgments interwoven with his detailed chronological account, it has been very difficult to extract selections that will be both brief and representative of this basic work.

Arthur Schlesinger's book is a sustained, subtle defense of the Kennedy Administration and a sensitive, brilliant portrait of the President. The author's reconstruction of events is in the grand style of a master craftsman and his ability to give historical underpinnings to the Kennedy ideas and programs is particularly valuable and insightful. I chose to reprint a part of Schlesinger's portrait of Kennedy and a chapter dealing with Kennedy's leadership.

All the selections in this anthology are my first choices. However, I would like to call to the reader's attention other significant writings which a longer book could have contained: Joseph Alsop, "The Legacy of John F. Kennedy," *The Saturday Evening Post,* November 21, 1964, pp. 15–19; David T. Bazelon, "Reflections on the Fate of the Union: Kennedy and After," *The New York Review of Books,* December 26, 1963, pp. 9–10; James MacGregor Burns, "The Legacy of the 1,000 Days," *The New York*

Times Magazine, December 1, 1963, pp. 27 *ff,* and "The Legacy of John Fitzgerald Kennedy," in *John Fitzgerald Kennedy . . . As We Remember Him,* New York: Atheneum, 1965, pp. 232–35; Harlan Cleveland, "Great Powers and Great Diversity: The Perceptions and Policies of President Kennedy," *The Department of State Bulletin,* December 23, 1963, pp. 964–69; Norman Cousins, "The Legacy of John F. Kennedy," *Saturday Review,* December 7, 1963, pp. 21–27; Henry Fairlie, "He Was a Man of Only One Season," *The New York Times Magazine,* November 21, 1965, pp. 28 *ff;* Joseph Kraft, "John F. Kennedy: Portrait of a President," *Harper's,* January 1964, pp. 96–100; Ernest R. May, "The Kennedy Presidency," *Frontier,* January 1964, pp. 16–18; Karl E. Meyer, "John F. Kennedy," *The New York Journal-American, Sun,* November 22, 1964, p. 17–L; Hans J. Morganthau, "The Kennedy Legacy: Significance in History," *The New Leader,* December 9, 1963, pp. 4–6; John P. Roche, "Kennedy and the Politics of Modernity," *The New Leader,* August 17, 1964, pp. 7–13; Arthur M. Schlesinger, Jr., "John Fitzgerald Kennedy," *Proceedings of the Massachusetts Historical Society,* January–December 1963, pp. 113–18; Diana Trilling, "Reflections a Year Later [On John F. Kennedy]," *Redbook Magazine,* November 1964, pp. 71–75; Tom Wicker, "Kennedy Without Tears," *Esquire,* June 1964, pp. 108 *ff.*

I have excluded articles that fall into the category of "eulogies" because they do not suit the purpose of this book. Many eloquent and moving tributes can be found in Pierre Salinger and Sander Vanocur, editors, *A Tribute to John F. Kennedy,* New York: Dell Publishing Co., Inc., 1964, and in Senate Document No. 59, 88th Congress, 2d Session. Most magazines printed tributes to Kennedy in late 1963 and early 1964.

Hugh Sidey's *John F. Kennedy, President,* New York: Atheneum, 1964, is a chronicle of affairs while Thomas A. Lane's *The Leadership of President Kennedy,* Caldwell, Idaho: Caxton Printers, 1964, is of dubious quality.